ILIUM

This book is a work of fiction. The characters, places, incidents, and dialogue are the product of the author's imagination and are not to be construed as real, or if real, are used fictitiously. Any resemblance to actual events, locales, or persons, either living or dead, is purely coincidental.

For more information, to inquire about rights to this or other works, or to purchase copies for special educational, business, or sales promotional uses please write to: Lawrence Strattner
2165 Foxwood Dr. Eureka CA 95503

FIRST EDITION

Published in Print and Digital formats in the United States of America

ISBN: 9781540526830

ILIUM
A Corporate Adventure Story;
Big Dreams, Big Business, and Big Money

Thomas J. Keller & Lawrence J. Strattner

Thomas J. Keller dedicates this novel to his wife, Adrienne.

Lawrence J. Strattner dedicates this novel to his wife, Janis.

They survived the dream.

Disclaimer: *This is a work of fiction. If you think any character or situation in this story is you, about you, or is modeled after your questionable behavior, it is not. Get a grip.*

Chapter One

Nick Jackson stormed into his office. *Bloody, but necessary.* He'd butchered several underperforming executives at his review meeting, leaving their résumés in need of updating and their entrails figuratively steaming. *I felt like Attila the Hun in there. The fucker knew how to lead. Constructive carnage.* He went to his desk, custom-sized to contribute gravitas to his diminutive stature. *It's good to be CEO.* He began reviewing possible successors to his moments-ago departed executives. His intercom buzzed. "Yes, Florence?"

"Turn on your television; something's happened to Nixon." Jackson flicked a button.

"…we have confirmation. President Nixon has been shot." As the words registered, Jackson pushed the files aside. "…the president had delivered a luncheon address at the University Club in Chicago to the Greater Faculty Congress, an educational organization known to be in opposition to the administration and its policies."

The pictures showed a street filled with police vans and security personnel. "It was here a large group of student protestors rallied. As he came down the steps of the club, the president made a surprise decision to engage them. A melee ensued. The crowd rushed him, overwhelming his secret service phalanx. Shots were fired. The demonstrators cheered. The secret service quickly formed a protective shield around the president, who lay on the ground, seriously wounded. In addition, one agent was killed and two others wounded. The demonstrators fled, scattering in different directions. No weapons were found or assailants detained. No members of the media witnessed the event. They had remained at the speaker's dais

1

to obtain quotes from the Congress' participants." The correspondent lowered the microphone. "This is Foster Park. Back to you, Claude…"

"This is Claude Howard in New York. Only moments ago the nation was shaken as bloodshed reached the highest office in the land." He paused, expression grave. "Once again, political violence further splinters a nation already sundered by dissent. Once again, the world of ordinary people in the supposed safety of familiar places is shattered. We hope President Nixon will survive and his administration will address the root causes of this unrest while maintaining the rights of those who might disagree. Now, these messages."

"Damn. This'll dominate coverage for weeks. The Apex deal is down the crapper." Jackson clicked off the TV and pressed the intercom. "Florence, get my direct reports on a conference call and then come in here." He tried, not altogether successfully, to keep the irritation out of his voice. He glanced out the window at the usual Manhattan Friday traffic backup.

"They're on the line," Florence said after a minute.

"Okay, Nixon's been shot and shit's hitting the fan. Opinions?"

"We need to consider the ramifications of this, Nick."

"Meaning?"

Another said, "The reaction to this will be enormous. The second US president almost assassinated in less than a decade. A direct blow has been delivered to authority. We can expect a countermove by the so-called silent majority."

"Thanks for the f-fucking lecture, Fred. What's in it for Ilium? How can we m-make money from this?" Jackson lapsed into his boyhood stutter, still a problem when he ranted at his inner circle.

A third voice spoke. "Expect a push for law and order."

"D-do you guys have anything in the f-fucking pipeline?" screamed Jackson. "S-something that'll m-meet the need for a step-up in law enforcement and national security? We are in b-business to make money, g-gentlemen. You should be able to identify a p-product or s-service to f-fill this n-need."

Throats cleared and papers rustled.

"W-well?" shouted Jackson.

"We'll get back to you, Nick," said an unidentified voice. Murmurs of agreement followed.

Jackson's face reddened and his hand shook as he leaned over the phone. "Y-your b-bonuses will depend on it." He mashed the off button, wiped his forehead, and turned to Florence.

"F-fucking ants, they're f-fucking ants, all of them. We've got too many doing the same stuff over and over. Paper-pushing insects. No original thoughts. We need game-changers, change agents..."

"You need soothing," Florence whispered. "You're the president and CEO of Ilium Electric." She walked up to him and unzipped his fly. "Oh, my," she cooed. "Mr. Winkie is coming out to play." She stepped back, removed her blouse and undid her skirt.

***

"Too bad about Nixon," said Burt Rawley. A cigarette dangled from his plump lips.

"Yeah," said Len Lovelace, suppressing a smirk, "we almost had President Agnew."

"Yes, well..." Rawley, the archconservative, frowned. "...So, Len, you actually hired those two trainees for the A&P Program?" He glanced at Lovelace's memo on his desk. "Donnelly and Collins? I see them on the new hire list." Years of Chesterfield straights and rivers of Kentucky sour mash put gravel in his voice.

"You may recall we discussed this, Burt," said Lovelace, staring at the nameplate on the desk. *It says General Manager; it should say Chief Horndog.* "You agreed to their being hired."

"Maybe I did and maybe I didn't." Rawley took a deep drag on his cigarette and exhaled. "At first I thought their colleges were seminaries: Duns Scotus and Roger Bacon. Schools neither I, nor anyone else, ever heard of." He tapped an ash. "What's their prior communications education or experience?" Another inhale. "Reading some wino his rights while slapping the cuffs on?" An exhale. "Mouthing the fire code while sifting through the ashes of some rundown tenement fire?"

You poseur. "Did you read their files?" Lovelace pointed to the personnel folders by Rawley's elbow.

"Skimmed them; saw what I needed to see. An ex-cop and an ex-fire marshal."

Don't extend yourself, Burt. Don't widen your vision. "Their sample portfolios were better than any we've received in the last several years. They're grownups who know what they want. We'd like to get some recruits on the program that aren't trying to molt out of their frat boy feathers. These are people we need."

"Okay, I gave the go-ahead for these experiments, as you called them on your referral memo, but for Christ's sake we're looking for giants, Len, not street trolls from Brooklyn and the Bronx." He stubbed out his cigarette and lit another. "You may also remember I questioned why we should lower our standards as to the class of people we hire. Have your two experiments arrived yet?"

"No." Lovelace lit a cigarette. "I expect them momentarily."

Rawley checked his watch. "It's quarter to nine. They're late. Your experiments are already in trouble. You're in charge of Personnel, Len. This is on your head."

"Uh-huh." Lovelace hedged. "I'll set them straight on the working hours and pack them off to Orientation."

"As far as I'm concerned they're already on a short leash. Now tell me again why you convinced me we should do this?"

"Fresh blood and a different outlook. If they don't work out we'll have learned a lesson. Meanwhile, the upside could be promising."

"True," said Rawley, leaning back and scratching his groin, "but Ilium's Advertising and Publicity program is an elite one, recognized as the best in the industry. Are Donnelly and Collins the kind of people Ilium wants?"

Keep fondling your nuts, Burt. "We'll find out soon enough, I suspect."

"Where are you going to assign them?"

"I was thinking of Joyce Locker's group." At Rawley's surprised look, he said, "It would be a good fit."

"Joyce Locker? Do these two need mothering?"

"If Joyce's so bad, Burt, why'd you make her a section manager?" *Take no crap; be firm.* "She's the only A&P'er to go to Kenoten." Kenoten was Ilium's executive management course. *Joyce Locker's the one A&P person to vaguely frighten Rawley. Probably because of her Nick Jackson connection.*

Rawley waved a hand. "Fine. Talk to her. You need me, I'll be at Exhibits."

Getting that itch relieved, I'm sure. "I'll keep you posted." Lovelace stubbed out his cigarette and walked out, closing the door, thankful to have survived the meeting with only a mild metaphysical flogging.

He returned to his office and left word for Joyce Locker that he'd meet her a little after five at the department hangout, L'Fey. *Donnelly and Collins better produce or my ass is grass.*

The potbellied driver sat on the fender of his cab engrossed in the Maqua *Gazette*'s coverage of the Nixon assassination attempt. "Ilium Electric," Frank Donnelly said, putting his luggage down. On the short walk to the cabstand he realized he was not warm enough in his suit jacket. *Number one on a long list of what they didn't tell me in the interviews. Maqua has to be on the same parallel as Nome, Alaska.*

"Not so fast, I need another fare," the driver said, his eye on a gangly redheaded man with two suitcases who came puffing up to the cab.

"Ilium Electric," the redhead said, flicking his cigarette ash and exhaling a monster drag of smoke. "This yours?" he asked Donnelly.

The New York accent registered. "Ours," Donnelly replied. "I'm heading to the same place."

As the driver loaded the luggage, Donnelly looked up at the leaden sky. "Are you expecting rain?"

"Snow," the driver said and got behind the wheel.

"It's the middle of May, for Christ's sake," Donnelly said. *I guess I can sign up for the Iditarod for something to do in my free time.* He and the other fare climbed into the back. *Shit, I hope working here on the Maqua tundra was a good decision.*

"New, eh?" the driver said, turning the ignition. "Summer begins June 15th and ends August 31st. You're gonna love Maqua." The cab rattled off through the dull landscape of unkempt lawns and piles of decaying leaves.

Donnelly turned and thrust out a hand. "Name's Frank Donnelly. You work for Ilium?"

"Jim Collins," the redhead said. "I think we were on the plane together coming up from LaGuardia. I start today."

"Really? So do I," said Donnelly. "Where?"

"Ilium's in-house agency, the Advertising and Publicity Department. I'm beginning the training program."

"Me too," said Donnelly. "Where'd you go to college?"

"Roger Bacon."

"So, a Bronx guy. I went to Duns Scotus," said Donnelly. "You from Brooklyn?"

Donnelly nodded. "How'd you find the Ilium job?"

"Probably the same as you. Stumbled on a blind ad in the *Times*. The wording intrigued me. It wasn't the CEO opening but…"

Donnelly laughed. "Me too. I was a New York fire marshal. Good job." He stared off. "But it was time to leave that behind." He sighed. "Anyway, I applied. Finished their assignment and sent in some stuff I wrote for FDNY magazines and our newsletter and what do you know? Before you could say better pay scale I got a letter to interview."

"Same for me," said Collins. "I was a cop and came to the same conclusion you did."

Donnelly looked over at Collins. "Sometime over drinks I suspect we might have stories to trade."

"I suspect you're right," Collins said. "My samples were little crime stories built around things I saw on the job. I made them into stories I sold to *True Detective, Strange Detective, Inside Detective*— magazines with tits on their covers. I had one nonfiction article about the Smith and Wesson Police Special in *The Shooter's Bible.*"

"I'm surprised the Ilium guys didn't write you off as dangerous."

"The interview cured that." Collins smiled. "I look respectable in a suit."

"You interview anywhere else?"

"Thought I had a job at *Time* magazine…"

"Let me guess," said Donnelly. "You got aced out by someone with old-boy connections."

"Sounds like you've been down the same road," said Collins.

Donnelly chuckled. "Oh, yeah. For me, it was at the *New York Times*. Looks like Ilium is another landing pad for the boys from top-tier universities." He shrugged. "Not the likes of us. Our suits may not be good enough for this party."

"I got the same impression, but we're here. You know what they say on the court: never up, never in. I plan to get lost in the crowd, do the three years, learn everything I can, and see what the career opportunities are. My dad knew a guy who went through it. We talked on the phone. He said it's a brass ring you're lucky to catch. He convinced me and I accepted Lovelace's offer. He also said not to think about this Ilium department as a formalized business. He stressed that it was an ad agency, with all the peccadillos and weirdness of same, tucked inside a major corporation. "

"Did he tell you about the classes?"

"Yeah," Collins said. "They were four to six in the afternoon when he did it; guess it's the same now. It's a three-year program: everything from electrical engineering to copywriting to finance to campaign planning. We learn it all on their dime."

Donnelly adjusted his long legs. "Did you get interviewed by the head of Personnel, guy named Len Lovelace?"

Collins nodded. "So how'd we sneak in?"

"Talent. Balls. Street smarts," said Donnelly. He winked. "And our accents."

"Right," said Collins. "Don't forget we went to Catholic colleges. Makes us morally superior. Ilium's reasoning is the same Harvard uses to accept minorities. We'll be the only people there who had a normal childhood, untainted by a flood of money and high-toned academic drivel. They must be having trouble with copywriters submitting text in Jane Austen English." The gray countryside rolled by, the skeletal trees bent from the harsh winters.

Donnelly checked his watch. "It's quarter to nine. We're pretty much on time."

"Be different working nine to five," said Collins.

Several minutes later the driver pulled up to a tall spiked-iron fence. He turned. "This is the Maqua Works of Ilium Electric. I'll get your bags."

They stepped out of the cab to face a seemingly endless stretch of monstrous buildings, dark, grimy, foreboding, like the movie *Metropolis* or the comic book Gotham of *Batman*. Smoke belched from several smokestacks. Across the top of a large building stretched a giant "Ilium Electric" sign complete with the ubiquitous "IE" logo. The air smelled of ozone.

Donnelly and Collins stared at each other with a "what did we get into?" look. Large flakes of snow began to fall.

The driver handed them their bags. "Report to the guards in the building over there. Before you go in you should be aware the hours are eight to five."

"Crap," said Donnelly. "Now I know how Nixon feels."

"At least he'll survive," said Collins.

***

At ten minutes after five Joyce Locker walked into an almost empty L'Fey. Tall and slim, her long overcoat emphasized her height. She brushed the snowflakes from the shoulders and hung the coat on a peg. Her blouse was unbuttoned at the neck, revealing the string of pearls at her throat. The few patrons greeted her with admiring glances.

Len Lovelace perched on a stool at the bar, Johnnie Walker at hand. He faced lots of wood and glass, a huge mirror, whiskey bottles, and ten beers on tap. The television was reporting on the hunt for the would-be Nixon assassin.

She slid into the adjoining seat and primly tucked her dress under her. "Bombay martini," she said to the bartender,

She acknowledged Lovelace. "What do you want from me, Len?" *Sniff.* Joyce Locker had a deviated septum that she treated with decongestants. She had procrastinated having the operation, fearing it might disfigure her. She'd learned to use her affliction over the years, quietly sniffing amusement, disdain, approval, or anger.

Lovelace sipped his drink. "I'm assigning two trainees to your section. They started today and are currently in the orientation course. They'll begin Wednesday." Lovelace was the perfect recruiter: tall, slender, well turned out, and with excellent diction. He was the graduate frat boy A&P trainees pictured themselves growing up to be. That was before they realized a meal at the Ilium Club was not a regular occurrence; and before they found themselves eating a plate lunch of suspicious meats and gravies in the Works' cafeteria.

"Do they have names? Why are you asking me? Most important, do I have a choice in this?" She lit a cigarillo.

"You have a choice, Joyce, even though you claim you don't. Their names are Frank Donnelly and Jim Collins. I'm asking you to take these two on because I think you and your section are the best fit. I suspect they'll be different from any trainees you've dealt with. They're tough, but so are you. You've got advertising and promotional smarts and they have the wherewithal to learn from you. You won't be disappointed." He took another sip. "I think your being a woman is a plus."

"Nice try at flattery, Len." *Sniff.* "They sound interesting. I'll assign them to Leeson." She puffed on the cigarillo.

"Leeson? Jesus, Joyce."

"Jesus has nothing to do with it. Leeson's an experienced guy, his drinking problems are behind him, and it's time he took on a larger load." She pushed her glass forward for a refill and pointed to Lovelace. The bartender started pouring.

"You don't want to know why they're different?" Lovelace finished his drink.

"It's May 1969, and we're finally getting around to hiring qualified minorities?"

"You haven't lost your sense of humor, Joyce. A dangerous one, I might add."

She nodded. "Nice job with Burt this morning. Agnew's the one, eh?"

Lovelace jerked his head back. "How?" A bark of laughter. "No secrets in this damn place, are there? Anyway, Joyce, back to my question: you don't want any information on them?"

"I'd rather get to know them as we go along, size them up. They're only trainees." She swirled her martini. "Now tell me who Rawley's banging over in Exhibits and when they'll finish the damn boat they're building for him. His hobbies are intruding on some trade show stuff I need."

Chapter Two

Four months later…

The phone rang in Burt Rawley's office.

"Mr. Rawley's office. Marsha speaking."

"Mr. Rawley, please."

"He's not available." *He's at the department's Exhibits Operation overseeing the final touches of the boat they're surreptitiously building for him. Spreading the costs across currently active, legitimate, projects that will absorb them.* "May I take a message?"

"Uh, my name is Harold Cox; I'm with the Low Voltage Small Controls Subsection and I have this new product…"

"I can transfer you to Mr. Blair. He's in charge of the publicity operation." *He'll bounce you faster than a hockey puck.*

Several clicks later Harold Cox was connected to the office of Sam Blair. Cox spoke for fifteen seconds. Blair deduced no personal political gain from Cox's babble and transferred him to the advertising manager in charge of the Low Voltage business.

***

Frank Donnelly fidgeted in his cubicle, doodling on a piece of paper. The idea of writing a brochure on inane and uninteresting industrial controls was causing brain arrest. Ilium had a great training program and promotion was Donnelly's first training assignment. He hoped things would get more attention-grabbing.

Aviator-framed glasses rose over Donnelly's partition. "Take this call, will you, Frank?" Dick Leeson hovered by his desk. "Some dork from the Low Voltage Department. Hear him out and let me know tomorrow. Get a charge number."

A dork calls a dork a dork. What's wrong with this picture? Donnelly punched the flashing button and picked up the phone. "Frank Donnelly, how may I help you?" Leeson waved and walked away.

"Uh, this is Harold Cox," Cox repeated, sounding resigned to his phone fate. "I'm with the Low Voltage Small Controls Subsection and…" He hesitated, expecting to be transferred again.

"Yes, go on," Donnelly said.

"Um, I need some publicity for a product I've developed. Brochures and stuff, you know?" Cox faltered. "I've never done anything like this before."

Donnelly flashed back to the first time he'd heard "I've never done anything like this before" spoken. He was twelve years old in the park in his Brooklyn neighborhood. All the guys had chipped in a quarter apiece and Donnelly's classmate, sexy Sue Costello, had agreed to go in the bushes and show them her tits. Her mercenary proposition had followed Frank into adulthood as an enduring suspicion of the "never done anything like this before" song and dance.

"…and the model LV228S-1 electric chair is portable and is effective even using normal household current…"

Sue's tits faded from memory. "Did you say electric chair? I presume you mean a chair that can be operated electrically?

"Well, yes, of course," Cox said. "But it is an electric chair, the kind they use…" He trailed off, "you know, to make you warmer on a cold evening."

"Electric chair? Portable?" Donnelly stifled a snigger. "Mr. Cox, we should get together and discuss this." He coughed, suppressing more laughter. "Are you free tomorrow morning? I and a colleague, Jim Collins, would like to meet with you."

"I have a Junior Chamber of Commerce meeting at eight but I should be in by nine-thirty. I'm in building 269, room 1265, cubicle 6. I'll meet you and Mr. Collins then," Cox said, and hung up. Donnelly sat for a moment, shook his head, and went around the corner.

Collins sat with his back to the cubicle entrance staring at a blank sheet of paper in his Underwood typewriter. He hadn't started to write seriously until he joined the police. He worked to shape his writing, journaling his days on the street. It proved an interesting challenge. *Not like the challenge of writing a goddamn brochure describing fast-acting limit switches.*

"You won't believe the guy we're going to talk to tomorrow morning and what he's selling," Donnelly said.

"Okay, I give up. Anything to relieve the tedium." Collins pushed some photos aside and swiveled. His chair emitted a thin metallic shriek.

"Would you believe an electric chair? Portable?" said Donnelly, in a Don Adams *Get Smart* voice.

"No, I wouldn't."

"Partly right," said Donnelly. "This engineer, Harold Cox, believes this chair can keep people warmer on cold evenings."

"And he calls it an electric chair?" said Collins. "How clueless is he?"

"Can't tell yet, but he is an engineer down at the bastion of innovation, Low Voltage Switchgear. Think of the opportunities for us, the fun we can have. We get him to jack up the voltage. Voila! A Captain America solution to the nation's crime problems."

"We could, couldn't we?" said Collins. "Jack-up justice for miscreants. A consumer product that fries the ass unworthy to sit upon it. Sounds like it has potential. Okay, when do we see Engineer Cox?"

"Tomorrow at nine-thirty in his burrow at Switchgear."

***

Donnelly leaned over the frosted glass partition screening Collins's cluttered desk. "Time to check out Engineer Cox."

"Whose car?" Collins put on his jacket and grabbed a monogrammed Ilium pad.

"Surely you jest," said Donnelly. "We go on foot. It'll take us at least as long to get to either of our cars out in parking lot four. If you don't come to work at 6:30 a.m. you park in East Jesus. So we walk or wait for the sometimes-running shuttle bus." They headed to the hallway.

They turned and left their creative cube farm, footsteps echoing. Moving carefully, they avoided the strewn paper covered with bad ideas and unapproved ad copy outside the stalls. Donnelly stared down the hallway. *The whole damn building is linoleum, all in ugly shades of green. Halls, walls, desk and table tops. I'm surprised they haven't done the ceilings in green linoleum. Or paved the parking lots with the shit. Ilium must own a piece of DuPont. Or they sell some transformer sludge by-product and DuPont uses the stuff and presto, thousands of little green squares become the interior design scourge of Ilium's Maqua Works.*

"We need gate passes so we can park behind the building," said Collins.

"We're not managers," said Donnelly. A trainee quickly discovered gate passes were a managerial perk.

"Who says real ones? I know a guy in the city who could forge one in a day."

"Might be worth it this winter," said Donnelly, mentally filing the good idea. *A phony gate pass is less likely to be discovered in the harsh Ilium winter when the gate guards and parking patrol would rather be in their*

15

warm little huts nestled in…their Ilium Electric Chairs! He repressed a laugh.

The shuttle bus passed dozens of sixty-year-old brick factory buildings. Smoke wafted through open doors and clanging overhead cranes manipulated huge pieces of industrial equipment. Dark sweaty men with hairy arms walked among the machines, looking as if they'd like nothing better than to barbecue a boss or two for lunch.

They arrived at building 269, passed through security, made their way to room 1265, and found Cox's cubicle.

Engineer Cox wore the whitest of socks and a plastic pocket protector, in which resided several very sharp pencils and a miniature gas-leak detector. His flattop crew cut, round-framed rimmed glasses, and hand-turned polka dot bow tie matched his sharp-creased, fresh-laundered dress shirt. His baby-smooth face was devoid of any facial hair.

Cox stared at a sheaf of diagrams and schematics. Without looking up, he glanced at his watch. "You're five minutes early," he said in a mid-range effeminate voice.

Donnelly remembered wandering into a gay bar on Flatbush Avenue once and hearing voices like this before he realized where he was. He looked closely at Cox.

"So we are. I'm Frank Donnelly and this is Jim Collins."

"Oh, and I'm Harold Cox," he said, turning toward them. "But I guess you already know that."

"Pleased to meet you, Harold," Collins said. "Dress in the dark this morning?" Donnelly choked.

"Excuse me?"

"I said we were a little pressed to find parking."

"Oh, yes, rather congested near the building," Cox said. "Let's go to the conference room."

16

The room was the size of four cubicles. They sat on uncomfortable steel chairs upholstered in green vinyl. Cox stood as Donnelly put some papers on the green-topped Formica table. "So, where'd you go to school?"

"I have my degree, a BSEE, from Southeastern Iowa State," Cox said.

Must've also been a cheerleader. "What electives did you take?" asked Collins.

"Every credit that I chose to take directly was a science elective," said Cox.

"Were you involved in any other projects before the electric chair?"

"Well," said Cox, "I worked for a year designing a gear meant to flush an electric latrine. We nicknamed it the Electric Can."

This guy does some weird stuff. "How'd that go for you?" Donnelly took his notebook out.

Cox chortled. "With horrible zaps, it would emasculate chaps whose aim wasn't terribly good. There was never a doubt our work was cut out as the current ran back up the spout and gave their equipment a clout."

Donnelly and Collins stared at each other. "Was that it?" Collins said. *Holy shit, this guy's gone loco in the rhymer's dungeon and we're stuck with him. Suppose he turns out to be one of the engineering geeks who wants to write the brochure himself? I thought all the weirdoes worked in the A&P copywriting section.*

"No," Cox said. His mouth curled into an almost smile. "After a bit of this and some of that, I rallied my flock so even a spastic could piddle without any danger of shock. We handed it over to Commercial Products. I understand the introduction will be in three months."

Again silence descended. Donnelly struggled not to snicker. "The electric chair?" he prompted.

"Yes, yes. The concept grew out of our effort with the Electric Can." Cox rose and stepped to a flipchart in the corner. He turned the cover page to a picture of a plain upholstered living room chair against a wall. Mouth loose, Cox wet his lips as he entered the euphoric trance of an engineering presentation. His blue eyes shone. "This is the electric chair, or as I would like to call it, the Electrified Comfort Chair. The chair operates on ordinary household current and provides the homeowner a warm, comfortable place to sit." He flipped a page. "I'm in the process of developing a motor-driven recliner model that will maintain a consistent level of warmth throughout its travel range or in any fixed position." Another page. "Here is a sample electric schematic…"

Cox dove deeper into the reverie of technical minutiae while Donnelly wrote obscene slogans and suggestions. Collins drew cartoonish pictures of high voltage chairs, with writhing stick figures sitting in them, arms, legs and hair straight out.

Donnelly imagined his grammar school nuns possessing chairs like these, wired with a somewhat higher voltage. *Jesus, Crucifixion would have been preferable with that tool in Sister Rafael's arsenal. None of us would have had our nuts intact.* His mouth opened and the question fell out. "Can you make chairs with a higher current?"

Cox, deep in detailing a minor electrical circuit, started. He contemplated his fifteenth diagram. "Of course, a simple matter of stepping up the voltage. Why?"

"Our job is to ask questions," said Donnelly. "It helps clarify. How high can you step up the voltage?" Collins swallowed a chuckle.

"Theoretically?"

Donnelly nodded.

"Two thousand volts, maybe more." He turned back to the flipchart. Donnelly and Collins scribbled notes.

Collins looked up. "What will two thousand volts do? Give us a perspective."

"Kill the person in the chair." Cox drummed his fingers on the conference table. "Two thousand is a voltage level used at Sing Sing prison. Not that long ago a criminal caught fire at two thousand volts. The president of Westinghouse said they would have done better to have used an ax." Cox smiled. "I guess he was embarrassed at the way his equipment performed."

"You can't be too sure if it's Westinghouse," said Collins.

Cox chuckled and waved a hand as if to forestall the next question. "Our superior solid-state step-up transformer technology is more precise. Our chair would be able to generate two thousand AC volts on ordinary household current." Cox stepped back. "Of course we have no intention of stepping up the chair so high. Chairs with that much voltage are one-offs; there's no mass market for them."

"How heavy is the chair?" Donnelly asked.

"Not very. The chair is self-contained and can be moved. We haven't addressed any miniaturization of the electrical components or optimization of the mechanical parts. Right now King Kong could plop down and it would probably function." Cox tittered. "We do have to reduce weight before we market to homeowners. We know the typical missus likes to rearrange her furniture occasionally." He tittered again. Donnelly decided Cox's titter was irritating.

The meeting went on for twenty more minutes with Collins and Donnelly promising to return with promotional suggestions and communication concepts. Cox appeared pleased with their progress. "Excellent," he said.

"Oh, one last detail," Donnelly said. "We need a charge number."

"Of course. Come back to my office."

***

They returned to their building through the endless linoleum corridors and enclosed bridges of the Ilium complex. "The guy is a nut job," said Donnelly. "I'm glad he's not in the nuclear division."

"A nut job?" said Collins. "Could be, but a bunch of these flakes are super smart. You know the Bentley parked in the lot behind our building?"

"Sure."

"A rotating equipment guy was on a computer markets evaluation team. The team decided Ilium had no future in computers. The guy with the Bentley cast the only dissenting vote. He remortgaged his house and used the proceeds to buy IBM at a dollar twenty."

Donnelly's eyebrows arched. "Holy shit! Why the hell is he still working?"

"His wife wouldn't let him quit. Would you want an engineer around your house all day every day?"

"Poor bastard," said Donnelly. "Anyway, this chair is no goddamn IBM."

"How about not just heat, but a gizmo in it to massage your back while you relax?"

"Are you climbing into the screwball bag with Cox? Do you have any idea of the price of a full-feature chair after this place built up the costs? Only an oil sheik could buy one. Next you'll tell me Cox should wire the chairs so they create sexual arousal. Call it the 'Dicky-do.' Or have it vibrate and call it the 'Giddit Up.'"

Collins grinned. "I suppose you're right, but I sense opportunity in this chair. Remember our conversation about frying the guilty?

The world is full of deserving assholes. There are enough of them to constitute an industrial-commercial market. Ilium might be more comfortable electrifying the world's felons than selling a portable Filipino massage parlor."

"Boy, Lovelace was right on in my interview." Donnelly laughed.

"About?"

"People in our department need to be kept in locked closets and their paycheck shoved under the door."

"I doubt he said it like that." Collins turned toward him.

"A slight exaggeration, but damned close. My ear put it into real-speak."

Chapter Three

"You going to L'Fey later?" Collins said as they walked to the parking lot

Frank Donnelly fished for his car keys. "Why?"

"Everyone'll be there."

"Everyone's always there."

"Yeah, but Fridays can be fun."

"What time are you going?" asked Donnelly.

"After I drop my car home." Collins lit up. "I can't get used to owning a car. Why can't this shithole town have a subway? Or at least a bus that runs more than every forty-five minutes?"

"Hey," said Donnelly, "this is upper nowhere, man. Our finishing school. Our trial by fire. If you can make it through here, you can get yourself recruited back to the city. To civilization. Manhattan. Screw up, they send you to Quasimodo, Georgia."

"There is that."

***

Rufus Hogg's snow-white buttocks pistoned in the pale moonlight to the rhythm of squeaking Ford seat springs. The blonde-haired head of the girl under him whipped from side to side accompanied by desperate squeaks, grunts, and moans. With a forceful final stroke, counterpointed by a female yelp, all went quiet. A moment later Hogg used the stick shift to leverage off a still-heaving Bonnie Bilbie, her legs spread on the front seat of his Chevy. He wiped himself with her skirt. *She musta come three times.*

Bilbie worked in the typing pool. They'd seen each other around the halls and here at L'Fey's happy hours. She had been walking and he'd offered her a ride. Hogg was a good presenter and the department used his talents for new account development. Those same skills got him laid a lot, like tonight.

"Gotta go now, babe. They're expecting me," he whispered to Bilbie, who reached for him. He pulled a white handkerchief from his jacket pocket and positioned it with a flourish against her fun box. She smiled coquettishly as he gave the cloth a gentle pat. He backed out, tucked in his shirt, buckled his belt, adjusted his tie, and closed the car's door. *Mr. Hanky scores again.* He strolled to the bar's front door.

Bilbie would find her way in when she was ready, he knew. She'd suck down a few drinks, get smashed, and likely leave to have a go with some bullpen artist. Hogg's intention was to have a couple of rounds with the dipshits, glad-hand around a little, and go home, smelling of whiskey, to his very proper Southern wife.

Smoke, noise, and laughter greeted Hogg as he walked into L'Fey. The men wore ties, the women, those who weren't out in the parking lot having sex, wore dresses. A few of the dresses were wrinkled in the front as if they had earlier been pushed up over willing hips. *As good a bar as bars get around Maqua. Ain't anything like the bars in Port Arthur. Lots of pretty sharp ladies in both places, but the corporate manufacturing Neanderthals made even the best of Maqua women into secretaries and meeting planners. They never got a chance to play with the boys no matter how competent. The women in Port Arthur were cowgirls. Took no shit from nobody and could ride you till you couldn't buck no more.*

"Rufie!" A puffed up, red-cheeked Duff Wall slapped him on the shoulder as soon as he entered. *Must have started early. He simply ain't a good ol' boy; always overdoes the chummy nicknames. I'll bet he wants us to be fifth graders so he can be the biggest cheese. I'm almost off the program. I'm digging up the new accounts and closing them and this dumbass still calls me Rufie. Jesus.*

"Yo, Duffster," said Hogg, slapping Wall on the shoulder in return. *A few more months and I'll be punching your arm and calling you doofus, you asshole.*

He wondered about the two New Yorkers, Donnelly and Collins. Those two appeared not to be folks to mess with. *Brooklyn and the Bronx, a nasty combination. How'd they get in the program? Have to check that out.* He'd been around long enough to recognize potentially dangerous people. He caught Donnelly's eye and waved. *You never know; I'll mosey over and say hi.*

Donnelly was well into a double Jameson with a beer chaser when Hogg came up on his right side, pivoting his hand on Donnelly's shoulder. Donnelly barely caught himself before he put a schoolyard elbow into Hogg's ribs. "Rufus!" he said, trying to muster good ol' boy bonhomie. "How's it going?"

"All raht, all raht!" said Hogg. He sucked on his drink, ready to unleash some shit-kicker witticism.

This is like Dogpatch without a sense of humor. Donnelly gave silent thanks when Collins walked up to them and did some "Howdies" with Hogg, disrupting his train of thought.

He turned to Donnelly. "We have been summoned."

"By who?"

"Locker."

Both knew Joyce Locker's reputation for chewing cowering subordinates to pieces for lunch in place of a sandwich. They had not yet been an object of her wrath. Three plastic olive toothpicks stood as mute testimony to her progress on her martini marathon.

"Well, well, my trainees. To what do I owe this honor?"

"Golly gee whiz, Joyce, we do believe it was you who asked us over." They put their drinks on the bar and bowed elaborately.

"Don't be such smartypants," said Locker. *Sniff.* She ran her hand through her tightly cropped hair, a sheen of sweat on her forehead. "I did, didn't I? So, you guys starting an agency?"

Where the hell did that come from? "Excuse me?" Collins reached for his drink.

"Your own agency. An enterprise." *Sniff.* Locker finished her drink and signaled for another. "Charlie Rokon told me you were working a charge number belonging to some poindexter engineer down at Low Voltage Switchgear Components. What's the product?

"The engineer called it an electrified comfort chair," said Donnelly.

"A chair? Electric? Hmmmf," said Locker. "Nobody in our group has heard a word about this project."

Donnelly leaned into Locker's face. "Hah! Our group? Newsflash, Joyce, nobody gives a shit about some small-change LVSC engineer with a budget to match. He couldn't get anyone to take his call for help." People began to back away as Donnelly's voice grew louder. "This engineer Cox called Rawley's office. Rawley must have been at Exhibits checking his boat. We guess Rawley's secretary, Marsha, passed him to Blair in Press Relations. As soon as Blair figured out Cox didn't have a million-dollar budget he got transferred down the food chain until he reached us in the depths of what Collins and I call the spiral binding section."

Holy shit, Donnelly sounds like he cares! Collins realized this was an uncharacteristic outburst. He and Donnelly talked about programs and marketing campaigns incessantly and Frank was not one for passionate diatribes.

"Who shoved the hot poker up your hindquarters?"

"Let me check," Donnelly said. He twisted. "Gosh, no poker, Joyce." He shrugged.

She turned crimson, veins throbbing in her forehead. *Well, these boys have spunk, I'll say that for them.* After a few seconds, she laughed.

Donnelly eyed his chaser. "It's not always a good idea to blow off these little shits without a hearing." He threw up his arms. Several barflies jumped, double-fisting their drinks. "Okay, it's a chair, an electric one at that. Maybe not a big deal, but who knows? But suppose he'd invented a new light bulb? Or something better than a light bulb? That's why we're here, for chrissakes. To sell the shit these guys make." He reached for his Jameson and drained it.

"That we are, that we are," she said, tasting her fresh martini and smacking her lips. "I like your style." *Sniff.* "We'll talk more in the future. Right now I have this martini to deal with." *Sniff.* "How about those Jets? And those Yankees too, huh?" She laughed again. *Sniff.*

"Screw the Yankees; I'm a Mets fan," said a straight-faced Donnelly.

"Cheeky son of a bitch, aren't you?" chuckled Locker. She called to the bartender. "Give these boys a round on me." *Sniff.*

"Will you respect us in the morning?" said Collins.

"Probably not," laughed Locker. "Probably not. You'll have to earn that from me, and it won't be easy."

***

Mike Drake and Austin Shepherd sidled up to an unsteady Rufus Hogg. Collins had wisecracked they rooted for football teams with campuses in swamps. "Get much tonight?" Shepherd nudged Drake in the ribs.

"Bonnie Bilbie from the typing pool," Hogg slurred. He made a wavy check mark. Drool leaked down his chin.

"Good on you, Rufe ol' boy. Where'd you nail her?"

"My car," Hogg wheezed and collapsed into a chair.

"The score?" Drake calculated the odds of getting seconds. A guy from Drafting was hitting on Bilbie. She leaned against a table, her breasts jutting forward.

Hogg lifted his head and drank. "On a scale of one to ten? Six, but enthusiastic. Not bad, considering the place. And I was a gentleman; she got my best hankie."

"Best hankie? Extra points." Shepherd leaned over. "In your car, you said?" Hogg nodded. Shepherd snickered. "Better air out the sumbitch before Anna May gets near it." Anna May was Hogg's wife.

"Good idea," said Hogg.

Shepherd looked down the bar and noticed Locker huddling with Donnelly and Collins. "What's them newbies doin' with Locker?"

"Sucking up," said Drake. "I think she called them over."

"How'd them boys get on the program?" Shepherd sucked on his drink. "They went to no-name commuter colleges somewhere in New York. Catholic, no less; no football or nothing.

"Wasn't Collins a cop," said Drake, "and Donnelly some kind of investigator? Program standards lowering?"

"I don't know," said Shepherd, "but Joyce is buying them a round of drinks. What're they working on?"

"We should take the trouble to find out," said Drake. "I suspect they're doing something above their pay grade. Or maybe she wants their young bodies for her own devices."

"Not likely," Shepherd said. "But one thing I do suspect is I'll get another drink."

***

"I should get him home. He's been like this for almost an hour. The boy ain't fit to drive." He walked over and tried to lift Hogg. "Give me a hand, Mike."

They carried Hogg out and poured him into the passenger seat of Shepherd's car. "Want me to come along?" said Drake.

"No, I can handle him," Shepherd said. In several minutes they were at Hogg's flat. They stumbled to the door and he pressed the doorbell. A minute later, Anna May, Hogg's wife, came out on the porch and stared at them.

"He's drunk, isn't he?" She moved aside, blond hair flowing down her shoulders, robe wrapped around her shapely figure. Shepherd dragged her besotted husband inside. He stood in the living room, catching his breath.

"We'll put him in the spare bedroom," she said, her Southern lilt soft music in Shepherd's ears. They each grabbed an arm and lifted him to the double bed. They backed out, closing the door.

"That son of bitch," she said, shaking. Shepherd didn't move. She wiped her eyes. "I'm sorry…It's just that…H-he's never home, he…"

Shepherd stepped forward and held her trembling hands. "If I had someone like you around," he murmured, "I wouldn't want to go to work, much less stay out after it." *The next move is hers.* As his eyes traveled across her body, Shepherd felt himself getting hard.

Her eyes glistened. She leaned into him and began to whimper. Pheromones flew. Her head came up as she felt his tumescence pressed against her. She moved into it and they kissed. The robe slipped from her shoulders.

The urgency of their lovemaking was punctuated by Anna May's moans. She writhed underneath, then above, Shepherd. *What a piece of ass.* Rufus Hogg's drunken snores sounded through the thin wall of the spare bedroom.

Chapter Four

Justin Hitchcock sat up straight in the soft leather chair, unblinking, magnificent, with his Hitchcock nose aloft. "Is there any progress on law-and-order matters with the administration?"

"No," the man said apologetically. "You must realize, sir, there has been a great deal of turmoil..." He twisted in his seat, "...but I'm pursuing several avenues, Mr. Hitchcock."

"Not any more. Jeffrey," Hitchcock said to the manservant who had appeared. "Please escort the gentleman out."

A moment later, Jeffrey returned. "Will there be anything else, sir?"

Hitchcock sighed. "Social order is breaking down, the judicial system is in shambles..."

"If you don't mind, sir, a suggestion. Perhaps Abe Floss might be helpful."

"The Democrat?"

"Yes, sir. Like you, he knows all kinds of people; they're just on his side of the fence."

"An intriguing possibility," said Hitchcock. "Abe can be reasoned with. I should talk with him.

***

"Mr. Floss, sir," said Jeffrey as he ushered in a slim, ordinary-looking man dressed impeccably in a stylish, understated suit.

"Hello, Abe, good to see you. Excuse me for not rising," said Hitchcock. "Do take a seat. Jeffrey, fetch Mr. Floss a libation. Abe, I recommend a pleasant single malt I've discovered. And, Jeffrey, I'll have one myself."

"Neat, if I may," Floss said, respecting Hitchcock's assessment of the Scotch's quality. He preferred some ice but that would not be polite. He noted the cane by Hitchcock's chair and the well-thumbed volume of *Prominent Families of New York* on the lamp table. He recognized the careless, well-bred accumulation found with old money: the Constable drawing, the Martin engraving, the Cooper watercolor, the paintings and sketches of various ancestors, the Chinese porcelains, and what he presumed were first editions on the bookshelf.

After Jeffrey served the drinks and Floss murmured appropriate appreciation for the single malt, both men settled back. Hitchcock adjusted the blanket on his lap. "I asked you here, Abe, to discuss a matter I feel transcends the usual political jousting."

Floss took a sip of his Scotch and nodded for Hitchcock to proceed.

"Although he's back on the job, the country is in a frenzy since Nixon was shot. The incident only adds to the turmoil caused by Bobby Kennedy's and Martin Luther King's deaths. Violent crime is rampant. Radical groups are becoming bolder."

"I'm sure the administration is sympathetic to your concerns, Justin," said Floss.

"Our cities and towns are in disarray, the judicial system is tied in knots by those perverting the legal system. The media gives voice to these radicals. The administration and Congress seem helpless." He toyed with his drink. "Although Mr. Nixon has never been one of our kind, his true persona is unknown to most Americans for a simple reason. His profanity. Even his mother said he had a mouth on him. His aides edit him as best they can."

Floss laughed. "Hannah Milhous, Nixon's mother, was a Quaker and knew a nasty mouth when she heard one. Nixon told Mike Mansfield he wanted to go after the gun lobby. 'Those assholes in the rifle association will be all over me like flies on shit but ordinary people should not have handguns. Kids usually kill themselves with the goddamn things.' Mike said the man can't communicate even well-meaning and constructive thoughts without lacing them in profanity. 'That son of a bitch has the right idea,' Nixon said of a radical leader promoting peace in the third world. 'Send the fucker a few million, and keep in touch.'" Floss chuckled. "What do you propose?"

Hitchcock's eyebrow lifted slightly. "We fix it," he said. "Quickly, before the streets are awash with blood. The problems need to go away, disappear."

"Are you talking about martial law, Justin?" said Floss.

"No, military intervention would send the stock market into a tailspin and transmit the wrong signal overseas."

"Any specifics?" Floss put his drink aside.

"Lean on Congress; you're in the majority. I'll do the same with the administration. Together, we'll deal with the judges."

"We should include the business community," said Floss. "Their advertising clout could apply pressure on the media to air stories that don't support these radicals and thugs."

Hitchcock watched Floss carefully. He said in an even tone, "You have someone in mind to spearhead an effort?"

"Yes. Nick Jackson, the CEO of Ilium and new chair of the Business Board. He's a lifelong Democrat."

"Nick the Zipper?" said Hitchcock.

"None other," said Floss. He laughed quietly. "He's called Nick the Dick by his employees."

The color rose in Hitchcock's face. "He can't keep it in his pants, he stutters, and he's practically a dwarf, for Christ's sake."

"Nevertheless, he can be quite persuasive, and the Business Board will follow his lead." Floss steepled his fingers. "I'll meet with Jackson and brief some people in Congress. You'll deal with the administration?" Hitchcock shook his head in the affirmative. "We should get together privately one or two more times as we set these things in motion, then go our separate ways, wouldn't you agree?"

"Yes." Hitchcock struggled to his feet. "We're doing what's best for the country, Abe."

Floss walked over and shook his hand. "If I didn't concur, I wouldn't be here. We are in perilous times, Justin. I'll see to Nick Jackson."

"I'd prefer to follow all this in the *Wall Street Journal* or the *New York Times* or on the evening news. Ideally, all three."

"I understand," said Floss. He and Hitchcock wanted distance from the events they understood would unfold. "Tomorrow night the financial community honors Jackson with the Pecunia Award. I'll attend and sound him out."

***

Nick Jackson gave a perfunctory wave to the tuxedoed crowd and walked off the main ballroom stage of the Waldorf-Astoria Hotel, the Pecunia Award firmly clenched in his hand. The applause and false camaraderie still echoed as Jackson handed the award to an assistant. The assistant, trained in the craft of craven submission, peeled off.

"He basically said, 'I deserve this,' didn't he?" said someone at a back table. "So much for the ethos of propriety, modesty, and caution."

A tablemate, an older man with a pink face and broken blood vessels in his nose and cheeks, rose, his mind wandering on capital cares. "I've worked for Ilium my entire career. Then Jackson arrived. He's clinical, lucid, cold, and strangely isolated. The man gives off no human heat; it's as if something had burned away any gentler impulses. Except, of course, if the something wears a skirt. I was ordered to attend this suck-up party but no one said I had to stay." He rose and stalked off.

Another lifted his drink toward the lumbering figure. "At least he knew some years of propriety, modesty, and caution before Jackson came on the scene."

***

The steps and sidewalk outside the Waldorf had almost disappeared, lost beneath the continuous movement of black tuxedo pants and silken gowns. A cold breeze whistled down the Park Avenue canyon as Jackson went through the door to the street.

A limo pulled up and a hand beckoned. Jackson recognized Abe Floss.

"Get in, Nick, your date can wait," Floss patted the seat. "This is important for you and Ilium. You know I don't waste people's time. Please sit."

Jackson settled into the limousine. "Okay, Abe to w-what do I owe this h-honor?" Jackson's lizard-like eyes, dull with lusterless self-absorption, sucked the vibrancy out of the moment. His climb up the corporate ladder had taught him to feign the appearance of rectitude.

The reality was somewhat different: selfish and cynical, full of secrecy and cunning charm.

"We need your help, both as CEO of Ilium but more importantly as the head of the Business Board. As I'm sure you recognize, society is cracking at the seams; the culture wars have gone critical. The media don't help. They showcase anyone with a contrary opinion and pay less than lip service to a civilized response."

Jackson did not respond, thinking back to his staff briefing on this subject.

"Well?" asked Floss.

"I'll be pleased to assist. Who knows, my company might even be able to offer products and services to help. Send someone to brief me. Now let me out; a woman who's better than a vacuum cleaner is waiting for me."

"While we work on this maybe you should buy one of those TV networks, Nick," said Floss as Jackson slid out of the car. "We'd be able to use some controlled media leverage."

Jackson stuck his head back in. "I'll have our guys look into it. Thanks, Abe."

Chapter Five

"Okay. Let's get started on the electric chair," said Collins. He and Donnelly sat at a green Formica table in a stuffy third-floor conference room. A small blacktopped parking area, a chain link fence, and railroad tracks made up the backyard of the building.

"Why the fence?" asked Donnelly.

"Keep the bums and perverts off Ilium property," said Collins. "Incidentally, that fence also keeps the bums and perverts working here from sneaking out of work early."

Donnelly began arranging some notes. "What do you think of Joyce Locker?" he blurted.

"Older than we are by a few years. Really good looking when you get past the bluster; wasting her time in this place." Collins ran his fingers through his hair. "Why? Where'd that come from?"

"It's been bugging me since the other night," Donnelly said. "I never saw a woman drink like that. Unreal. Then I saw what the bartender was doing."

"You noticed it too?" said Collins.

"He keeps what I guess is gin bottle filled with water," said Donnelly. "At least every other drink she gets is water."

"Helps her retain her aura. You need to do something when you live in this tundra. But if you want to discuss the unreal," Collins snickered, "there's Engineer Cox, who I believe is gay, nonjudgmentally speaking." He reached for his notes.

"How could you tell with all that male mufti he was wrapped in? Where did Cox being gay come from?"

"I don't know, he's just weird. Kind of a femme. He makes me nervous. I don't get a very strong guy-vibe from him. He's always excited. First, the dumb poetry session when we interviewed him about the chair. I mean how much faggy shit do you have to see before the verdict is gay?"

"Maybe he's effeminate? He does have those sloe eyes and parted lips."

"Think back," said Collins. "He's on the tall side, with skinny arms and a pedestal neck. Being gay's fine by me. Don't misunderstand, I'm okay with it as long as he stays where I can see him."

Donnelly laughed. "Going for the manly man award, eh?"

Collins stared out the window. "We've got bigger worries than at which end Cox gets laid."

"On another subject," said Donnelly, "I have some very good stuff here, obtained by stroking little Thelma down in the department library. She researched her garage-sized ass off."

"Thelma? Jesus. Will the sliminess never stop? She's preposterous: beetle-browed, high-waisted, and misshapen. I hope you didn't touch her."

"No. I didn't want to cut in on your action."

"Ha, ha," said Collins. "What do you have?"

Donnelly spread out some papers and transparencies of the United States. "First, the population demographics of the US." He pushed one sheet forward. "Next"—he overlaid a transparency on the sheet—"the higher income areas within the population. Next"—he laid on a third transparency—"markets where for more than five months of the year the temperature hovers around thirty degrees."

"All of upstate New York is crosshatched," Collins said. "Tell me again why we live upstate?"

"Because we enjoy freezing our asses off for five months," said Donnelly. "To relieve the tedium during the two-week changes of seasons, it'll either rain or snow or hail, the wind will blow, and every damn dog within fifty miles will howl. If you're a certain personality type, you get a perverse visual enjoyment. Oh yeah, don't forget our jobs."

"And don't overlook the smoke, the ugly women, and the sleazy bars."

"Hey, Jim, you're being judgmental during brainstorming. Didn't they teach you in brainstorming class to leave your mind open?"

"I must have been out that week."

"I have shown you, without piling on a bunch of SIC codes or any other industrial research crap, the target market map for the warm, snuggly, adjustable Ilium Electric Comfort Chair."

"Can you and Thelma's ass both fit in it at the same time?"

"No. But since you're being hypercritical again, I'd bet you and Harold Cox could." Donnelly shifted the transparencies around. "Think about this. The weather is cold in certain places. Many of those shivering folks have financial resources, always necessary to acquire Ilium products." He overlaid the transparencies again. "And we now know the locations of the cold places with affluent people." He snapped his fingers. "I just thought of another market. Old-age homes. Those poor bastards are always cold."

"Brilliant, Einstein," said Collins. "We can sell Electric Comfort Chairs up the wazoo at excessive margins." He rubbed his hands together. "Lots of profit for the Ilium till. A two-level jump in our pay at our next review?"

"In your dreams, pal." Donnelly spoke briskly, as if aware he needed to finish his thought before it vanished. "I've figured out one thing. We're junior woodchucks in this place. As a Brooklyn boy and all-around cynic, I perceive others close by who will want to claim not only our ideas but also our pay raises for their own." He pumped his fist. "We must trounce them." Fist pump. "Piss on them while they are down." A double fist pump as his voice rose. "And stomp their asses if they try to get up."

"Rah, rah," Collins said. His sardonic grin narrowed his eyes and lit up his shrewd Irish face. "Let's find a way to get to Rawley with this. Establish our promotional strategies and ideas and make this project our baby regardless of markets. Needless to say, we'll have an immediate problem with at least one pack of department jackals."

"Golly, I wonder who?"

Collins ignored the heavy-handed irony. "The consumer group, led by Bob dot-dot-dot Dingmann." Dingmann, the manager of the consumer section handling small and large electric appliances, various gadgets, lawnmowers, and hedge clippers, was notorious for pushing ad campaigns that featured ellipses. He used people as a ladder. He called industrial advertising trash and boring. According to him only his carefully selected group could write and produce an effective advertising idea. He recruited Ivy leaguers almost exclusively.

"Bingo. Dingmann," Donnelly said, with a bitter distaste. "No one here wants to see the other guy succeed. Everyone will realize this is an opportunity to raise their profile. Dingmann will pounce, once he figures it out. His assholes will come up with twenty-five reasons why we sub-educated industrial retards can't handle the chair. I've already heard multiple recountings of newbies being burned by this guy. Might be hard to shake them off, don't you think?"

"We need air cover," said Collins. "After four months here we know Leeson is useless."

"Leeson avoids conflict of any kind," said Collins. "'In late, leave early' is his motto. He spends the day drinking endless cups of coffee, going to the men's room, and recounting past glories when he was a hotshot copywriter and notorious skirt-chaser.

"Joyce Locker," they said simultaneously.

Donnelly absent-mindedly brushed off another transparency. "If we get tight with her on this, two things will happen. One, we'll present to Rawley because Locker likes to develop and support up-and-comers. Two, she's got enough political muscle to push off Dingmann and his consumer guys before they can storm the wall and take us down. Everyone knows she's tight with Nick Jackson. Dingmann will think twice about messing around with her."

"Good idea."

"Yeah, well. Answers to complex problems like this are why they pay me the big bucks."

"Problems?"

"You'll agree the last several years in America are all about passion and confusion?" Collins pushed his chair back.

"Uh huh. Do you mean the spasmodic barbarisms of the advantaged upper-class kids who shut down their elite universities with no consequences? What's that got to do with anything?"

"Everything," Collins said. "The vast majority of people need certitude, not immature acting out. The Nixon Administration appears to be coming down on the side of certitude."

"Is all this going to result in the title of our brochure?"

"Maybe. Remember the bullshit with Cox, the stuff we discussed when we busted Cox's balls about the voltage he could put through the chair?"

"We called it the Captain America solution to the nation's crime problems."

Collins opened another folder and pushed a transparency forward. "Exactly. The black dots are all the maximum security and violent offender prisons in America." He took Donnelly's transparency and overlaid his. "You'll notice a bunch of the markets these prisons serve are adjacent to your primary electric chair markets. Most crime is where the money is." He pointed with his pencil tip. "The yellow hatching on the map shows the location of unexecuted outstanding warrants for violent or predatory crime."

"Where did you get this info?" Donnelly sat back.

Collins shrugged. "My uncle runs the Manhattan FBI office."

"Jesus. Show me you're not wearing a wire."

"Funny. We develop the quote-unquote Industrial-Societal market for the chair, use the chair to fight and crush crime in a high-profile public way. We position ourselves industrially in a consumer market before Dingmann's idiots know."

"Clever. But," Donnelly said, "would a consumer want a crime-buster chair they've seen fry some criminal on TV?"

"Yes. The kind of people who can't shoot but buy guns. The people who buy fad electronics. The people who install elaborate security systems. The people who see our campaign exhorting them: Relax in the chair that brought law and order to America! Deadly to those who transgress. Relaxing to you who deserve. Stuff like that. Everybody wants to be a cowboy, Clint Eastwood. We'll sell the shit out of the chair."

"Let me offer an alternative," said Donnelly. "Think a Cadillac and a Nash Rambler. They're both cars but no one thinks they're the same. Different audiences, different messages. Besides, the home-use chair is a chair, not an execution device. I must say, though, your proposal could make sense. Are you sure you're not from Brooklyn?"

"This'll work. The country is out of control. We should hash out your dual-audience approach. People are sick of anarchy, rising crime rates, violence, all that crap. An item that settles the mess down will be in big demand. People will want to be a part of it."

"Televise the executions." Donnelly stood. "Imagine some three-time loser, the current ripping through him, screaming desperately, the spasms jerking his body as he fights the bitter struggle, shitting his drawers and pissing his pants as the death agony finally overcomes him. Message: crime does not pay and no corner-cutting lawyers or lefty judges will get you off."

"You are from Brooklyn, you sick son of a bitch." Collins skipped a beat. "I love the idea. We'll make those chairs the altars of dread. Spin the shit out of it; give the publicity guys something to do instead of writing AC vs. DC articles for IEEE magazine."

Donnelly waited while a freight train rolled noisily past on the tracks behind the building. "You'll agree," he said, raising his voice, "the deluxe Ilium Electric Comfort Chair is an engine of coziness for the advantaged. In the hands of the forces of law and order an up-voltage version transforms to an engine of justice."

"How do we get this to Locker without looking like scheming backstabbing attention-whores?"

Donnelly laughed. "Aren't we? Before we do, how about we consider a third market for this chair?"

Collins frowned.

"Parents and schools. I'll bet only a slight upping of the voltage from the Comfort Chair level would prove effective in disciplining kids."

Collins whistled. "Holy shit, to coin a phrase. Would it be legal?"

"With the way the Nixon Administration is headed? I'd say yes. This country will be increasingly run by vociferous pressure groups." Donnelly gazed out the window. Some kids had climbed the fence and were chasing each other down the tracks. "Yesterday, the lefties were committed to the proposition their views were correct, self-evident, and based on fact and reason. Anyone else's positions were not just wrong but illegitimate, ideological, and unworthy of serious consideration. Today, the conservatives. Same deal. You'll agree the last several years have been all about fervor and misunderstanding?'

"True enough. We've got the beginnings of a plan." Collins wiped his forehead. "We done? This is a good start."

"When do you think we should talk to Joyce? Here or at L'Fey?"

"Well," said Collins, "we can always corner her at L'Fey. Nah. Too many ears. I'll bet she'll not only like the plan but will add her own twists. For one, she's not a fan of Dingmann. She's called him Dot-Dot."

"You could, of course, go to the library to do more research and hit on Thelma," Donnelly said

Collins' face reddened. "Asshole."

They laughed.

***

The sound of the phone jolted Collins. He dropped the report he was reading and fumbled for the receiver. "Collins."

A thick and phlegmy voice. "Uh, Jim, this is, uh, Thelma, uh, down in the library, you know? I tried Frank's line and he's not around."

"He'll be back this afternoon."

"You work with him, right?"

"Yes."

"That'll be fine. Next time you're, uh, down this way, could you drop in?"

"Sure," said Collins. He picked up the report he'd dropped. He checked the internal phone list. "You're in B-25, right?"

"Right."

"I need to read over something and I'll be down in a couple of minutes. See you in a few." He disconnected. *Thelma, the last of the motor mouths. Something's up; better find out what.*

***

A few minutes later Collins had descended to the library. Shelves stacked with reference materials and periodicals, all neatly filed, extended into the immediate horizon. He knocked at Thelma's open door.

She looked up and waved him in. Her oval face was framed by a graying Prince Valiant hairdo. A yellow sweater covered a shapeless blue and pink floral dress, which barely contained her considerable bulk. Thelma had buried two husbands and was now married to her job. She had a doctorate in library science and a gold medal in company gossip.

As he sat she said, "Do you know Quentin Rhodes?"

"He's one of Dingmann's guys. Why?"

"The other day Rhodes and I were chatting in the hallway and I mentioned the type of research you and Donnelly were doing. He asked more questions…maybe I shouldn't have said anything to him; I thought it was harmless talk"

"Not to worry, Thelma." *Like hell.*

"I just received another call from him. He wants to know whether you two were doing more research…did I do something wrong?"

Oh shit, intruder alert! How did Rhodes glom onto this? Play it cool; don't show any concern. "Don't worry," he said and went to rise.

"You and Donnelly work for Joyce Locker, don't you?

"Technically we work for Dick Leeson, who works for Joyce." He smiled and sat again. "But yeah, we do." *Give us the dirt, Thelma.*

"What do you think of her?"

Boy, Thelma's really plain. No makeup and the lipstick looks like an afterthought. Could her glasses be any bigger? "I don't know much about her except she's smart, seems fair, and is attractive. Can you fill me in?"

Thelma's vice went lower. "Her father was the general manager of the entire Maqua Works. So was her grandfather. They're an old line Ilium family."

"I haven't heard of a Works manager."

"Oversaw everything. They eliminated the job some years ago," Thelma said. "It was Nick Jackson's suggestion—he worked for her father—Mr. Locker did it and took early retirement. Nick has gone off to bigger and better things. Joyce has known Nick Jackson since she was a child."

Now that's a dainty morsel. Wonder how many people know? "How old is she?"

"Not sure, early to mid-thirties. She's the youngest section manager in department history as well as being the first woman. And yes, she's very smart. She has a dual degree, with high honors, in English and Electrical Engineering from Rensselaer Poly and an MBA from Rochester Institute."

Thelma may not be a beauty but she sure is a fount of knowledge. "Stayed upstate?"

"Close to home; not sure why."

"Boyfriend?" said Collins. "Given her looks you'd think so." *Shit. Never thought of her that way, but she is a looker.*

45

Thelma paused. "She keeps her private life private. Except," she chuckled, "she works out two hours every morning before she comes to work. She has a black belt in one of the martial arts."

So that's why she's so trim and why she survives the martini regimen. "Impressive." *Come to think of it, it is.* Collins stood. "Thanks for the info, Thelma. Let me know if Rhodes or any of the others ask about us." He smiled. "For relative newbies, people sure are curious about us."

***

Collins climbed the stairs and went to Donnelly's cubicle. "Frank," he said, "Rhodes is on the scent." He told him about Thelma's conversations with Rhodes. "We better talk to Cox, ask if anyone's sniffing around."

"In person or by phone?" said Donnelly.

"In person, don't you think? We can check to see if Cox hedges. If not, we can bring him up to speed on where we are."

***

They sat in Cox's conference room. "So, no one from our department has been in contact with you?" said Donnelly. "People like Quentin Rhodes or Chase Winchester or Bob Dingmann?"

"No," said Cox. "The only person I've talked to, other than you two, is your boss. Dick Leeson is your boss, isn't he?"

"Unfortunately," said Collins. "What did he want?"

46

"Not much," said Cox. "The usual, I guess. Checking the charge number, what you guys were working on, what I thought of your ideas and so on."

"Shit," they both said.

"Huh?" said Cox. *They don't trust their own boss? What kind of a cutthroat department are these guys in?*

"Leeson doesn't care about any of our projects," said Collins. "Let's go over some of our ideas."

***

Donnelly and Collins had finished presenting their strategy. "So your proposal," Cox said, "is to take the chair from being a consumer offering into a crime-stopper solution?"

"Good summary," said Collins. "The consumer chair would have a separate identity, of course." He and Donnelly gathered their materials.

I'm an engineer. I'm not trained to consider these kinds of consequences. Are we heading for a police state? "Do you think things are getting so desperate in this country we'd go this far?"

"Don't know," Donnelly said. "We examine social trends and match them with applicable Ilium products and services. We extrapolated the chair's crime-fighting capability for a possible fit." *Besides, we were bored and this seemed like a neat idea. I doubt this'll ever get far, but better us than someone else.*

"Interesting," said Cox. *These two are quicker and sharper than I figured. They sound like straight shooters; might be worthwhile to listen to them. Could be good for my career.*

Time for a preemptive maneuver and an early warning system; this should tell us if Cox trusts us. "Do us a favor?" asked Donnelly.

"Such as?" said Cox, a note of caution in his voice.

47

"You may get other calls from our department regarding the chair. Jim and I would appreciate limiting your comments to the Electric Comfort Chair, and not today's discussion." Collins signaled agreement.

Cox thought for a minute and then thrust out a hand. "Deal."

***

"Did you get the memo about the department Christmas party?" Collins said to Donnelly on the way back to their office.

The shuttle bus let off some passengers and started up again. "Tomorrow night, if I remember correctly. Why?"

"I was told attendance is mandatory."

"So?" Donnelly said. "Where the hell else can you go in this town on a Thursday night two weeks before Christmas? Is the booze free?"

"Yes, according to Austin Shepherd."

"That I'd believe; it'd be the only way to get anyone to go." The bus stopped and they jumped out.

***

Harold Cox sat in his cubicle. *Finally some free time. Need to review yesterday's strategy bombshell. What do Donnelly and Collins want to do with my Comfort Chair? What did they say? Social trends and the chair's crime-fighting capability?* He started doodling on a piece of paper. *Jack up the voltage? Turn it into something different? Kill convicts? What's in it for them? What's in it for me?* He stopped. *If what those two say is correct, we might have a winner. I might have a winner.* The doodles turned to circuit diagrams.

An hour later Cox pushed the papers aside. *We can ramp up the voltage and use the Comfort Chair framework. So, no retooling for the chair per se, just the electrical.*

Cox's phone rang. "This is Harold Cox."

"Cox, this is George Kelso…"

My new department manager. What's going on? "Yes, sir, how can I help you?"

"You're the engineer in charge of the Comfort Chair project?"

"Yes, I am." *Now what?*

"I got a call from Burt Rawley. He's General Manager of the Advertising and Publicity Department. Burt is aware of this Comfort Chair and asked if we could get him one for their Christmas party tonight. I presume we have one…?"

Cox paused. "We have a prototype I guess they could use."

"Good. Burt's people will be over in an hour. Please have it ready. Oh…and Cox…?"

"Yes, sir?"

"I want a full briefing on this project tomorrow morning at eight."

The dial tone sounded in Cox's ear. *Great. I don't need this. Need to call Collins or Donnelly and find out what the heck happened.*

He was told they were gone for the day. He left no message. *I'll talk to them tomorrow.*

Chapter Six

2:30 p.m.: It was the Thursday afternoon of the Ilium Advertising and Publicity Department's annual Christmas party. Inside the Proteus Room of the Old Town Hotel the Exhibit Operation's Special Projects Team beavered away hanging the decorations. On an elevated platform they had constructed were a Christmas tree, a box of party favors, and the recently delivered prototype electric comfort chair for Burt Rawley to sit in during the introduction.

4:50 p.m.: Their work finished, the Special Projects Team adjourned to the hotel bar.

5:20 p.m.: The dwarfs who were to distribute the party favors and man the Christmas display arrived at the hotel dressed as elves. They found the door to the Proteus room locked and went to the bar, where they joined the crew from Exhibits.

5:30 p.m.: Clare Duckett, the Exhibit Operation's secretary, was bent over a conference table, butt high, panties on the floor and dress up on her shoulders. Burt Rawley pumped away behind her. As he thrust, one hand reached around and stroked her heaving breast. With his other hand he slapped her buttocks and yelled, "Giddyap." She flared her nostrils and whinnied in response and had an orgasm. Burt snorted and had one too.

Clare Duckett's relationship with Rawley was an open secret to everyone except her husband, Cal, a recently returned Vietnam vet and the manager of Electrical Installations for the Exhibit Operation. He had come back from the hotel to Exhibits to pick up Clare.

Hearing sounds coming from the conference room, he cracked the door open. A moment later, face burning, he shut it quietly and went to sit by her desk.

5:47 p.m.: Rawley departed for the Maqua Curling Club to fetch his wife, Portia, from a lady's lunch. Rawley was late and Portia seethed. They left the club in a stony silence.

5:55 p.m.: Cal and Clare Duckett left together for the party. Cal was uncharacteristically quiet on the drive over.

6:00 p.m.: The doors to the Proteus Room swung open. A group of early attendees surged forward. The bartenders braced for the onslaught.

6:02 p.m.: Bob Dingmann, head of the Consumer Group, arrived with a group of his followers. His face was long and smooth with a pendulous lower lip and unblinking brown eyes magnified by oversized horn-rimmed glasses. His lengthy black hair was combed straight back.

6:03 p.m.: A drunken art director from the industrial operation forgot his ticket. Spencer Holdsworth, one of Dingmann's charges, demanded ten dollars for a baggage tag he claimed was a ticket.

6:07 p.m.: The drunken art director gained admission by sketching a profile of the door attendant on the back of the baggage tag. The attendant informed him that there was no charge for tickets and Holdsworth had screwed him.

6:10 p.m.: The dwarfs and the Exhibits people remained in the hotel bar. Coming back from the men's room, the Exhibits supervisor glanced into the Proteus room and realized the party had begun.

6:12 p.m.: The Exhibits supervisor forged Burt Rawley's name on the hefty bar tab while the crowd stumbled into the party. The dwarfs circulated, coming on to every woman in the place.

51

6:15 p.m.: No one had booked a band. Agitated finger pointing ensued, followed by frantic phone calls. They found a DJ in the lounge, set to work a wedding the next day. Fortunately, he'd hooked the room up for sound.

6:16 p.m.: The group from Technical Publications sat at a table. Thick and meaty with a hoarse, loud way of talking, they resided at the bottom of the department food chain.

6:18 p.m.: Cal and Clare Duckett arrived. They settled with the group from Exhibits. Cal herded the dwarfs out of the party and behind the stage curtain. They insisted on bringing a round of drinks with them. Cal checked the work the Special Projects team performed onstage and in setting up the chair. He spent ten minutes making some adjustments and left with a satisfied smile on his face.

6:35 p.m.: Burt and Portia Rawley arrived. Behind Portia's peevish face lurked a shrewish tongue and the withering flesh of an old woman. She strutted by the table where the department secretaries sat. She clutched her mink shoulder wrap to her throat and ignored their existence.

"Would you look at those hands? Knuckles like a stevedore," snickered one brunette.

"Probably knocks Burt around to keep him in line," said another secretary.

"Done any good?" said another, cradling her 7 and 7.

"She's the queen and he's the knave," said Dingmann's secretary, Helen. "I'll bet she's remained loyal out of spite."

"He's just another sexual buccaneer grown old," cackled her friend, puffing on a cigarette.

"Ask Clare Duckett," said Marsha, Rawley's secretary, tipsy after three quick scotches. "She used to be like Snow White, but she's drifted." Realizing what she'd uttered, she put her hand over her mouth. Everyone laughed and hoisted their glasses.

"Egotistical bastards like him tend not to be hated," said Locker's secretary, Pat. "Their antics are respected for the sheer self-delusion that accompanies them." Her fingers were exquisitely arranged around a cigarette.

6:36 p.m.: Watching Burt Rawley's arrival, Dick Leeson casually mentioned to Joyce Locker he'd briefed Rawley on the Electric Comfort Chair and Rawley had indicated it might be more appropriate for Dingmann's group.

"You idiot," she hissed, running her hand along her Pucci scarf, resisting the urge to wrap it around Leeson's neck. "Why the hell did you do that?" She took a restrained sip of her martini and glared at Duff Wall and Opie Tarant, her go-to guys and general factotums. They rolled their eyes.

"Umma umma umma," stammered Leeson, grabbing his coffee cup and spilling half on his pants, "he told me he was meeting Nick Jackson and he asked me what was new." He swallowed the coffee. "I sort of told him about the chair and we had these two hotshot trainees working on it."

Rawley doesn't trust trainees. Sniff. "Did you tell Donnelly and Collins any of this?"

"Er, no."

"You know anything about those two?"

"Not really. They were assigned to me and they're sharp...that's about it."

"Those are two trainees you don't want to mess with," said Locker in a cautionary tone. "They're not the ordinary ex–frat boys you're accustomed to. They are a hard-nosed ex–New York City cop and a fire department investigator." She glared at Leeson. "So, Dick, anything else?"

"Rawley told Dingmann to get him one of the chairs for the party tonight." Leeson was sweating. "He'll be onstage sitting in the chair when the favors are distributed."

"Rawley told Dingmann to get a chair?"

Leeson nodded.

She finished her martini and mulled ways she could throttle Leeson's scrawny neck. She fingered her scarf again. Wall and Tarant waited for the explosion. Instead she held out his glass. "Get me another drink, Duff."

"Sure, Joyce." Wall went to the bar.

6:37 p.m.: Rawley left Portia to get a drink. His face was tied into a knot, indicative of an unfinished argument. His eyes were dark slits, his mouth partly open and twisted.

6:38 p.m.: Portia walked over to sit with the secretaries. False welcomes and shuffling greeted her as she approached.

After several minutes Portia blurted, "Just two nights ago Burt met with Nick Jackson and a group of very senior executives."

The secretaries stared at her.

"Oh yes, he did, didn't he?" Marsha said, and sipped her scotch.

6:40 p.m.: The buffet line opened. It appeared to have once been expensive food. Tonight it appeared to be presented for its second offering. A long line quickly formed.

6:45 p.m.: The DJ arrived and set up. Soon "I Heard It through the Grapevine" blasted through the speakers.

"Is it a realistic condition of life," said Rufus Hogg, "to ask a man to stick to one pair of tits, one pussy? Forever and ever and ever, just the one?" He raised his seventh drink and toasted his tablemates, Shepherd, Drake, Donnelly, and Collins. He inclined his head to where several women from the typing pool sat. "They're practicing their pouts. I'll fix that. Take notes."

He stood somewhat unsteadily and approached their table, drink in hand. "Hi, ladies," he said in his Texas drawl. "I'm Rufus Hogg, superstar; how do you like me so far?"

"I do," said a large-breasted woman named Wanda, who had been downing shots and beers. She came over to Hogg and put her arm around his waist.

Hogg blinked, his bluff called. He stared at her; Shepherd and Drake snickered. His drink spilled as he slurred in his best Rhett Butler imitation, "Frankly, my dear, I had someone a bit more elegant in mind." A tear slid down her cheek and she slapped him so hard his head turned 120 degrees.

Shepherd and Drake laughed the loud laugh of the inebriated. "Hogg's added another image to the ugly picture album behind his eyes," said Shepherd.

7:00 p.m.: "Ah, the company courtesan," Shepherd whispered as Bonnie Bilbie came toward their table. "Her breasts are the stars; the rest of her is the entourage." He downed his bourbon. "She's a highly desirable sexpot with exploitable curves and fine thighs."

"She's the epitome of slut chic," said Drake. "She's banged so many people she'll be buried in a y-shaped coffin."

Bilbie asked Hogg if he wanted to dance. The DJ played "Honky Tonk Women." He tottered and meandered with her to the floor.

"How'd you like to check out the adventure playground behind the zipper of my trousers?" he whispered, halfway into the song.

"After the party maybe," she said, "if all of you is still standing." 7:10 p.m.: Collins, bored, rose and wandered around the room, taking in the scene. He noted Joyce Locker staring off while conversations went on all around her. He went up behind her and said softly, "Are we having fun yet?"

She turned and laughed. "Duty," she murmured.

"Care to dance?" he said, as "Hooked on a Feeling" played. She slid into his arms as they moved slowly around the floor. *Nice, she fits really nice. Am I crazy? She's my boss.* The song ended and he escorted her back to her table and returned to a smirking Donnelly. Collins gave him a surreptitious middle finger.

7:20 p.m.: The room grew overheated, filled with people, whiskey, beer, and the smells of fried food. The hollow shout of voices echoed everywhere. Outside, the snow swirled.

Donnelly was drinking Jameson while Collins consumed gin martinis with beer chasers in an atmosphere of ruthless jocularity.

"Behold the entitled," said Collins, gesturing toward Dingmann's table. "They sit like crows on a fence, feigning conversational interest, forcing tiny laughs, and exaggerating their gestures. Bunch of posers."

"I worked for Dingmann on my first assignment," said Drake. "He possesses all the vices of a bad boss and none of the virtues of a good one. He's an irony-free zone plus a dour, humorless personality."

"Them boys worship at ol' Dingmann's feet," said Hogg.

"Benefits of a privileged education," muttered Donnelly. "They're looking for the best place to stick the knife."

"You New York guys sure have a cynical attitude," said Shepherd, tossing back a shot.

"Realistic," said Donnelly and Collins simultaneously.

"Fill us in on this hush-hush project you two are working on," said Drake.

Hogg and Shepherd held their drinks at their mouths, a raptor's look on their faces.

56

"Hush-hush project?" said Donnelly. "We're here but seven months, mere trainees, not big-shot almost-finished-the-program hotshots like you slobs."

Microphone feedback squeal diverted their attention to the makeshift stage and Dexter Warren, the manager of Technical Publications. His lame opening joke brought the place to stunned silence. He attributed the dearth of laughter to the PA system. Warren had a tiresome habit of giggling and shaking his shoulders up and down when he laughed. He launched into a long-winded introduction of Burt Rawley in his whiny up-and-down voice.

The curtain rose to an empty stage, save for a Christmas tree and a lump covered with shiny cloth. Rawley walked out, surrounded by the elf-dressed dwarfs, loaded with party favors. They were obviously drunk, an assembly of pantomime imps lit up with laughing gas.

Rawley waved. The dwarfs took this as a cue and ran off the stage, throwing the party favors at the various tables. They continued to the back of the room and went out the door to a raucous bellow.

"Merry Christmas, everybody!" Rawley roared. He stepped back and removed the fabric from the lump sheet. "New, from Ilium Electric, the Electric Comfort Chair!" he yelled, to a round of applause.

Collins and Donnelly glanced at each other. Donnelly's face darkened and he and Collins turned to Locker. She mouthed "Leeson," who studiously avoided their gaze. "Later," Locker murmured.

Rawley launched into a three-minute monologue on the merits of the Comfort Chair and how Bob Dingmann and his team would be promoting this latest consumer product.

Donnelly and Collins fumed. Quentin Rhodes, from Dingmann's section, slid in between them. He had the thinnest lips

Donnelly had ever seen. "We'll need a briefing on the chair from you fellows," he said. "For the weeks after that you can continue the polite deception of reasonable activity. Shall we say Monday?"

"If we're in the office," said Collins and drank his martini. "Goodbye." He turned his attention to the stage.

Shepherd, Hogg, and Drake watched Rhodes depart. "I guess your secret project ain't so secret anymore," said Drake. "And for shit-sure it ain't yours either. Good going, rookies."

"…and the controls for the Electric Comfort Chair allow you to customize your comfort level." Rawley grasped the control, ostentatiously punched a button and plopped into the seat. He squirmed as he tried to adjust his position. "Uh, it appears I'm pinned here. I don't seem able to move." He began to twitch and a soft moan escaped his lips. The moan quickly turned into forty-second high-octane scream, which abruptly ceased.

People rushed to the perimeter of the stage and skidded to a halt. They wanted to see the car crash but no one wanted to be in the car.

The smell hit them first, leaving them gasping. "Whew, who cut one?" someone said. "That's on the triple-flutter blast scale."

"That was no fart, man. Look at him." Rawley sprawled in the chair, head back, face gray, yellowed teeth clearly visible.

"The full Vesuvius," another said. "Open mouth in rictus."

"Somebody better call an ambulance," said Shepherd.

"Appears like it's too late," said Collins.

"They'll likely pin this on Cox," murmured Donnelly

"Bet on it," said Collins. "Let's tamp things down."

Applying skills learned as police and fire professionals they spent several minutes reassuring people and affirming matters would be efficiently conducted. Their unspoken mission was to try to find out what happened.

***

"It couldn't be suicide," Portia Rawley said to a detective. "Like I told the girls, Burt said he'd had a successful meeting with Nick Jackson this past Monday. "Wouldn't the future seem bright?" The translucent creases around her eyes looked like cracks in an ice cube."

The Maqua police had finally arrived. A detective made a note.

After he left, Portia continued to shudder, an elaborate body spasm with a hand on her ample breast and the other fanning her face, like a Victorian matron having the vapors. She wiped a tear, in shock now. "He was kind, but his vast responsibilities made our marriage difficult."

Clare Duckett returned with her colleagues to their table. "They say Mr. Rawley is dead," she said to her husband, a tremor in her voice.

"Oh?" He nonchalantly sipped his beer.

"He's dead, Cal, he's dead." Her body shook.

"I figure he won't go horseback riding no more," he said, and finished the beer. "Can I get you another drink?"

Fear seized her as realization dawned. "No," she croaked.

Elsewhere, the room buzzed with comments and observations.

"Do you think all of a sudden Rawley is the Ghost of Relevance Past?"

"I hope they haul the body out of the casket at the viewing, prop him up in a chair, put a drink in one hand and a cigarette in the other. If he doesn't take a drag or a swallow we'll know the son of a bitch is dead for sure."

"There goes the curling club."

"Yeah; the suckups will have to find a new hobby."

"These corporate training programs are all the same…hire top-shelf college graduates, even advanced-degree people, and put them in jobs supervised by thirty-year veterans. These time-servers, out of fear for their own positions, lock them in cubicles and slip their checks under the door every two weeks. In the meanwhile they intimidate and oppress them long enough to hold still for the company logo to be tattooed, metaphorically, on their forehead."

"Quite a mouthful."

"True, but I describe reality. Name someone around here who likes their boss, much less the imperial manipulators two levels up. I strongly suspect any of the senior managers would stab a peer without a second thought. And they all know it. Welcome to Ilium."

"Welcome to corporate America."

The police sealed off the Proteus room and began interviewing. Most had sobered up. A car was dispatched to the dwarfs' hotel. Three hours later, the partygoers were released. The chair needed to be scrutinized before they could draw any conclusions. The search for the dwarfs failed to locate them.

Donnelly and Collins made their way over to Locker's table, drinks in hand. "Where's Leeson?" they asked.

"Saw you two coming and hightailed it out of here."

"Are we screwed on this?" asked Donnelly.

"I don't think so," Locker replied. "Dingmann pulled a fast one, thanks to Leeson's stupidity. I don't take kindly to that." She gestured to the platform. "Any ideas?" Police still swarmed around the chair.

"It's hard to believe, but did you consider he might have been *murdered?*" Collins asked calmly.

Tarant and Wall looked surprised. Locker didn't. "What makes you think that? Are your ex-investigator skills coming into play here?"

"For one thing, Rawley appeared to be pinned in the seat before the electric current got him." Collins sipped his drink. "Only a serious design flaw or tampering would cause something like that to happen."

"Rawley was struggling and he yelled something about being stuck," added Donnelly. "I'm sure the locals will follow up. Getting the perp is another matter."

"The dwarfs?" ventured Wall.

No one gave the remark the dignity of a response. Wall flushed.

Locker stood. "Homage may be tasteless so soon, but one is sometimes moved to a wave of sentiment for a flawed man. To Burt Rawley!" They all followed. "Past the lips, over the tongue, down to L'Fey, here we come!" She downed the drink and headed into the snowy night, everyone trooping after.

The after-process began at the already crowded L'Fey. The evening's events were broken down, chewed, and reduced into complicated indigestible morsels. "Terrible, I'll never forget it…tragic…" The reactions of the authorities were explored. Before long they had beaten the tragedy to death and the snake swallowed the pig.

***

The Ilium logo pierced the haze of the Manhattan morning, a swirl of letters glowing from the tall, sleek building sporting the company name. On the highest floor Nick Jackson sat in his office, a phone in one hand and a pen in the other. "You're telling me Burt Rawley was electrocuted last night? In one of the Electric Comfort Chairs he was nattering about in Maqua on Monday?"

"At his department's Christmas party, no less. The police say it was murder."

"See to it that Rawley's death stays a local story," Jackson said and hung up. *A general manager position to fill. What about this Comfort Chair? Does it have consumer potential like Rawley said it did?* He pressed the intercom. "Florence, get me the new general manager at Low Voltage Switchgear."

A minute later she buzzed him. "George Kelso's on the line."

"Kelso, are you up to speed on the Rawley situation?"

"Yes, terrible..."

"The matter could be serious. We'll keep the publicity local. Is the chair safe?" Visions of lawsuits flitted through Jackson's head.

"Yes. It's undergone rigorous testing. My understanding is someone, somehow rigged the chair to glue Rawley to it. The voltage was somehow then amplified to provide a killing current. A nasty way to go."

"How difficult is it to rig the chair to produce that kind of result?"

"The glue part? Not at all. The electrical? Very. Whoever did it is highly knowledgeable."

"Okay, we'll get back to you." A muted lamp cast a soft shadow on Jackson's balding head. His pallid complexion was lined with wrinkles that congregated about pale blue eyes framed under thick black brows. As he mulled over the situation he tugged at the cuffs of his Savile Row suit.

***

Harold Cox trudged through the almost-empty Ilium parking lot, searching for his car in an igloo village of snow-covered vehicles. He bent over against the cold, protecting his eyes with his arms. Circles of white light advanced out of the ice-white dust toward him. He jumped aside as a car whipped by. *Another contented Ilium worker wanting to get away from the place as fast as possible.*

Car at last located, Cox brushed the three-inch deep layer off the car, painfully scraped the ice from the windshield, broke the frozen wipers away from the glass, chipped the car lock free, climbed in, and started off. Stores, streets, cars appearing like charging Yetis burst into vision, then vanished, swallowed by a swirling white storm. Cox drove slowly, the wind howling, the snow piling up in drifts, his headlights weak white cones in the blinding night.

As the car sluiced though the snow, Cox examined the day. *Possibly a career worst. The 3 a.m. phone call about Burt Rawley's death at the A&P Christmas party. Dragged over to examine the chair and talk to the police. Cretins. Hearing the obvious: Rawley glued down, the chair rewired. The son of a bitch knew his onions. Thank god they took the body away. What a stench. Worse than the men's room on a Monday morning. Didn't realize there could be a smell as bad.*

From the crime scene into the office. Meeting with the new general manager, George Kelso. Implied it was my fault. But Kelso was the one who authorized the chair be sent for Burt Rawley to use at the A&P party. Wonder who gave the cops my name? Donnelly? Collins? Have to tell them I had nothing to do with any of this.

Okay, I'm home. Let's be careful in the driveway. Golly, more snow here than in Iowa. Christmas is in two weeks; maybe I can go visit the family, see mom and dad. Need to call them. They're getting on in years. Park here. Right. Get my stuff and go into the flat. God, I'm tired. Cox carefully climbed the icy steps.

The key jammed. Cox muttered and wiggled the lock and pushed. The door did not give. Stuck again. Finally after more finagling the door popped open. Cox stumbled in and immediately began to sing. "Doff we now our guy apparel." Off came the coat, the shoes, the tie and the pants. As the shirt was shed a tight binding around the chest appeared. Still singing, Cox undid the binding and a pair of size thirty-four breasts appeared.

Harold Cox, the undistinguished caterpillar, became the butterfly, Harriet Cox. She breathed a deep sigh and rubbed her chest, massaging it as if to restore some life. "Don we now our gal apparel," she continued, rummaging in a drawer for her nightgown, "fa la la la la la la la la."

After a microwaved meal Cox flopped on her bed, exhaustion claiming her. As she drifted off, the phone rang. She picked up and her mother asked, after the usual pleasantries, what was new.

"Oh my, you've had some day." her mother said, after she finished.

Cox let out a long slow breath. "I certainly have, Mom."

"Are you still posing as a man?"

"I've no choice, mom. Women engineers are a nonexistent species at Ilium. It's amazing the deference with which Harold Cox is treated by men and women. If they knew I was a woman, they'd slot me as a secretary and I'd be brewing and serving coffee in no time."

Her mother made appropriately sympathetic noises. "Have you met any nice young men, dear?"

Not likely. This is a company town. The men are all married or raving idiot trainees who get transferred out as soon as they can put their shoe on the correct foot. Rather than get into an extended discussion, she said, "Not yet, Mom. Tell Dad I love him too."

Her mother caught the tiredness in her voice and the call ended.

The phone was barely back in the cradle before Harriet Cox was sound asleep.

Chapter Seven

Abe Floss's intercom buzzed. "Justin Hitchcock is on line one."
"Justin, how are you?"
"I'm fine," said Hitchcock. "I have to confess, though, conditions worsened faster than I thought."
"I agree," said Floss. "Construction workers attacking student demonstrators."
"The students are out of control, as are their teachers and administrators," said Hitchcock. "Those students never did anything productive in their lives. They take their tactics from Fidel Castro and their cash from daddy. It was these same radicals who tried to assassinate Nixon, and look where we are now."
Floss sighed. "Congress fiddles and fights and the country burns. Riots in Detroit, Newark, Memphis, and Stockton. Few arrests and those have been overturned. The police are hamstrung. Civil order is deteriorating at a rapid pace. We need laws passed to deal with this."
Hitchcock sipped his afternoon tea, an estate Assam. "Or judges with backbone. To be honest, Abe, Vice President Agnew is not helping matters. Nixon's people are prodding him; he's dividing when he should be uniting. Not the time to throw around emotion-laden statements in public like calling enemies of the administration 'vicars of vacillation.' You can't call opposition Democrats 'ideological eunuchs' or say the press is dominated by a 'tiny and closed fraternity, elected by no one.'"

Floss stared off into the horizon from his K Street office window. "I don't think either one of us want the vice-president of the United States sounding like a half-loaded barfly."

"We need to turn up the heat," said Hitchcock.

"Agreed," said Floss. He disconnected and made another call.

"Al," said Floss to a senior Democratic senator, "we're in stasis when we shouldn't be." He cradled the phone with his shoulder. "You need to get things going."

"Abe, we're just too intellectual," the senator said. "We like to read and think. We thrive on policy debates, arguments, statistics, and getting the facts right." He paused. "Unlike the opposition across the aisle and those yahoos they represent."

"America's in serious trouble, Al." Floss pressed his lips together in aggravation.

"Our views are correct and self-evident," said the senator, "based on fact and reason. Their positions are based on emotion, not just wrong but illegitimate and unworthy of serious consideration…"

Floss breathed out in exasperation. *Windbags like Al are causing the country to shatter like a broken window.*

"…and we dump all those right-wing reactionaries into the Texas Panhandle, create, if you'll pardon the expression, the state of Dumbass Fuckistan, and build a wall around it to keep them from coming back into America."

End this now. It's clear he's become a populist since his views are less accepted. "Well, thanks for your perspectives, Senator," said Floss. "I'll be approaching you regarding some legislation that we'd like passed. I trust you'll cooperate?"

The senator understood. One did not cross Abe Floss. "You can be assured of it, Abe."

***

Later in the afternoon the Republican Senate Minority Leader entered Justin Hitchcock's Washington office. He scanned the surroundings. Understated, like the man himself. Extremely functional. Neat, too. All his business dealings and his workplace communicated that message very clearly. Hitchcock greeted the senator with a warm smile.

"Good to see you, Lloyd. Please," Hitchcock gestured to an adjacent table, "make yourself comfortable. You take your bourbon neat if I remember correctly. I'll join you in a glass."

The refreshments served, Hitchcock quickly got down to business. "The Congress is in gridlock and the country is going up in flames. How do you think we can deal with the issues that are ripping us apart?"

The senator drummed his fingers and weighed his response. "Any appeals to bipartisanship, those fellows on the other side of the aisle join in a chorus of intellectual condescension. They think they are entitled to save people from themselves. There is no private discussion. None. Publicly they bludgeon our views with public assertions on television and through their allies in the media." He sipped his drink.

"Can we find common ground?"

"I don't see how. If you are one of the select, which includes my liberal colleagues, you are entitled to always be right. They characterize themselves as intellectuals; meanwhile, criminals and looters run rampant and go scot-free in the cities. Murder rates have quintupled. Nothing happens. We have an effete corps of impudent snobs who defend these dregs."

Hitchcock sighed, realizing this as the truth.

Chapter Eight

"Hello," Len Lovelace croaked after the sixth ring. *Where the hell is Shirley? I should never have downed that Manhattan last night. Thought I'd ordered a martini. The Real Man's rule is no gin and vermouth, no martini. Brain-mouth coordination went haywire. The wife didn't help with a half-hour harangue in the car on the way home. Never stops. OK, I pulled over and hurled. That damn Manhattan was something from Preppie Hell. What I get for fraternizing with the strivers. Good-looking women, though.*

"Len, Joyce Locker here."

"Hold your voice down, Joyce. I'm trying to snap back from the weekend." Lovelace had the blinds drawn in his office to keep out the cheerful sun.

"A martini with tomato juice and bitters on the side usually works."

Lovelace groped for a cigarette. "Don't even say the word martini to me. Damn bartender slipped me a Manhattan for my last."

"The pity party will be Wednesday at L'Fey," said Locker. "To the matter at hand." *Sniff.* "When you hired Donnelly and Collins for the program did you delve into their backgrounds? Why hire them? They're outside the usual mold."

"We conducted an experiment. We wanted people who had work experience, who didn't think the office was an extension of the frat house. As to how deep we went? Much more than usual. Why?"

"They're working on a project that could become high profile. Possibly even get in front of Nick Jackson. The last part is for your ears only. You've done a thorough sneak and peek on those two?"

"Yes. After lunch?"

"See you at my place, okay?" she said.

***

Locker's intercom buzzed. "Mr. Lovelace is here."

"Send him in." Ten seconds later Lovelace steamed in.

"You sure as hell recovered fast."

"I followed your advice on the bitters and tomato juice." He took a puff on his cigarette. "But I changed the formula and laid in a couple of snorts of rum."

"You trying for the hitters club?"

"I'm not in your league, Joyce. Unlike you, I didn't have them all together."

"Try not to puke on my rug, Len."

Lovelace took another drag and opened a folder. "No reason to get snotty. I'll begin with Donnelly. The man has more going on than an episode of *Hogan's Heroes*; Collins does too. You need to know this if you're putting these guys with Jackson."

"Okay."

"Francis Dylan Donnelly, born May 11, 1945, at Lutheran Hospital in Brooklyn. His father, Sean Donnelly, was in the New York Fire Department, working his way up to captain and was in charge of a firehouse in Red Hook, Brooklyn. That's a tough neighborhood, Joyce. Mother, Ruth Dillon Donnelly, housewife. Six kids. Frank is in the middle. One of his two sisters is a nun; another brother was a seminarian but dropped out. All of them whip-smart. I have their names and ages on file if you want them."

"Catholics," said Locker. "Like Groucho said, 'I love my cigar too, but I take it out once in a while.'"

Lovelace took a deep drag on his cigarette. "Ha, ha. Family lived in Crown Heights section of Brooklyn until right before the neighborhood exploded in the mid-fifties—a rising incidence of weapons-related stuff in the area, including shotguns and machine guns. Place was getting overly dangerous for those unarmed. Father moved the family when Frank was about twelve from Crown Heights to Flatbush, still in Brooklyn but out of the hot spot."

"Sounds like Crown Heights was a war zone."

"To continue, no record of any delinquency." He looked up. "Not surprising. Donnelly had all kinds of relatives on the police force so unless he committed a major crime, he probably got a pass. A ton of kid gangs were in the city then but Donnelly doesn't appear to have been in one." He took a puff. "That's significant. Donnelly and whatever friends he had must have been tough cookies to avoid that kind of pressure. Okay, a few minor scrapes, several street fights."

Sniff. "Fists only?"

"Usually. Zip guns were common but no record of Donnelly having one. And he appeared to always be the winner." Another puff.

"Go on."

"The usual for a city kid. Some trespass, got caught in a bar at fourteen. The sin was getting caught. I'm sure he got it worse from his folks than at the precinct."

"Talk to any neighbors on those?"

"Yeah. My lady Maureen canvassed the neighborhood. She looks like a St. Patrick's Day queen. Good blarney, motherly. People take to her and she got plenty of feedback. Said he was clean. No strong-arm stuff, B&E, or anything."

"Where'd he go to primary school?" *Sniff.*

"The parish elementary school, Crucifixion. Okay student until sixth grade; seemed to get interested in science and literature. Marks took off on an upward curve. Minor disciplinary. Couple of fights."

"High school?"

"Cardinal Mothoin. College prep curriculum. Concentrated in the physical sciences. Good grades. All-city in baseball and third team in basketball. Full academic boat to Duns Scotus College. Did it in three years and graduated cum laude. Triple major in English, math, and philosophy. Marks could have been a little better but he also majored in fun seeking. Once, he wound up standing in the lobby of the Plaza Hotel at eight in the morning, a girl on each arm, clueless on what happened. Another where he and two buddies climbed on a stage at a parish dance. The friends held up Ws and Donnelly spread his cheeks and mooned the crowd. Said they spelled 'wow.' Drunk as skunks. Couple of minor infractions; typical party problems."

Locker half-smiled. "Define party problems."

Lovelace stubbed out his cigarette and lit another. "You know. Cops broke up a loud neighborhood party or two. Some substances on premises. No known origin. No one holding. Our boy looks innocent."

"I doubt Donnelly has ever been innocent."

"Right. But he wasn't close enough to any liquid or solid refreshments to be besmirched."

She leaned back. "Good pilot too; adept at flying below the radar."

"I concur. He's a 'do-a-lot-but-don't-get-caught-a-lot' guy."

"I see him in the same light."

"So"—a drag on the cigarette—"graduated at twenty and into the army's communications and electronics program." To Locker's quizzical glance, he said, "CECOM Fort Monmouth, NJ, rank, private first class. Turned down Officer Candidate School based on length of commitment. Good service record. Liked by fellow soldiers and command. One disciplinary action, a giant bar brawl in Asbury Park. So many detainees the army slapped everybody with leave cancellations and unpleasant detail assignments and wrote it off. The army team won the fight. Like the city parties, our boy was present and accounted for but not an identifiable participant."

"The Shadow."

"Check."

"Given his specialty, why no Vietnam service?"

Lovelace leaned forward. "Seems Donnelly got his records lost." He tapped an ash. "Instead of sending his records back to his reserve unit, Donnelly somehow contrived to have them sent to the army records operation, which is where your records go when your obligation is finished." He took a drag on his cigarette. "That last one was a bitch to find out."

"So Donnelly is an operator." *That is an epic achievement. How the hell was he able to get them lost? On another day.* "Then?"

"After the army he joined the fire marshal group at FDNY investigating origins and causes."

"Tell me about them."

"The New York fire marshals are armed police officers with full powers of arrest. They generally work in pairs and investigate serious fires. Donnelly received comprehensive police training that included annual weapons qualification with all firearms available to the police. He also underwent special training at the FBI Academy in Quantico."

"Impressive training." *More than impressive.* "How'd he wind up at Ilium?"

"He was paired with a grizzled vet and together they made a name for themselves closing a bunch of investigations, some of them implicating connected people."

"Connected how?" *Sniff.* "Be specific, Len."

"Political bosses, rabbis, the mob. All of them slumlords, and all of them publicity-averse. In a way, good for Donnelly, but he became a marked man. His partner didn't give a damn; he was nearing his twenty years of service, eligible for retirement, and could go out with a flourish. Right before his partner retired a slumlord burned down an entire building while five families slept. Donnelly and his partner went after him. Turns out he was a top aide to the mayor, who had to publicly disown him. Given the way things work in the city, powerful forces aligned against Donnelly's advancement."

"Ouch," said Locker, understanding.

Lovelace nodded. "The situation developed into an issue in the subsequent election. Not-so-subtle pressure was applied for Donnelly's partner to retire immediately and for Donnelly to be transferred as far away as possible."

"What happened?" Locker reached into her desk and pulled out a cigarillo.

"Some old bulls caved and Donnelly wound up in Tottenville, at the southernmost end of Staten Island. He served six months and then quit."

"He went quietly?" Locker lit the cigarillo and sent the first plume upward.

Lovelace shook his head in admiration. "Within three months everyone involved in his transfer found themselves in violation of various department rules. Each was serious enough to force their resignations."

She put the cigarillo in the ashtray and laughed. "How very Irish. 'Don't get mad; get even.' Exquisite. And?"

"He almost got on at the *New York Times* but some guy from Yale used his family links and landed the job. Ilium was his second choice, and he wouldn't be here if we'd hired on our old criteria."

"Hell of a background."

"To summarize. Fighter. Quick study. Planner. Disciplined. Technically competent. Risk-taker. Chameleon qualities when they suit him. Good writer, good communicator. Fit. Self-assured." Lovelace took a drag and winked at Locker. "Watch out, Ilium Board of Directors."

"Amusing."

"I knew you'd agree. Let's get to Collins. He's as much fun, trust me." Lovelace put another file on the desk.

"Once more, with feeling," said Locker, puffing.

"James Brian Collins, born November 14, 1944, at Our Lady of Mercy Medical Center in the Bronx. His father, Martin Collins, was in the New York Police Department and rose to the rank of inspector. He spent his career mostly in the Bronx. Mother, Mary Margaret Treanor Collins, a housewife. Four kids. Jim is the third. One sister, the younger one, is a rookie cop. A brother works for CBS; the other is career military. A major, currently stateside. Like Donnelly's family they're all smart. I have their names and ages on file if you want them."

"Well," said Locker, "not as fecund as the Donnelly family."

"Noted," said Lovelace. "They lived in the Tremont section of the Bronx until things began to change, similar to Crown Heights. Mr. Collins moved the family to the Norwood area, an Irish enclave in the upper Bronx, when Collins was in third grade.

"Sounds like Tremont was another war zone." Locker took another pull on the cigarillo.

"Things were changing in the city; some areas faster than others." Lovelace lit a cigarette and took a puff. "In fifth grade a hit-and-run driver knocked Collins over while he was riding his bike. He broke a bunch of bones and incurred some internal injuries. He lost a year of school recuperating." Another puff. "He recovered fully."

"Good. School?" *Sniff.*

"The parish school, Crown of Thorns. Okay student until he lost the year. Apparently his convalescence triggered an academic turnaround."

"High school?"

"St. Sebastian, a quasi-military high school in the Bronx. Outstanding academics, pretty strict discipline, and sports."

Locker frowned. "Why a military high school?"

"We think Collins was involved with a gang; they called themselves the Norwood Boys." He looked up. "We couldn't ascertain for sure. The Norwood Boys did some serious shit, Joyce. Many of them are still in jail. I'm guessing his cop father got tipped off and put the clamps on young Jim. Going to a place like St. Sebastian's probably saved him."

"So Collins became a straight arrow?" Locker placed her cigarillo in the ashtray.

"Not exactly." Lovelace blew a smoke ring. "St. Sebastian's had a college prep curriculum. Excellent grades. Played football, all-city at end. Didn't play baseball or basketball but was a top-flight pitcher in an industrial league. Rumor had it he couldn't stand the St. Sebastian baseball coach so he wouldn't play for the school. Approached by several teams but the father said no way, you're going to college." He shrugged. "Must be an Irish attribute, education before cash. Had an academic scholarship to Roger Bacon. Like Donnelly, graduated summa cum laude in three years with a triple major."

"The straight arrow part?"

"In his last year of high school and first year at Roger Bacon, Collins and his buddies ran monthly beer blasts. They'd rent a hall, charge ten bucks a head, provide tight security, and make a respectable piece of change."

Sniff. "Entrepreneurial. Why'd he stop?"

"The mob tried to muscle in. He was a college student with a lot to lose, so he walked away." He chuckled. "But not far."

"Details?"

"Six months after the mob muscled in, a series of articles ran in the *New York Post* naming names and detailing the mob's illegal drinking parties with underage drinkers. The *Times* and the *News* picked it up, as did the local TV guys. Pictures of the police raids; multiple indictments."

Locker shook her head. *Sniff.* "He and Donnelly make an ideal pair."

"Oh, yeah. He also did the same kind of stunts as Donnelly; you can check them out if you want…"

"No," said Locker, "I get the hang of their plot. After college?"

"He graduated and signed up for the Navy's six-month reserve program. Received cryptology training. Good service record. One disciplinary action. Told an officer to, if you'll pardon the expression, go fuck himself when the guy wanted him to leave his station during a training exercise. The ensuing hearing deemed Collins correct and the officer out of line. This did not make said officer Collins's new best friend."

"Obviously something happened," said Locker.

"The lieutenant ran into him in a crowded off-base bar, both in civvies. The lieutenant, who considered himself a martial arts expert, tried to take Collins out. In two minutes Collins beat the living crap out of him. Someone phoned the MPs and the net result was no one bothered Collins anymore. Shortly afterward Collins's enlistment was up."

"Why wasn't he called back?"

"Because he's like Donnelly," said Lovelace. "He had an angle. Apparently a petty officer in personnel liked what Collins had done to that officer. He sent Collins's records to the navy records center in Bainbridge, Maryland, where they won't surface for eight years. No reserve duty, no call-ups."

"How'd you find this out?"

"Had someone dig real deep; all the way to Bainbridge and back. Discreetly, of course. Did the same with Donnelly. My guy left no fingerprints."

"So, Collins is another operator." *Not bad to dance with either.* "These two are real pieces of work." *Nick has to hear about this.* "After that?"

Lovelace looked down. "The New York City Police Department. Top of his class at the Academy."

"Where did he get assigned?"

"Midtown South, primo duty. Collins took advantage of the opportunity. Within a year he had several citations and been targeted as a real comer." Lovelace consulted the file. "Six months later he was seconded for what is called in his record, 'special assignment.' Unclear as to the training he got, or where, but he came back and was promoted to detective in a unit that reported directly to the commissioner."

"What did they do?" *What's the deal with this guy?*

"Unknown. We suspect it combined his NYPD experience with his cryptology training but we can't be sure."

"Obviously on the fast track." Locker shrugged, palms up.

"New mayor and his new commissioner disbanded the unit. Collins went to a precinct. That's when the sharks took a run at him. His group had done too well and indicted scores of people. There were accusations they ignored people's rights. They made a bunch of enemies among the bad folks and within the department. Same types as Donnelly ran into, only harder guys. Collins took all his unpaid leave and quietly left the force."

Sniff. "How'd he get even?"

Lovelace laughed in recognition. "Anyone who went after him who was bent found themselves under IRS investigation for hidden financials. Several of the cases received publicity. Interestingly, nobody ever considered Collins; he'd just faded into the woodwork."

"Was he behind it?" She stifled a sniff.

"Oh, absolutely. We talked with his ex-partner; he called Collins, got his permission, and told us."

Locker shook her head. "Brilliant. He who laughs last, laughs best."

Lovelace checked the file once more. "Like Donnelly, someone with old boy connections aced him out of a job. In Collins's case it was *Time* magazine."

Locker puffed on her cigarillo, saying nothing.

"To summarize briefly. Similar to Donnelly. I'm hearing they're stirring the pot in the A&P Department." He tapped an ash and winked at Locker. "Once again, watch out, Ilium Board of Directors."

Locker grimaced while chuckling.

Chapter Nine

"Mr. Jackson, Joyce Locker is here."

Nick Jackson pushed the internal report on Burt Rawley's death aside and came out from behind his desk. "Send her in, Florence, and bring us some coffee, please."

The door opened and Florence led Joyce Locker into the office. She was dressed in an understated Givenchy suit. Jackson had known Joyce Locker all his life; she was the closest thing to a younger sister that Nick Jackson had. He kissed her chastely on the cheek and gave her a hug. "Joyce, thanks for coming down here. How's your dad?" Jackson's first boss and subsequent mentor had been her father.

"Annoying my mother," Locker said, "something he has refined into an art form."

Jackson, knowing her parents, laughed. After several minutes of small talk he said, "Tell me about Rawley. I'm tempted to accuse all you people of barbecuing him."

"Rawley's death isn't worth your time, Nick. The police inquiry is ongoing."

"They have anyone yet?"

"They're trying to find some dwarfs who were backstage just before Rawley got juiced." She muffled her sniff.

"Dwarfs?" *Is this what's going on up in Maqua, an alternate reality Ilium?*

81

Locker held up a hand. "The dwarfs were part of the Christmas party program." Jackson stared at him. "Nick, it was like Disney on acid with those little bastards. Then Rawley fried and the dwarfs— they were all drunk, someone said—vaporized. That's why the cops are looking for them."

"I have a question for you, Joyce," said Jackson. He pressed his lips together and leaned back. "With Rawley gone, his job is open. It's yours if you want it. I'd like nothing better than to appoint a woman as a general manager."

She smiled. "Thanks, Nick, but no. It's a bit too soon. I'd probably punch someone; too much bullshit." She reached for her coffee cup. "And it would interfere with my social life."

Jackson nodded. *The only social life she has these days has been with a drink.* "I'm not surprised, but you were the obvious choice. On to other subjects. I want a presentation on this Comfort Chair, its possibilities, and the promotional plans for it. Is your gang on the project?"

"First off, thanks for the nomination. If you ever need anything up here let me know and it'll be done."

"I know. Thanks, Joyce."

"Back to the chair. For a while we were developing a full-bore rollout with some exciting ideas but Dingmann, the consumer guy, convinced Rawley to put his people on it."

"Dingmann?"

Locker sipped her coffee, wishing it was a martini. "Dingmann's a mama's boy with a Harvard degree and all the smarmy suckup skills to get ahead in life. He takes only like people in his group and is a limp-dicked backstabber." He pushed the cup aside. "In other words, Nick, he's an asshole."

If Joyce Locker thinks he's an asshole, he must be a first-rate one. "Get you and your people in my conference room next Friday. I want anyone who has touched this chair project down here. Who've you got on this?"

Locker peered over her coffee cup. "Two trainees." She sipped. "But they're unlike any trainees you've ever seen."

"They better be," said Jackson. "Who knows you're here today?"

"Only my secretary and she keeps her mouth shut."

"Okay, I'll see you at the presentation. Make sure these trainees are ready. I look forward to seeing Mr. Dingmann." He stood. "Regards to your dad."

"One suggestion, Nick?" she said, pausing by the door.

"Yes?"

"Have your Washington guy here for the meeting. Trust me on this." She chuckled and stepped out.

***

Donnelly and Collins walked down Third Avenue after setting up for the next morning's presentation at Ilium's headquarters. Once again New York was theirs, the chill nighttime air welcoming them. They were back, albeit briefly, from exile in Maqua.

"Where'd Locker go?" said Collins. Their hotel was a small, quiet place of the better sort, tucked on a side street away from the noise and the traffic.

"Said she'd meet us in the bar in about an hour," Donnelly said. They climbed the three steps and through the brass-bound plate glass door, savoring the moment, and surveyed the scene. The lobby table lamps illuminated the patterned carpet, shading the walls into an inky remoteness. The chairs were empty, with a three-elevator bank on one side and the reception desk on the other. The clerk eyed them and yawned.

"Drink?" Collins said.

"Oh, yeah," said Donnelly, heading to the elevators. "Meet you in the bar in fifteen minutes. Are Dingmann and his folks staying here?"

"Don't care," said Collins and pushed the button for his floor.

***

"Center stage tomorrow," said Donnelly, sipping his beer. "Do you think we're ready for prime time?" He reached for the bowl of nuts.

"We're prepared, you know that. But we're on the back bench, the players to be named later," said Collins. "We'll be wall ornaments while Dingmann and his overeducated eunuchs present their 'dot-dot-dot' Electric Comfort Chair concepts to Nick the Zipper and his lackeys."

"I hear Dingmann threw a shit-fit when Jackson's office made it clear that he wanted all hands touching the chair in the meeting." Donnelly pushed his glass to the side. "He told Jackson's office that he wasn't aware of anyone else who'd been involved with the chair. Jackson's office essentially said 'think again' and Dingmann blinked."

"Not an auspicious start," said Collins, reaching for his martini. "Locker's hand is in this. Who's presenting for them?"

"Dingmann himself," said Donnelly. "He wants the spotlight. Dot-dot has a career enhancer. Rhodes will be the slide feeder and Winchester the flipchart flipper. "

"Benefits of a privileged life and education," said Collins, looking around the half-empty bar. "A thundering asshole talks over flipcharts and slides."

"Unimaginative concepts presented by a preening stiff," added Donnelly. "Here comes Locker with Dingmann and his entourage."

"Sleeping with the enemy?" said Collins.
"Or softening him up?" asked Donnelly.

***

Drinks furnished, the six of them sat around a table. After a half hour of conversation, Dingmann turned to Collins and Donnelly. "Didn't notice your presentation materials in the conference room. Did you boys bother to bring them?"

"We took the precaution of locking them away, Bob," Donnelly said. "We're merely relaxing and waiting."

"Waiting is the hardest kind of work, don't you think?" said Dingmann. He picked up his fourth drink and drained it empty. "But you boys won't have much to wait for, sitting against the wall tomorrow. Too bad Joyce"—he turned to Locker—"dragged you down here. Kind of a waste of company resources, I'd say."

"You're a funny guy, Dingmann," said Donnelly. "How come you're telling us this?" A miniature of a smile worked at the corner of his lips. He rubbed his fingers gently together, cracking his knuckles. He sat relaxed, his blue eyes calm.

"I'm just trying to help you two along, this being your first occasion in a pressure situation. You're in New York, the big time." He turned to Rhodes and Winchester. "Right?" They gave Dingmann bobblehead-doll nods. Locker sniffed.

The bar waitress, wearing her pert uniform and clothed in late-evening exhaustion, took their orders for another round of drinks.

"Gee, Bob, you and your boys," Collins said as the waitress walked away, "wouldn't be trying to intimidate us, would you? I mean we're nothing but lowly trainees along for the ride, honored at the privilege of sitting by while you knock Nick Jackson on his keister with your dazzling dot-dot-dot concepts. We are present only to imbibe from the vast cup of your ivory-tower-infused knowledge and expertise."

Locker's eyes crinkled in amusement.

Dingmann didn't turn his head. He frowned, anger building. *I shouldn't be subject to this. These two smart-mouth trainees annoy me.* He rose with a surprising litheness and leaned into Collins's face. He pushed his hand against Collins's chest and shoved. "Slow down, boy. You're heading for trouble. Learn to behave when with your betters." Another shove.

Collins's hand whipped around and caught Dingmann's arm in a vise-like grip and pushed him back into his seat. With his other hand he slithered his drink along the hard wood of the table and the contents splashed across Dingmann's lap. In a toneless voice Collins said, "You ever pull a stunt like that again, you condescending ponce, I'll stick your head so far up your ass, you'll shit it out your dick."

Donnelly glanced at Rhodes and Winchester. They stayed rooted to their seats.

Locker drank her martini and turned to Dingmann. "Bob, why don't you and your fellows get yourselves rested for tomorrow? I'll pick up the tab." She smiled.

Dingmann sat, not moving. Collins and Donnelly scanned the now mostly empty room, a half-smile on their faces. After a full minute, Dingmann coughed to camouflage the bile rising from his throat and signaled to Rhodes and Winchester. He rose, nodded to Locker, weaved, steadied himself and shuffled out, his cohorts in his wake.

The waitress came to their table and smiled sadly, sensing what had taken place. "Will that be all, gentlemen?" she asked. Locker asked her for the check and less than a minute later she returned.

"Here," said Collins. He looked the bill over, added an overly generous tip, signed it, and handed it back to her.

"You two outdid yourselves tonight," said Locker. They went to the elevator and punched in their floors.

"He asked for it," Donnelly said with a shrug.

"You better have your act together tomorrow," Locker said. "Dingmann will have the long knives out for both of you." She got off at her floor. They did not see the grin on her face as she walked down the hall.

"Whose name did you sign to the check?" said Donnelly as the door shut.

"Dingmann's, of course," said Collins. "He was bitching about his room and I caught him mentioning the room number. In for a penny, in for pound. Meet you in the morning."

***

Donnelly and Collins walked into the black-walled conference room. Rectangular tables were positioned to form a U with seating on the outside. A credenza with pastries, bagels, coffee, and water was against one wall. Against the other were several metal chairs.

Joyce Locker was talking to Dingmann, Rhodes, and Winchester. A large screen at the unclosed end awaited the output of a slide projector. Two flipchart easels were positioned next to the screen.

The door burst open and Nick Jackson strode in with several associates, including Tyler Doremus, manager of Ilium Corporate Communications and Marketing, and Stan Schuyler, in charge of the

Washington operation. Introductions were made and everyone settled in.

"All right," said Jackson, "ground rules: no bullshit, keep things short, don't leave anything out, accidentally or on purpose. Confine your pitch to the chair, what it might do for the business, the company and any other near- or long-term benefits. Understand?"

"I believe so," said Dingmann with the beginnings of a smirk on his lips. He turned to his minions and winked.

Dingmann stood next to the screen. "I have twelve slides here. They'll give you the whole background and bring the story right up to today." He nodded to Rhodes. Click. "Slide one is the R&D projects down at Low Voltage Switchgear Components. Those projects have evolved into the Electric Comfort Chair we're here to discuss." Click. "Slide two is the LVSC profit contribution graph for…"

Jackson put up his hand. "Hold it, hold it, Dingmann! Stop! This is exactly what I don't want. Are you deaf? I sit through this shit day in, day out in every dumbass business review from every dumbass manager in the company." He leaned forward. "For Christ's sake, Rawley fried in this chair. People are talking about this chair in every building in Ilium's Maqua Works. I don't give a shit about LVSC. Who are these two drones with you again?"

"Quentin Rhodes and Chase Winchester."

"Good. Need to keep the scorecard straight." He nodded at Doremus and Schuyler.

A muscle twitched on Dingmann's upper lip. He moistened his mouth. "Uh, right, we've, uh, worked up a promotional campaign for the Comfort Chair…" His mind whirled. He took two steps across the floor to where the ad layouts were stacked. He grabbed them and put them on the conference table. He looked up with forced courage into the penetrating eyes of Nick Jackson.

"Onward and downward, Dingmann. Continue."

Dingmann felt a flickering unease, a spark threatening to ignite the dread growing in the pit of his stomach. He lifted the first layout, featuring a richly upholstered chair with a middle-aged woman sitting with a book in her hand. The over line read, "New from Ilium"; underneath that was the headline, "The Newest in Home Comfort (three dots) Electrically."

Jackson glanced at Tyler Doremus, who wrinkled his nose. Doremus asked, "Are the other ads along these lines?'

Dingmann nervously sorted through the layouts. "We have this one," he said, showing a layout with a row of Comfort Chairs of different designs with a variety of people sitting in them.

Before he spoke Jackson cut in "W-what's your f-fucking strategy for all this?"

Dingmann's mind raced. "Well, we do these ads and some brochures and they'll sell the chairs and..."

"That's a strategy?" screamed Jackson. "J-Jesus fucking Christ." A fallen-away Catholic, he crossed himself. "If you A&P people call this a strategy I'd b-better shut the department down and fire you assholes."

"I'm sure, Nick, we can develop an approach to support this campaign," said Dingmann in a strained voice.

"Really now?" Jackson's voice dripped with scorn.

"Tell us," said Doremus.

"Those are just pictures," said Schuyler.

The staff joined in, sensing blood in the water. The questions flew; the answers didn't.

Dingmann's bladder let go. As the stain spread across his pants and down his legs, he cringed and began stuttering uncontrollably. Rhodes and Winchester didn't move.

Donnelly watched, fascinated. *The piranhas are hungry today. Even Dingmann doesn't deserve this.*

Collins's mind raced. *Now I know what it's like when sharks feed. Hope Dingmann has a change of pants.*

Jackson said softly, "Go back to Maqua, Dingmann; take those fellows with you and think about this. We'll reconvene in five minutes. Locker, can I see you for a minute?"

Locker rose and turned to Donnelly and Collins. "Set up and make sure you have your act together."

***

"Are these the two you told me about?" Jackson was off in a corner with Locker. She nodded. "Are you letting them present?"

"I'll do a thirty-second setup; after that, they're on."

"Good," said Jackson, slurping his coffee. "Let them talk. Christ, Joyce, you've known me a long time. You know I don't like drab shit. Steer 'em while they tell me about the goddamn chair!"

"I'm not sure I'll need to, Nick."

***

Locker returned her flipchart to the cover page and motioned to Collins and Donnelly. "Okay, you two, you're up."

Donnelly walked to the middle of the room. *Holy shit. Throw my ass on the conveyor belt to the chipper. This is gonna be the ultimate "motherfucker" conversation. No way out but straight ahead.* "The Ilium Electric Comfort Chair is, to coin a cliché, a wolf in sheep's clothing," he said, looking at Jackson. "Not only is this chair an overpriced, over-engineered, obscenely high-profit place of refuge for upper-middle-class Americans," he stopped and smiled. "But beneath its benign surface lurks a dispenser of swift and merciless justice to those who do evil."

Jackson shifted in his chair. "This is what I mean, Joyce." "The relationship of the chair to criminal justice may not be readily apparent, but we will show how every law-abiding American consumer will want to own an Ilium Electric Comfort Chair."

"I'm dying to learn about this scheme," said Jackson. "Glad to hear it," said Donnelly. Collins clicked a slide. "First, the population demographics of the US" Another slide. "The higher-income areas, within the population. Next, markets where the low ambient temperature average is at least forty degrees for more than five months of the year." Donnelly took a pointer and touched the screen. "Voila! The target market map for the warm, snuggly, adjustable Ilium Electric Comfort Chair.

"Consider the weather in certain places. Many of those shivering folks have strong financial means, always necessary to acquire Ilium products." Another slide. "Here's where the cold places with affluent people are." Another slide. "Don't forget the senior living enclaves…"

Jackson began shuffling papers. Donnelly rubbed his hands together. "Okay, enough of the consumer stuff. Yet another high potential market for this product awaits." The audience sat straighter.

"Let's start with a premise," Donnelly said. "Many major urban areas are becoming war zones with the possibility they will spread to the more affluent suburbs. The vast majority of people want assurance and order. This is not happening. Instead radical and often violent dissent happens in demonstrations and in America's courtrooms." He stepped forward. "Favorably reported, I may add, by a press that has lost its objectivity. The Nixon Administration is ready to change that." He turned to Collins.

Sounds like Floss and Hitchcock, Jackson thought. Wonder if these two have an answer.

Collins began, "The unfortunate demise of Burt Rawley…" Jackson's head snapped up. "…called our attention to an aspect of the chair's lethal capability."

Collins paused. "With only a couple of minor adjustments the high-priced, high-margin Electric Comfort Chair can carry up to two thousand volts." He smiled. "Sing-Sing hot-squat quality, folks. With some simple modifications, the chair becomes a reasonably priced, industrial-grade, lightweight, fully portable electric chair in the true sense of the phrase." He tapped the chart. "With volume potential."

Jackson's laugh did not sound pleasant to Donnelly and Collins. "This is a little off the wall, but you two have piqued my curiosity. At least I haven't decided to fire your asses for conduct unbecoming an Ilium manager."

A *sniff* came from Locker's direction.

Donnelly stirred. *Did he say manager? He also said fired. We could be on our way up. Or out.*

Collins continued, not missing a beat. "Today, the bad guys thumb their noses at society. Riots and anarchy everywhere. In the movies and on old TV shows, the marshal rode into town, found the bad guys, and strung them up or shot them down. Ta da! Everyone knew who was who and that the bad guys deserved it. No problem. Perhaps the country needs an example or two of frontier justice. Our idea is to encourage this market, the market simpatico to the marshal."

Jackson smiled. This gets better every second.

"Accordingly," Donnelly said, "we identified the worst crime pockets in the US, places with the most outstanding warrants for heinous felonies." A slide appeared on the screen. "With federal support, track-down squads could get put on the street with a judge, jury, and executioner assigned to each." The screen displayed a picture of a large van. "We catch these bastards, try them, and fry them in an Ilium Portable Electric chair." The screen now showed the interior shot of a van with an Ilium Portable Electric Chair mockup. "Right on the spot."

Donnelly's eyes swept across the room. "Ilium could be like every frontier hero who ever lived. An icon for the long-ignored 'silent majority' of law-abiding folks. They will make a quiet statement by having the symbol of justice in their den—the Ilium Electric Comfort Chair," he said quietly, "the 'Captain America' solution to the nation's crime problems." He gestured to Collins.

Doremus interrupted in a nasal voice, "What consumer is going to want a chair they think kills people?"

A shark tries for its first bite. "They won't know," said Collins. "Different audiences, different messages. The home-use chair will look like a comfortable recliner, not an execution device. The chair made by those folks who brought a safer society to America! Relaxing to you who deserve to relax." He stepped away. "People who can't shoot still buy guns and install elaborate security systems. These same people will see our campaign and want to be part of it in some way."

"There's a third market for this chair," Donnelly said, "a slightly higher voltage version than the Comfort Chair."

"Go ahead," said Jackson, now fully engaged.

"Parents and schools. I'll bet a slight upping of the voltage from the Comfort Chair level would prove effective in making kids behave and provide much-needed discipline in America's schools."

Donnelly's eyes twinkled. "Anyone who went to Catholic school would immediately understand."

Jackson sat back. *These goddamn rookies are on to something.*

"How will you extend this high-voltage chair?" said Schuyler. "And the legal obstacles?"

"The legal obstacles would be your task, Stan," Jackson said.

Right across the son of a bitch's bow. "Eventually, they'll televise the executions," Collins said to a stunned silence.

Jackson made a note. Better speed up buying that TV network.

"Think about it," Collins said, enthusiasm building in his voice. "All of America watching some vicious, violent, three-time loser, the current ripping through him, screaming desperately, the spasms jerking his body as he fights the bitter struggle, shitting his drawers and pissing his pants as the death agony finally overcomes him. Message: crime does not pay. No corner-cutting lawyers or lefty judges to get you off."

Unfuckingbelieveable. Jackson almost rose to his feet but caught himself. *It wouldn't do to give these trainees too much approval.* He was secretly envious. *To be like these assholes again! Enthusiasm! Damn the torpedoes! Full speed ahead! Take the hill!*

"Shouldn't we be concerned about the racial aspects of this?" said one of Doremus's acolytes.

Collins walked over to where the man sat: a thin, bow-tied staffer with round-rimmed eyeglasses. He began to blink nervously as Collins approached. "Here's an unpleasant truth you never hear in the public media." He laughed. "Doesn't fit their worldview. Seventy percent of the people who get arrested for violent crime are Negro in areas where seventy percent of the population are Negro. Ditto, for Puerto Ricans. Ditto, White Trash too." He loomed over him. "Not discrimination, my friend. It's the Law of Probability." He spun and walked back to where he had been standing, put his hands on the conference table and said, "I'm sure we'll find deserving white candidates."

He put that little twerp down; these boys don't take prisoners. Locker was right; they aren't your usual trainees. Who are they?

"What about a strategy for all this?" said Doremus, sensing Collins and Donnelly on a rapid ascendancy concurrent with his own possible descent.

Okay, the sharks and piranha are still circling. Donnelly stepped to the flipchart and went to the next page. "First, the concept of the Electrified Comfort Chair. Include TV, radio, print publications, and newspapers…the usual suspects." Doremus found himself nodding in agreement.

"Second is the political sell: create the legal environment where an electric chair can be used in the smallest of communities, providing the defendants receive a swift and fair trial with an accredited judge and an appropriate jury.

"The education market is a more specialized channel."

For another fifteen minutes, he and Collins spoke, fielding questions with concise, prepared answers.

These two have their shit together big-time. "Anything else?" Jackson said.

Donnelly tapped his watch. "We might discuss the work required to shift public attitudes to something supporting an effort like this. Review the various sales channels employed, the role of our lobbyists and outside political consultants. Look at the need for complete, airtight legal air cover…" He handed Jackson a thick binder. "Or you can look at this; it's all in here. Other copies are on the credenza. We're at your disposal."

"Good work," Jackson said. "Your guys are *It*. Needs a little fine-tuning, but you're in charge. I'll give you my corporate counsel to grease the track. Joyce'll watch over you. She knows the ropes.

She's the best, seen it all. She'll keep you out of trouble. Screw up, you're gone. Get upside-down, you're gone. Embarrass us, you're gone. But this is the flipside: a success, you're superstars. You've made your bones. You're in," Jackson smiled.

Hard to read that smile. Donnelly took Jackson's smile and nodded back.

Collins let the corners of his mouth turn up.

They understood. They were *It*.

Jackson shook hands, grabbed two more binders, and left the room. *Schuyler and Doremus should have come up with this.*

***

Jackson returned to his office and told Florence to hold all calls. *What a freak show. Dingmann, the heavyweight manager, pisses his pants. Can't play in the bigs; back he goes to the minors in Class D Maqua. His guys sat on their hands, looking like feral cats waiting for him to topple over to make feeding easier.*

He took the binder Joyce's guys had left and went through it. *Impressive. She can pick 'em. Smart alecks, but confident ones. Those two fuckers covered all the bases. Their ideas about societal changes and the mood of the majority of the electorate sound dead on. They have balls; I'll give them that, unlike the lardass stonehenges I had in the room. Love the idea about a school version.* He laughed to himself. *I wouldn't have an ass if the good Sisters who wrestled me through St. Ethelred had one.*

He closed the binder and hand-wrote notes to Abe Floss and Justin Hitchcock. "Take a look at this proposal about a possible way to address many of the issues under discussion. Draconian perhaps, but the thrust of what is said here is the times demand draconian solutions. For this to work, intensive political and public preparation will be needed. Let me know your thoughts and when we should

96

discuss." He signed them "Nick" and attached them to the extra binders.

He buzzed Florence and told her to get them to Floss and Hitchcock as quickly as possible.

***

On the following Tuesday Abe Floss's private line rang. "Hello," he said, putting aside the large binder he had just finished reviewing.

"Abe, Justin Hitchcock here. Did you receive the material Nick Jackson sent us?"

"Yes. What do you think?" Floss employed the tactic of not giving anything away, holding his options to gauge which way the wind was blowing.

Hitchcock, as much a game player as Floss, said, "Best discussed face-to-face in a private setting, given the nature of its contents."

Floss chuckled to himself, acknowledging the ball had come back over the net. "I agree. Your place or mine? I'll be in New York next week. Would that fit your schedule?"

Hitchcock appreciated Floss's consideration for his physical problems. "A proper repast and appropriate libations will be available." He coughed lightly. "How much do you know about Nick Jackson?"

"The usual corporate bio stuff," Floss said.

"We need to learn more," said Hitchcock.

Floss stared out his K Street window. He pushed the binder aside. "I can go through the FBI. Wednesday next week at your place? We'll compare notes.

"Sounds good. I'll talk to the NSA. Anything said between us stays between us," said Hitchcock. "You have my word."

"Agreed," said Floss.

Chapter Ten

"Are either Jim Collins or Frank Donnelly there? This is Harold Cox."

"Hi, Harold, this is Jim. How can I help?"

"I want to go over some convertibility factors with both of you."

Christ on a crutch, more engineering esoterica. Our job is to promote the damn chair, not build it. "To do...?"

"Swap the chair from one application to another," said Cox. "I've integrated some functions which positively impact our cost structure. They might suggest other possibilities. I get stalled occasionally, just working by myself."

"No problem. When?"

"Within the next hour would be best. I'm making some materials decisions on the frame and mechanicals. I don't want to overlook anything glaringly obvious."

Ha, Collins thought, *the mind of the engineer. We wouldn't pick up the subtle, only the glaringly obvious.* "We'll be down in fifteen minutes. I need to locate my scrutiny glasses."

"Excuse me?"

"Make certain nothing on my end is approaching critical mass."

"Oh. Okay. I'm out in the lab area," Cox said. *Those guys have odd senses of humor, but they're fun to work with. They think I'm a dork. If they only knew.*

99

***

"What's the next step?" said Donnelly on their way to Cox's office. "Aside from tightening our plan? Should we worry about Dingmann?"

"We need to be proactive regarding him," said Collins. "Jackson bumped him off the glory road at the presentation."

"A day to remember," said Donnelly.

"Bad enough Locker witnessed his mortification," said Collins. "Worse, we were present."

"Which must drive him nuts."

"Dingmann will not leave this alone," said Collins. "He'll try and grab back this prize in any way he and his toadies can conjure."

"Sounds like conflict," said Donnelly.

"No doubt," said Collins. "Should we tell Cox?"

"Maybe. I'm pretty sure he likes working with us. Let's play it by ear."

***

"Any more questions?" said Cox after the briefing.

Donnelly and Collins glanced at each other. "There's something else we want to share with you," said Donnelly. They described the events of the last weeks and their concerns.

100

"You two think this Dingmann person and his people are looking for ways for you to fail?"

"In a word, yes," said Collins.

Cox sat, weighing several factors. *Should I aid them in their departmental political battle or stand on the sidelines and deal with the winner? I hadn't liked my new department manager, George Kelso, bypassing me, sending the chair to be used at the A&P Christmas party. He rather unsubtly tried to pin Burt Rawley's murder on me after the issue heated up, even though the chair was verified to be in good working order before and after it left my chain of control. I know now they defended me without even having that knowledge, told the police the chair had been rigged. I owe them. Do I tell them I'm Harriet Cox, not Harold Cox? Not right away on that last one, but help them in their fight with this Dingmann? Yes.* "How drastic do you want to get?"

"Whatever's necessary," said Donnelly. "No bodily harm."

"Are you in building twenty-two?" Cox asked.

"Yes, why?" said Collins.

"You'll need information," said Cox. "I'll be back in fifteen minutes." Cox left the conference room.

"What's going on?" said Donnelly.

"Do we have an ally?" said Collins.

"Let's see what he gives us," said Donnelly.

***

Cox held a sheaf of blueprints. "Years ago, buildings like the one you're in were used for heavy manufacturing. Giant boilers and furnaces provided the heat. In the last two decades several were converted to offices, yours among them." She unfurled the blueprints. "Check this out." Donnelly and Collins stepped over. "Here's what they did on your floor." She ran her hand over a section. "They dropped the ceilings to accommodate more efficient heat and power options and the ducting and electrical runs."

They studied the blueprint and the maps.

"Where is Dingmann's office?"

They pointed.

"Okay." She made a mark. "Anything else?"

"His people are housed here." Collins designated the area.

"His conference room is here," Donnelly said, indicating another space.

"Got them," Cox said, marking the spots. "That's it?"

"Yeah," said Collins, "build a hide above the ugly white acoustic panel grid. I'm thinking box ends glued to a cardboard sheet attached to a duct. Of course we'd be dealing with bacteria, flying insects of assorted capabilities, rare but deadly allergens, and aggressive rodents. We'll need to be up there when they are in any of those three rooms."

Cox's lips turned up in a slight smile. "Or obtain some advanced voice-activated eavesdropping equipment that would feed into a remote tape recorder. Listen to the conversations at your leisure."

"We're aware such stuff exists," said Donnelly, "but those are highly specialized electronics. Above our capability to acquire, even in our former lives."

Former lives? What did these two do before Ilium? Curiouser and curiouser. Cox leaned over the blueprints. "But I can." She rolled them up and handed them to Collins. "You'll also need phone taps; I can get those too. I'll need the blueprints back. You two are in a war."

A war neither Donnelly nor Collins planned on losing. With their street and work backgrounds they recognized solid intelligence underpinned the most successful attack. "We can be au courant on their plans, thanks to you," said Donnelly.

Collins nodded. "One detail. Even with Dingmann wetting his pants in New York, they still think we're both stupid." He began to pace. "I'll have to work at keeping them thinking that."

"Simple," Donnelly said. "Act normal."
Collins couldn't help himself and laughed.
As did Cox.

Chapter Eleven

"Thank you, Jeffrey," Hitchcock said. "Please close the door. Should we need additional refreshments, I'll ring you."

Hitchcock waited a full minute and turned to Floss. "I trust you found the meal satisfactory, Abe." He gestured. "A postprandial libation?"

Floss shook his head no. "You serve a fine meal, Justin." He patted his stomach and took stock of Hitchcock's drawing-cum-conference room. *Elegant but functional.* They sat in comfortable leather chairs next to a rosewood dwarf bookcase. In front of the mirror a French clock rested on a white marble mantelpiece. No house or traffic noises intruded.

"Nick Jackson is a complex man," said Hitchcock as he unzipped a file folder. He spread documents marked Confidential on a Honduran mahogany table.

"That, Justin, is an understatement," Floss said, opening his own document bag. "Some wag once noted 'business executive is the perfect job for any psychopath not already otherwise involved in death and dismemberment.' Nick Jackson fits the bill of particulars rather well, I would say."

"Indeed," said Hitchcock, adjusting his glasses.

"Jackson," said Floss, "doesn't spend time worrying why he is the way he is. He's perceived that raw genetics, enhanced by a solid foundation in aggressive thinking, shaped his mature personality." Floss checked his notes. "Which has contributed to his more disturbing habits."

104

"From what I've gleaned," said Hitchcock, "he enjoys those behaviors and considers wrestling with them time poorly spent. Anything on his stutter?"

"Made public settings a nightmare at school." Floss produced a slim, bound document. "I obtained the report by the psychologist the family retained. During the process the seventeen-year-old Jackson seduced her. They had a three-month affair. His sexual voraciousness, magnetic aura, and feeling of menace left her exhausted and confused. Afterward, she sought therapy for herself in Switzerland, for which Jackson's family paid.

"The therapist's notes," Floss held up several pages. "Jackson's psychologist was in a quandary over a number of items. Did taking it in the ear and the armpit make her deviant? Open a numbered account in Zurich with her fee? Go back to Jackson? The Swiss psychiatrist, being sensible, recommended she buy a vibrator and calm herself."

"Ever practical, those Swiss. And the psychologist?"

"I believe she moved to the Midwest, went into another field, and married a hotshot Ilium exec"—he searched the text—"by the name of Willets."

"Anything more on Jackson's therapy?"

"Lots," said Floss. "The therapy made him understand his father's role as the source of many of his issues. One evening, Jackson had just turned twelve, he somehow sensed his father was having intercourse with one of the ewes." He coughed. "They kept a small herd of sheep in the backyard of their Pawtucket mansion."

"Did you say sheep?" Hitchcock checked his paintings and antiques, pleased they hadn't fallen.

"I did."

Hitchcock looked offended. Floss continued, a sly grin on his face. "They used the sheep to keep the grass shorn on their front and back lawns. Jackson soon confirmed his suspicion and before long young Nick was giving it a go into their curly glory." Floss slid a paper over to Hitchcock. "Lamb's wool sweaters are still an aphrodisiac to him."

"Thank you for sharing."

Floss continued reading. "...word spread concerning the lamb's wool. Any hottie who wanted to get noticed wore one." He adjusted his glasses. "I'm surprised they didn't use a hose to cool Jackson down."

"So he has an active libido and perhaps we now know why." Hitchcock smiled. "How many paternity suits and sexual assault complaints?"

"I can't count high enough," said Floss. "However, we can infer that the discipline he applied to curbing his stutter gave him the ability to communicate clearly with investors and customers."

Hitchcock checked his notes. "As he climbed the Ilium ladder he demonstrated an ability to choose products and businesses to bet on. Jackson is a cash flow and business development genius. He evaluates any opportunity based on margin potential greater than seventy-five percent and the chance for bizarre rush and mental and physical triumph. Born into prosperity, his Ilium success has made him obscenely rich."

"Even with these standards he still can shake the sand and produce a stunning nugget."

"Jackson thinks the Ilium chair could be a winner," Floss said. He read again. "He senses not only success but excitement, power plays, enticement, and self-aggrandizement. Plus, Justin, lots of new pussy." He lowered the pages. "I can visualize the beads of sweat on his forehead."

"Is this what Ilium stands for these days? Pussy and profit?" *Maybe I should buy more stock.*

"Well," said Floss, "his corporate and life strategy are beginning to intertwine, which is a concern. He punctuates his business triumphs by spotting women, preferably someone new, who would be more than pleased to satisfy him."

Hitchcock limped over to the table and poured two Jack Daniels, neat. "Enough of Jackson; we know his strengths and weaknesses. What about the chair?"

Hitchcock handed him his drink. "The political situation is severe, we agree," said Floss. "Does the country institute a form of martial law to contain this civil unrest?" He took a sip. "Do we suppress due process to allow executions, at the local level, of guilty felons?"

"Personally I don't believe due process would be suppressed," said Hitchcock. "A reforming, perhaps, to match the direction in which society is heading. Everything immediate: information, gratification, and results. Of course only the truly horrendous must be targeted."

"Until the public becomes more comfortable with reduced due process, I think they will." Floss waved the Ilium document. "Jackson's plan contains a degree of cynical sophistication both fascinating and disturbing. The portable electric chair could be the means to our end."

"Every poll I've seen says, by a margin of eight to one, the country is out of control." Hitchcock toyed with his glass. "People are afraid to leave their houses, the economy is growing at a negative rate for the first time since the Depression, and we are seen as weak overseas. And they hate the administration."

"They hate the Congress more," said Floss. "Given all this, is the Portable Electric Chair the answer?"

"I'm thinking yes," said Hitchcock. "You, Abe?"

"Unfortunately. Harsh times call for harsh measures." He sipped his drink.

"Can we trust Nick Jackson? Is he a loose cannon?"

Floss sighed. "Good question. For all his peccadilloes we can trust him when it comes to Ilium, the chair, and rallying the support from the business community so we can return society to a semblance of order."

"It is a matter of belief, isn't it?"

"Yes," said Floss, "but sooner rather than later there will be a reckoning. The pendulum always swings back, and the left can be shriller than the right. They're also better at retribution." He drummed his fingers. "On a related subject, are you hearing anything about Vice President Agnew's activities when he was Maryland's governor?"

Hitchcock put his drink down. "Not a peep." He waited for Floss to elaborate. Floss was too smart to show any of his cards. Hitchcock realized a reeking heap might lurk in Agnew's woodpile. *There were irregularities in the Veep's Maryland ledgers and allegations of bribes. Need to look into that later, possibly signs of the atmospheric rotation preceding a tornado.* "Back to the matter at hand," he said.

For an hour they discussed their next moves.

Chapter Twelve

"I've obtained the equipment we talked about," said Cox. Donnelly adjusted the phone and smiled. For the last week he and Collins had been fine-tuning their plans and keeping tabs on any maneuvers by Dingmann and company. So far, nada. Soon Dingmann would stop licking his wounds and make a move. "When do you want to do this?" asked Cox.

"Good question," said Donnelly. "Are you around tonight after work?"

"Of course. Where else would I be in this social wasteland?"

"Okay, let me talk to Collins and I'll be back to you in ten minutes or so," he said and disconnected. He leaned over the wall and motioned to Collins to hang up. Thanks to Joyce Locker, he and Collins now sat in adjoining cubicles.

Donnelly pulled up a chair next to Collins's desk. "Cox has our stuff. We can do this tonight. You around?"

"For that? Yes."

"I'll tell Cox to meet us at seven. The place will be clear by then."

***

"Push it to the right. To the right," said Cox, standing on a ladder, head poking through the dropped ceiling where they'd pushed out an aged acoustic tile.

109

We're not laying down the transatlantic cable, just going overhead across five offices. Collins stubbed his cigarette, and he and Donnelly continued installing their clandestine equipment. A half hour later they'd wired Dingmann's conference room, office, phone, and the offices and phones of several of his key people.

"Anyplace else?" asked Cox

Donnelly thought hard. *Damn, never up, never in. New guy coming in, you just don't know.* "Burt Rawley's former digs," Donnelly replied.

This one'll cause a shitstorm. Oh well. "Joyce Locker's office," Collins said. To Donnelly's sharp glance he said, "Hey, I like her too, but better we come first."

Donnelly shook his head slowly. "Yeah, I guess you're right."

Cox listened to the interplay. *These guys are cautious. What's the term? Street smart? They're covering all their bases. I like that.*

Another half hour and they were finished.

"Where do you want the voice activation hardware and recording boxes? They're small and can fit almost anywhere in an office."

They settled on a lockable lower drawer in Donnelly's desk.

"This calls for a celebration," said Collins. "Tomorrow night?"

"We'll meet at McGarry's. Nothing fancy, have a few pops, relax," said Donnelly.

"Sure," said Cox. "Where's McGarry's? I haven't had the time to get around that much." *I can't go out as a woman and I'm tired of posing as a man.*

"On Reid between Insley and Hammond. You can't miss it," said Collins. "Seven?"

"This'll be our coming-out party," said Cox. *And Harriet Cox will be joining you.*

***

McGarry's was the closest thing to a New York neighborhood bar in Maqua. Great beer, generous drinks, and acceptable food. A non-Ilium clientele made it attractive to Donnelly and Collins. Jimmy "Mac" McGarry, an ex–New York cop, presided. He'd won the place in a Bronx poker game ten years ago, promptly put in his retirement papers, and moved.

Donnelly arrived early. He sat on a stool nursing a Schaefer. The last gasp of the day cohort, the shot-and-beer locals and pensioners, had ended an hour or so ago. Vestiges of their smoke haze remained. They had taken their comfort from the honor of sucking up the day's first rations. McGarry's evening clientele, dribbling in now, was a slight improvement. They were employed.

This is one of the few bars in this godforsaken town where guys like Collins and I can drink and talk and smoke, even. We're lucky to have found such a place. Collins's father was one of McGarry's early patrol partners. Donnelly felt comfortable here, with the mahogany bar, sawdust floors, and bowls of peanuts and popcorn.

In the large mirror he saw Collins come in, speak to McGarry, and wend his way over. "Cox here yet?"

"Not yet."

"Grab a table in the back," said Collins. "I'm gonna grab a beer and some glasses. Should I get a pitcher?"

"Good idea. Hope Cox likes a brew."

***

Harriet Cox got out of her car and walked to the door of McGarry's. She checked her blond wig and reflection in the window, inhaled and pushed into the entry. *Not many women. Early times, I guess. I'm so nervous and lonely. Can I trust them? I'd better, considering that I helped them wire their offices. Although after seeing what it looked like above the dropped ceiling I doubt anything will be discovered in my lifetime. Should I have come here? They're looking my way. They don't recognize me. No whitest of socks or plastic pocket protectors for me tonight.*

Donnelly poured himself a beer. "Any sign of Cox?"

"No, but the babe quotient in this place just quadrupled." Collins puffed on a cigarette. "Check out the blond at the door."

"She's waving to us," said Donnelly, "and heading our way. Do we know her?"

"I don't think so, but who cares?" said Collins. He stubbed his cigarette.

"What'll we do when Cox gets here?"

"Ignore him?"

"Hi Frank, hi Jim," Cox said and pulled up a chair and plopped herself down.

Who the hell is she and how does she know who we are? "Would you like a beer...?" Collins asked.

"Harriet," Cox said. "Thank you, I'd love one." She grabbed the empty glass and Collins poured from the pitcher. *No idea, Cox thought.*

"Sláinte," Donnelly said.

"Sláinte to you, Frank," Cox said. "Figured it out yet?"

Identification registered. "Harold?" Collins shifted nervously.

"Don't worry, Jim, I'm really a girl. I don't swing from the other side of the plate." She smiled. "How many female engineers do you know? How many female anythings who aren't secretaries or tea servers or some other subservient role do you know?" She laughed. "Other than your own Joyce Locker?"

"I take it you're wearing a wig?" said Donnelly. "And contacts?"

"Right on both counts," she said.

Harold? Shit, no, Harriet. She must be lonely. No social life to speak of.

"Why us?" Donnelly picked up his beer.

"I trust you two. I can be myself. Since you now know, why don't you tell me more about yourselves and how you plan to promote the various versions of my chair?"

"We should eat first," said Collins.

For the next two and a half hours they talked. Donnelly and Collins were candid, as was Cox.

"Let's do this again," Collins said and paid the bill. *Christ, she's attractive.*

"Absolutely," said Donnelly. *What a looker.*

Chapter Thirteen

Walt Sukeforth, Nick Jackson's personnel manager, sat opposite him. "Who is this guy?" said Jackson, pushing aside the file.

"Lou Willets. His most recent assignment's been running an operation that builds demonstration houses under various government programs. A sales bonanza. He's used the houses to feature cutting-edge Ilium products and systems. He was able to convince a bunch of Ilium divisions to cooperate and run all kinds of customers, distributors, wholesalers, through the place. He's also displayed a knack for working with the government to get more demo contracts."

Jackson leaned back and read Willets's file, which described a high-potential executive. "You talked to him?"

"Oh yeah," said Sukeforth. "I flew out to Dayton and met with him for the day. He's high energy, high tech; he'd be ideal for the A&P job; the perfect smoke-and-mirrors guy while we get ready to come out of the blocks with the chair."

"Princeton, eh?" said Jackson, moving the file aside.

"With full preppie credentials; went to Cornwallis. After Princeton, on to Northwestern for his MBA."

"You have other candidates?"

"Many. This is the guy."

Jackson scanned the file again. "Been with Ilium nine years. Young. Married?"

"No kids. Wife's a college teacher; psychology." He pushed the papers aside. "He's a pussy hound."

Jackson smiled inwardly. "Any idea on the wife's reaction?"

"Nothing. She's several years older; probably gets some on the side, too."

Jackson sat back, decision made. "He looks good on paper. Bring him in next Tuesday."

Five minutes after Lou Willets left his office, Jackson called personnel. "Does he want the job?"

"Enough to tell me he can start in less than two weeks."

"Outstanding." Jackson hit the intercom. "Florence, get Joyce Locker on the phone."

***

"Joyce? Nick. I've got the man for the GM slot at A&P. I'm gonna give you a little more insight than usual about what I'm up to here. I want you to feel comfortable how this is going. Okay?"

Sniff. "Okay."

"Good. His name is Lou Willets. You know him?

"No. Where's he from?"

"Ran an operation in Dayton. Incredibly successful. Fucker's dynamic, Joyce. I gotta tell you. Could sell shit to a goose, for Chrissakes. You with me?"

Sniff. "With you?"

"Excellent; we sing from the same page. You're now plugged into some heavy stock options. This whole chair deal will make you rich. Nobody puts themselves on the line for me and walks away poor. Those two trainees of yours are signed up too, but don't say anything to them yet. This chair is gonna go nuts. You've done a big thing here, Joyce. You dug up two good ones in Stronnelly and Mullins. This outfit needs fresh blood like them."

"Donnelly and Collins."

"F-f-fucking whatever. Y-you understand my meaning. We are all of us g-gonna be right on t-top of this wave," Nick yelled. "Ridin' high!"

Christ, she thought, *Nick is into this one. Hope those two are ready.* After the latest Jackson blitzkrieg hundreds of battered executives pursued other interests. In his wake were strewn countless secretaries with sore pussies and stretched lips. *Nick is on a roll. The chair has everything: money, pain, turmoil, pandemonium, and executions.*

"You can smell a wild one, can't you, Joyce?" *Sniff.*

Later in the day, Donnelly and Collins listened to every word.

Collins turned to Donnelly, "Who the hell is Lou Willets?"

"No idea," said Donnelly. "Seems he's our new General Manager. Sounds like he'll be here soon."

"Okay, kemosabe," said Collins. "Next?"

Donnelly pulled the Dingmann tape.

A minute later Donnelly signaled Collins. "Catch this."

"Mr. Dingmann, a Mr. Lou Willets is on the line. Shall I put him through?"

"Yes." A click sounded.

"Lou, how are you? It's been awhile."

"I wanted you to be the first to know, Bob, that Nick Jackson has offered me the General Manager's job at A&P. I start a week from Monday."

"...congratulations, Lou..." said Dingmann.

Willets spoke over Dingmann's words. "Jackson waxed enthusiastic on the subject of something called an Electric Comfort Chair. I'm on my way back to Dayton. Once I'm in Maqua on Monday we'll get together and you can you brief me on this product."

"Sure, Lou. You say when. Congratulations. It'll be like old times at Cornwallis."

"Look forward," Willets said and disconnected.

Dingmann sighed before adding a muffled "shit" and punched a button.

"Helen, tell my senior staff we're meeting tomorrow at 8:00 a.m. Attendance is mandatory and promptness is expected."

Donnelly spoke first. "Trespasser alert."

"Man battle stations. They're going to plot against us."

"You think so?" said Donnelly, voice dripping with sarcasm.

"We eavesdrop live, right?"

"One of us, anyway. I nominate you." Donnelly closed his file drawer, locking the recording equipment. "Too conspicuous for both of us to do. You can have the privilege of listening to the nose-wrinkling fusspots with permanent 'do-you-mind?' expressions on their self-congratulatory faces."

"My bet is Dingmann uses the Willets news to restore his face to normal from the imprint of Jackson's stomping."

"Witnessed by Locker, you, and me."

***

Bob Dingmann's staff meetings usually consisted of rants, raves, self-serving plaudits, and directives. They didn't last long, unless someone wanted to do extended bragging. *Not this morning.*

Fifteen minutes early, Collins's audio microphone hissed to life. The usual suspects had begun to arrive. They prattled on with office gossip. Another two arrivals and they shifted into a discussion of some must-see movies. They went on and on about two pictures: *The Strawberry Statement*, about the Columbia riots in 1968, and *Harry Munter*, a Swedish film directed by Kjell Grede. Both had received rave reviews at the Cannes festival. *Reason enough to never watch them. Why don't they ever screen a movie like* Bambi Meets Godzilla *or the Bond flick with Diana Rigg?* Harry Munter *sounds like poker-faced Swedes looking up a dead rat's ass.* Strawberry Statement *is self-congratulatory propaganda glorifying those pampered students as God's gift to the righteous way. Horseshit.*

The conversation in his earphones changed to sports. *Jesus, Fencing!* Collins thought his head would pop. A door opened. "Gentlemen! Let's get this under way!" Chairs scraped with the sounds of the group taking seats and the rustling of paper.

"We will dispense with the opening prayer," Dingmann said, to obsequious chuckles. "I'll get to the matter at hand. Let me foreground this. Our chair presentation suffered an unfortunate, er, hiccup, in New York." Collins chuckled at the coughing and clearing of throats. *And you, Dot-Dot, needed to buy new underwear and send your pants to the cleaners.*

"You may close your notebooks," Dingmann said a moment later. Sounds of notebooks snapping shut. "I want no physical record of this meeting. I chose each of you to work for me because you are intelligent. I trust that will extend to your remembering the events of this morning.

"Since Burt Rawley's unfortunate passing the general manager's slot has been empty. That is no longer the case. The new general manager is Lou Willets, who comes to us from a high-profile public-private operation he ran for the company in Dayton. Nick Jackson himself appointed him. Lou called me yesterday and asked to get together on his first day here so I could brief him on the Comfort Chair. For your private information, Lou was my roommate at Cornwallis. Even though he went to Princeton and I to Harvard, we have stayed in touch. This is our chance to step off the down elevator. We are back in the game, gentlemen," he said, to a round of polite applause. *Damn cheerleaders.*

"This product's ad budget is currently in the hands of Joyce Locker's section."

"They couldn't craft an ad to sell a pristine Rolls-Royce to a Saudi prince, let alone a high-end piece of multifunction furniture." *Sounds like Chase Winchester.*

"Not for discussion," said Dingmann. "Today we discuss and lay out action items on how to convince Lou Willets that extracting the Electric Comfort Chair from the grasp of the Locker group benefits Lou Willets and the A&P Department. Comments?"

"Perhaps if we changed our creative approach; less, um, 'dot-dot-dot electrically' and no 'New from Ilium'?"

Whoa, who's the ballsy fucker?

"Thank you for your comment," said Dingmann in a clipped voice.

Dingmann's voice could freeze boiling water. Good luck on your next assignment, pal, whoever you are. Collins laughed to himself.

"What did Locker's group propose to Jackson?" said someone else.

"No one is forthcoming," said Dingmann. "We need to know."

"Who's the engineer behind the product?"

"Cox," said someone. "Harold Cox, I believe."

"I'm sure Cox is introverted," said Dingmann. "Perhaps one of you could befriend him and turn the conversation to the subject of the chair?"

Collins imagined Dingmann gazing around the room, looking for a candidate. "Who wants to be the new best friend?"

"I will." *Kiss-ass Quentin Rhodes rides to the rescue, lips puckered. We'd better clue Cox in.*

"Any way to discredit Locker?"

"Dozens," laughed someone. "Drinking, irreverence, crudity, foul language…"

"I mean one that will work," said Dingmann, annoyance in his voice.

"I say, no need for a fire," said a voice Collins didn't recognize, "With the new general manager, a little smoke should be enough. What if Joyce gets caught in a compromising position with a young trainee? Smoke enough for the puritans around here, I say."

Another silence descended as the group seemed to ponder the idea.

Who's that? Holy shit. Might work if they tried it.

"Should we try to have some of Locker's people on our side?" said an unidentifiable voice. "Promise them transfers into our section when we get the project?"

120

"A distinct possibility," said Dingmann. "Have you anyone in mind, Duncan?"

Ah, Duncan Peters, Collins realized. *He's such an annoying turd Gandhi would want to punch him out.*

"Rufus Hogg, Austin Shepherd, and Mike Drake," Peters said. "They are not overly happy with curb creatures like Collins and Donnelly getting recognition beyond their station."

Curb creatures? Not a bad line. We better keep tabs.

A chair scraped. "Some good ideas, gentlemen," said Dingmann. "Let's hold off on them until after Lou Willets comes onboard. Except Hogg, Shepherd, and Drake. Drake's first assignment was with us before he rotated out. Duncan, would you explore?"

***

Bob Dingmann's journey to Ilium had been an unusual one. He'd graduated from Harvard, a degree in history, a minor in English, and vague ideas of teaching. But the draft loomed. Harvard had taught him to avoid military service in any way possible, so he joined an early draft resistance movement.

Dingmann realized his physical was coming due and he couldn't go unprepared. He obtained the name of a shrink from a friend in the movement who guaranteed, "He'll write you a letter to show them." This particular antimilitary Boston psychiatrist wrote many letters to help graduating students get deferments. Dingmann had one fifty-minute session, during which he told this well-dressed, emotionless man about himself. The psychiatrist gave him a letter and said keep it sealed until he went to the draft board.

On the day before his physical, Dingmann steamed the letter open. The text unsettled him. The psychiatrist declared Dingmann was homosexual, with the letter stating that he "doesn't act well in group situations or interpersonal relationships." Dingmann recognized he had a surefire deferment but worried that the shrink believed his own words. He presented the resealed letter the next day at the draft board. Not exactly the way Dingmann had hoped, but it did the job. He was declared 4F: physically unfit to serve.

The draft deferment and a Harvard diploma got him a job at Ilium and helped him achieve his current position. However, Dingmann grasped, somewhere in a government file he was branded a homosexual. The "compromising note" reference had a certain negative resonance for him. He preferred to keep that particular tactic off the table.

One subject did not come up at the meeting. Two, actually: Donnelly and Collins. In a way, they frightened him. They were outside of his experience and unlike anyone he'd met at Ilium. The night before disgracing himself at the Jackson presentation he'd tried to intimidate them. Collins's reaction had caused him to piss his pants. No one had noticed, fortunately. Locker wasn't the issue; Collins and Donnelly were. He couldn't imagine Lou Willets wanting them in the department. Not their kind of people.

Chapter Fourteen

"Now we sting Dingmann's ass without letting him know we have an ear on them." Donnelly and Collins had reviewed the tape of Dingmann's meeting and had shared it with Harriet Cox. They sat at a back table in McGarry's ready to feed on a stack of burgers, fries, and a pitcher of beer.

"Do we bait Shepherd and Rhodes with false information?" Donnelly took a bite out of his burger. "Any ideas?"

Collins picked up a French fry. "The electric urinal?"

Cox sipped her beer. "Commercial Products will take the urinal to market. But," she set her glass down and chuckled, "I can fill this Quentin Rhodes's willing ears with disinformation about the Vibrating Electric Toilet."

Donnelly sputtered, beer spraying, as he laughed.

"The Vibrating Electric Toilet," Cox repeated, deadpan. "Let me explain. Quentin Rhodes wants to provide Dingmann with 'scoop' on the hot new product you presented to Nick Jackson. Am I right?'

"Yes," they said. Collins lit a cigarette.

"Rhodes goes away thinking the VET is a unique product in the annals of bathroom fixtures and a market changer."

"How so?" Donnelly finished his beer and poured himself another. "What're you going to say to the poor guy?"

Cox lifted her glass in a mock toast. "Appealing to both sexes. Warm to sit on. Prevents unpleasant odors from escaping from its immediate environs. The vibration effect adds to 'the complete bathroom process.'" She smiled. "An extra-cost feature enables the vibrating aspect to cause sexual stimulation."

"For when the wife's away?" laughed Collins.

"When the man's not up to it," Cox said dryly, to a ripple of laughter.

"Convents and rectories and single-sex schools," said Donnelly, "would love this product. Relieve the tension, wouldn't you think?"

"Feed that to Rhodes," said Collins, "but warn him the product may be banned by the Legion of Decency."

"From what you told me," said Cox, "he'll probably want to call it the Wizz."

"'Nobody beats the Wizz' will be his tagline," said Donnelly.

"We shall see," said Cox. *Enough of this.* "The lowdown on Rhodes, please?"

"Burnside, one of the lesser preps," said Collins. "Cornell, one of the lesser Ivies. A&P program, with the company six years, minimal advancement. Best talent is sucking up."

"I anticipate meeting him," said Cox. "Let's get another pitcher."

Chapter Fifteen

"We interrupt this news broadcast. We have a verdict in the Half Moon murder case. Here's Bill Barlow at the courthouse." "Thank you, Floyd. The defendant, Gwanzelle Half Moon, is coming down the courthouse steps to a flurry of shouted questions and flashing cameras."

His lead attorney, Clinton Pearson, civil rights lawyer and supporter of progressive causes, stepped forward. He was dressed in a bespoke suit, his long hair tied in a ponytail falling halfway down his back. The crowd quieted. "The standard of our legal system," he said, "assumes you are innocent until proven guilty. In Gwanzelle's case," he turned to his client, "the power structure declared him guilty until proven innocent. Which is why we have trial by jury. Gwanzelle, a member of two persecuted minority groups, is acquitted of all charges. As a lawyer I can't countenance the oppression that has affected my client." Pearson leaned into the microphone. "And I commend Judge Bruce Wigler for his handling of the trial. His ruling to disallow all police testimony against my client was a courageous declaration by an enlightened jurist." He stepped back. "Thank you."

Across the street the student demonstrators cheered.

Justin Hitchcock switched the station. Behind the reporter, buildings burned and looters broke into stores. *Yet another urban riot. How many were killed this time? Why are these animals roaming at will? The situation is getting worse.* He turned off the set, reached for the phone, and dialed Abe Floss.

125

"…for crying out loud Abe, don't be naïve. It's the American justice system."

"I would agree, Justin," said Floss. "At the least we need to be able to try an offender, come to a verdict, and then act without endless appeals, stays, and higher court dithering."

"Amen," said Hitchcock. "In your observation is a kernel of an excellent idea. Not wholly original but as with all worthy thinking, perhaps the time is now?"

"Such as?"

"States' rights," said Hitchcock. "To change the law and adjudicate capital cases at the local level without federal courts' review or interference."

"Do we have the votes? I believe this is doable but the effort must be bipartisan."

"Point well taken." *We should quickly turn this issue into a platform.* Hitchcock mentally counted heads. "We can do this. We whisper words in the right ears and sit back."

***

Senator Jeffrey Marshall's chief of staff walked the wealthy constituent to the door. "I understand your outrage, sir, and I'm glad you appreciate our position. The senator is supporting a new way to deal with these criminals." *The senator is looking for a topic that puts him on the tube. Shazam! Issues of law and order are top of mind with the electorate these days.*

The constituent continued, "An attempt to assassinate a president and no one was caught. The cities are burning and no one is convicted. The students laugh at the cameras. Even putting the Nixon shooting aside, the country won't stand for this kind of dealing. Scum like Gwanzelle Half Moon walk because of an unethical lawyer and a corrupt judge." He paused to take a breath.

"Yes, we share your concerns, sir," said Marshall's chief of staff, "and we appreciate your contributions to the senator's efforts to make our nation a safe and just place. Even as we speak, the senator is drafting legislation to put rights to these egregious wrongs." *And we want to be at the front of the pack when the issue goes to the lead on the networks and to Senate hearings.*

Senator Marshall lacked the height and angular features Hollywood frequently offered as their movie-theater rendition of the prototypical national legislator. He was short, pudgy, round-faced, and beginning to lose the last of his hair.

Marshall hung up the phone, an annoyed and perplexed look on his face. He reached for his intercom. "Sencha, please page Norman and tell him to see me as soon as he gets back." Yet another debate on judicial reform was under way. He chuckled. *All the hand-wringing in the world is not going to change the essential dynamics of the political game. It costs money to join, it costs money to play, it costs money to stay, and it costs money to climb. Information is power and one needs its leverage to gamble at these stakes. Knowledge justifies our position and place in the dealing, trimming, and not leveling, within accepted bounds of course, with my colleagues and other "in the know" people.*

Two minutes later, Norman, Marshall's chief of staff, stuck his head in the doorway. "I'm here, Senator."

"What did Mr. Green say?" "Mr. Green" was code for a big-time contributor.

"He's concerned about law and order. The judges, the perps, et cetera. He was particularly upset with the Gwanzelle Half Moon decision, his lawyer Clinton Pearson, and the judge, 'Turn 'em loose Bruce' Wigler."

"Like everyone else these days." Senator Marshall sighed. "I just got off the phone with someone I'm not even going to name. The message came through loud and clear: do something about the law-and-order issue: craft a bill giving more control to states and localities."

"The Half Moon decision may not be the catalyst, Senator," Norman said. "Egged on by various groups, the minorities will scream discrimination. Next, the students demonstrate in support, followed by more riots in the urban areas."

Marshall motioned to Norman to close the door. He reached into his desk drawer and pulled out a cigar. After fussing, he lit it and puffed. The smoke swirled coolly down his throat. He exhaled; the thick, rich haze breached the air and hung high before wobbling into odd shapes and tapering away. "You're right," he acknowledged, taking a further puff. "We'll stage a press conference and say we're working on ways to deal with this crisis."

"With the result being?" said Norman, searching for breathable air.

"Some high-profile reprobate will create an uproar and we can pass a local-powers bill without any significant protest."

Norman nodded. *And you'll have a carefully crafted track record as you shoot for the big one. All the law-and-order Mr. Greens will flock to your corner.*

***

The press conference was on the steps of the Capitol building. Hitchcock and Floss had quietly spread the word, and the legislators had listened. It was a bipartisan moment with the perfect photo-op backdrop. Many of Senator Marshall's colleagues on the Senate

Crime Committee joined with Representative Alan Pomfret, chairman of the House Crime Committee, and a dozen other members.

Marshall stepped forward, scanned the assembled journalists, and spoke, "I'll make a short statement and afterward Congressman Pomfret and I will take your questions. Some years before joining this august body"—he gestured to his colleagues and the building behind them—"I was an attorney general in my home state of Massachusetts. I fought for the rights of the underprivileged and for the maintenance of an acceptable standard of law and order. In this new decade, those standards are dissolving as our cities burn and ordinary citizens huddle in terror in their houses. Yet nothing is done. We are forming a bipartisan study group to address this issue and come up with concrete proposals to bring before the Congress."

Chapter Sixteen

An exasperated Nick Jackson switched off the TV. "Florence, get me Schuyler in Washington."

A minute later his intercom buzzed. "He's on line two, Mr. Jackson."

"Stan, what the fuck are Marshall and Pomfret and their pals up to?"

"Staging a holding action, Nick," said Schuyler. "They feel they need a mechanism to get the local communities the right to try and convict locally for capital crimes."

"What the hell do those bastards want besides our money?"

"They want certain justice, promptly delivered, not a minority getting off like Gwanzelle Half Moon."

"I'm holding you responsible, Stan. I want something benefiting our products passed. Soon. Let those guys on the Hill know the cash spigots dry up unless they do." Jackson slammed the phone down. *The results will come, especially since I lit a Bunsen burner under Schuyler's ass.* He pressed the intercom. "Florence, get me Marty Spiegel."

Thirty seconds later Spiegel was on the line. "Marty, where are we on the Global deal?" Ilium was in negotiations to buy the Global Broadcasting Corporation.

Spiegel filled him in. "...so we followed your guidelines and then chewed them down another twenty percent. Schuyler is greasing the wheels in Washington, so no flak from them. We can do the deal in the next few days."

"Excellent! Great job, Marty," Nick shouted. He hung up, made a note to deliver a sizable bonus to Spiegel, and instructed Florence to reach Abe Floss.

***

"Abe," said Jackson, "we're finalizing the Global deal. Any obstacles?"

"None I am aware of, Nick. We had a word with the key committee people who might voice a concern over antitrust implications. Your DC folks covered the rest."

Jackson smiled. *Beautiful. Prime time. Prime twat. Lots of actresses to bang.* "I'll make my gratitude known by a check to the committee."

"Much appreciated," said Floss.

"Before you go, Abe, where are we on the crime issue? That was a nonsense press conference Marshall and those other guys staged at the Capitol this afternoon."

"Once we get a case that outrages all the citizenry, it'll pass both houses faster than shit through a goose. Good talking with you, Nick. Thanks for the check."

Chapter Seventeen

A supporter of progressive issues, Clinton Pearson was a power in the liberal wing of the Democratic Party. His wife, Beatrice Arbuthnot Pearson, was an old-money Republican descended from Mayflower stock. Upon graduation from Columbia, Pearson joined a white shoe law firm and advanced to partner. Then a college friend convinced him to participate in an early Freedom Ride down South. Radicalized, he began to support left-wing causes, angering his firm's partners.

Pearson had recently moved into the limelight for a different reason, defending accused rapists, terrorists, and mafia bosses, sparking hatred from the wider community. He became adept at getting his picture on TV and in the print media. This approach took a toll on his family. His son Guy didn't see much of him. Pearson's eldest child, Wilma, was in and out of rehab and his wife, Beatrice, subsisted on her horses, prescription pills, and sherry.

Guy Pearson was exposed to the brightest and best from an early age. He attended the finest primary and prep schools and quickly learned privilege didn't amount to much unless you had power. The way to power was money. As a fifth grader at Eton Hill Country Day he began selling prescription medications filched from his mother and Wilma. At Dalrymple Prep he dealt weed and hash as a freshman and sophomore. Junior year introduced Pearson to the wonders of dealing and using coke. It was clean and people paid for it in large-denomination banknotes.

In the summer between Dalrymple and Harvard, Pearson found the mother lode: heroin. He avoided its use but learned supplying was the gift that kept on giving. During his time at Harvard he discovered girls with habits would do anything for it. This enhanced Guy Pearson's sex life.

Coke remained his personal drug of choice: controllable, just-in-time exhilaration. In dealing heroin, Pearson put layers between himself and his clientele. He became a careful but brutal businessman. Miss a payment or otherwise cause concern, you'd disappear. He personally overdosed eight customers in his sophomore year with no one the wiser. As a junior he saw to the death of anyone appearing to show turncoat tendencies. Killing provided Guy a better high without coke's runny nose, loss of appetite, and septum damage. By senior year he was raping his hardcore female customers. Life was good.

The Massachusetts State Police and the Boston police knew of a large heroin dealer and more than a dozen unsolved rapes and murders. The parents of the students who died were in an uproar. No connection with Pearson; he'd had some close scrapes but was never caught.

***

The Cauldron pounded with Harvard undergrads twisting and swaying to the DJ's playlist. Pearson headed to his "office": a table in an out-of-the-way corner where his lieutenants received a steady stream of visitors. In exchange for obscene amounts of cash, they left with discreet packets of a substance variously called horse, scag, dragon, and, more familiarly, heroin.

After a side conversation concerning the evening's take, Pearson set off to the bar.

A minute later she came in the door with several giggling friends. *A townie. New talent. An innocent. First-rate tits. Fresh face. A nobody. Perhaps a little more.*

Her name was Mary Jane Davisson; she and four of her friends had come from nearby Salem. Pearson turned on the charm for Ms. Davisson. Shortly thereafter, the parasites descended and swooped up her pals.

A half hour later he and Davisson were in a storage room. Pearson had force-fed her a line of heroin and she lay, clothes strewn beside her, sprawled on the floor. His silk underwear, Gucci loafers, pale blue Armani blazer, sweat-soaked Sulka pima cotton shirt, and Hermès tie lay neatly stacked on a crate. Drops of perspiration slid down his forehead; his erection was rock-hard. She didn't move as he lowered himself on top of her. *A little stiff maybe, but still good enough to be a fine piece of ass.*

Suddenly the door burst in and police pulled him up. He did not resist. The light made the drool dripping off his chin sparkle. He smiled and his eyes danced. "I'd like to call my lawyer," he said.

Another officer checked for vitals. He looked up at his partner and shook his head. He dug out her wallet and pulled out her driver's license. "Her name's Mary Jane Davisson." He went silent as he dug through other documents in the purse. "Oh shit, she's Ike Davisson's daughter. Read this douchebag his rights and get him the hell out of here."

"I repeat; I want to call my lawyer," said Pearson, a little more loudly.

"Better be a good one, pal," said one of the policemen. "We're talking homicide and she's the daughter of the superintendent of state police."

"My lawyer is Clinton Pearson," he said. "He's my father. Good enough?"

***

Clinton Pearson used his influence to get Guy's bail hearing in front of Judge Bruce "Turn-'em-loose-Bruce" Wigler. Though the police considered Guy a flight risk, his father argued that the evidence leading up to the assault was largely circumstantial. Remand would be punitive because the state had no case other than the compromising position they found Guy in. Judge Wigler agreed; he freed Guy on $25,000 bail.

Within twenty-four hours Pearson jumped bail and vanished.

***

Three days later Justin Hitchcock received a phone call. "Holy Moses," he muttered after he hung up. He quickly dialed Abe Floss.

"Abe, are you aware they arrested Clint Pearson's kid two days ago and he jumped bail?"

"Shit no," said Floss. "What did they arrest him for?"

Hitchcock described the circumstances of the capture. "Because of Mary Jane Davisson's father, the full investigative resources of several police agencies and the FBI are mobilized on Guy Pearson and his activities. As you can imagine the law wants his head on a skewer above the city gates."

"I don't doubt it," said Floss. "I know the girl's father. Ike Davisson is a good man, well-liked."

Hitchcock sipped his coffee. "The police have been busy, particularly since Guy Pearson escaped. Apparently Guy has dealt drugs since grade school. He started with pills. At Dalrymple he moved to cocaine and then heroin. They've found out he had a huge network in Boston and as far south as Providence and as far north as Portland, Maine. The authorities are rousting anyone. They've found he rose by killing anyone he knew, or at least that's what the rumor is. More than that, they've discovered he's a rapist many times over. Whether his father is aware of any of this remains to be seen."

"Do they have proof?" asked Floss.

"Witnesses are coming out of the woodwork. His dealers and associates are plea-bargaining—if you'll pardon my French—their *asses* off. Appears that Guy Pearson was a lead suspect in a number of crimes, but they could never prove it nor had enough evidence to formally charge him. The worst case they've linked him to was when he killed an entire family with a machete. The father owed Pearson money; he zip-tied the father to a bed and brought his family into the room. Pearson raped the heroin-addicted wife and their eleven-year old daughter. Hacked them to pieces. A four-year-old sister listened in a closet. She's now seven."

"Jesus," said Floss, "the kid's a monster. Is his father his lawyer?"

"Indeed," said Hitchcock. "Clinton Pearson is one of the leading lights of your left wing, isn't he? Turns out his son is rich, hard to touch, clever, and an ogre."

Floss considered his answer. "The American system guarantees legal representation for the accused. Clint Pearson earned his fame and reputation working for the poor and the powerless. In the last couple of years he's shed the brand he so compellingly created. He's lost standing with the party because of the dregs he now defends. They call him a 'publicity hound' and a hit-and-run lawyer who 'brings cases on page one; the public defender eventually wins them on page sixty-eight.'"

"Harsh folks, your lefties, Abe," said Hitchcock. "If we jump on this fast while it still has maximum grisly, stomach-churning impact, Guy Pearson could be the catalyst for speedy and local justice. He is such an extreme case we should have little difficulty rallying everyone in the Congress who matters."

Floss sighed. "You're right. Let's get on it."

***

The press and the television networks jumped on the story and played up the lurid aspects of Pearson's criminal activities. Largely circumstantial evidence, Clinton Pearson explained.

Public reaction began to set in. Shocked such a twisted freak could be walking among them triggered a massive manhunt. His picture appeared everywhere.

A tsunami of negative opinion followed. Since Clinton Pearson had turned to defending low-life defendants, his son was presumed guilty by association. Pressure grew for laws that would allow decision and action at the local level.

Into the gap jumped several lawmakers, led by Senator Marshall and Congressman Pomfret. In their joint announcement, covered by the major networks, they reminded everyone of the bipartisan study group they'd formed to address the issue. "This effort has produced concrete proposals to prevent even more social disruption. We will work to enact them into law."

Marshall stepped forward. "All justice should be local; it is time to shuck off federal interference and indecision. Our bill allows officials to deal at the local level with aggressive criminal elements, up to and including capital punishment. The judiciary has taken the idea

137

of social and human rights too far off track. We are dealing with monsters."

Pomfret added, "We expect swift passage of our proposal."

Of course the draft was leaked. Everyone even remotely involved pored over it, searching for irregularities or passageways to crawl through. The media, unsympathetic to the purpose, parsed it word by word. Editorials thundered. Unusual for legislation, the language was tightly woven. One short understandable phrase moved to the next, the warp and the weft simple but tight. Several legislators tried to attach riders and were promptly swatted away by their party elders.

The bill passed by a large margin in both houses.

Chapter Eighteen

Donnelly sat, listening in on the sounds coming from Dingman's office, imagining Dingmann sitting back in his chair in his faux William Buckley posture, wearing the de rigueur dark blue silk suit with the little random nubs complemented by a Brooks Brothers tie in the pattern of some regiment.

Donnelly could hear someone compliment Dingmann on the tie as his subordinates assembled for their staff meeting. He recounted its provenance. Donnelly snickered. He mentally pictured *The Blue Painted Balls Hanging Out Queen's Regiment.* Being Irish, he could never figure out where all the Brit history came from. *Between starving ancestors, beheading wives, staking out heads of dissenting nobles, and smothering royal heirs in their cribs, I guess they spent any extra time they could find naming Regiments.*

"Harrumph." *Dingmann. Probably pursing his lips and making an mmm sound prior to his pontification.* "This Comfort Chair situation has gotten out of control and is currently in the hands of incompetents with not the slightest glimmer of the intricacies and standards of Ilium consumer product marketing."

"Hear, hear," rejoined a voice Donnelly couldn't identify. *An asshole.*

He did recognize the next. "We gotta discredit those peckerwoods." *Rufus Hogg. The son of a bitch.*

Only a matter of time before Hogg, Drake, and Shepherd threw in with Dingmann. He and Collins appreciated the tempting combination of the chair and Nick Jackson's attention. *Danger versus career payoff.*

139

Dingmann took a beating at the first Jackson review. A key ingredient to corporate success is staying power. Creatures like Dingmann never stop simpering back. We won't know how many Judased us unless they speak up, but our assumptions about the rats have been solid. Donnelly chuckled. *Not bad corporate politics for curb creatures.*

Dingmann continued, "After some reflection I asked Quentin Rhodes to invite the lead engineer on the chair project, Harold Cox, to our meeting. Mr. Rhodes says Cox is technically adept but unwise in the ways of the world.

"No aggressive probing or comments, please. They might alert Mr. Cox to our intentions. I want a pleasant, upbeat conversation subtly flattering Cox's technical skills and soft pushes on him directed at finding out where this is and what's next. Once we obtain some concrete information we will formulate our interdiction. Quentin, please escort our guest in."

Donnelly then heard the sound of a door opening and Dingmann say, "Good morning, Mr. Cox. We are pleased you spared the time to brief us on your project."

"Thank you for the invitation," Cox said. "I'm always excited to talk about our chair."

Paper crackled as Cox affixed a flipchart to a stand.

Clever, using the collective to make them feel included in his project. Donnelly smiled. *Cox was a techie, true, but once clued into the political web, a formidable player. Now to bait the trap.*

"The chair is the epitome of Ilium technology coupled with a practical market application. As you can perceive in this intelligent circuit"—sounds of a flipchart page turning. Donnelly drifted a bit. He and Collins were briefed on the big technical design picture when they first met Cox. At the moment it was being applied to Dingmann's folks as a soporific. Next would be the hook for them to swallow.

Cox droned on long enough to lull the audience. A final crackling flip of the chart: "But the impact of this will be minuscule compared to the Vibrating Electric Toilet." Donnelly heard the intake of breath from everyone in the room. He imagined Dingmann bolting upright. Possibly even accidentally shoving his finger up his nose in surprise.

"A vibrating electric toilet?" *So, Shepherd. Bastard.*

"Yes. Top secret, as you'd expect. We're all Ilium folk here so I don't see why you shouldn't be told. Think about it for a moment. Toilets"—Cox paused for effect—"are ubiquitous! Especially compared to the limited market for the chair."

"My god!" some minion exclaimed. *Cox is a regular Jimmy Stewart with the bullshit delivery. We need to step up the use of her skills.*

"Tell us the difference between this electric toilet and an, um, everyday such device?" *Drake this time. Christ, they're all Benedict Arnolding. Bastards. Don't get mad; get even, I say.*

"Well," said Cox, repeating what she'd concocted in their meeting, "the toilet is warm to sit on, with the capability to prevent unpleasant odors escaping from its immediate environs. The vibration effect assists the, ah, 'complete bathroom process.'" Donnelly imagined Cox smiling. "We've added an extra-cost feature to enable the vibrating aspect to cause sexual stimulation."

No comments? A throat cleared and Dingmann said, "Thank you so much for your time and this very informative update, Mr. Cox. I trust you are being well served by others in our department, but if there arises anything else you need, we stand ready to assist you. I will have our Mr. Rhodes stay in touch to maintain contact."

"Thank you, gentlemen." Sound of a flipchart rolling up and the conference room door opening and closing.

"A goddamn vibrating electric toilet!" Drake's voice. "Can you believe it? In this kind of housing-start market? Into even only the

141

top-tier residences? The volume would be enough to drive the price down as fast as electronics. This goddamn toilet could be a monster!"

"How about Watt Shit as a name," said Hogg.

"Make the tagline 'Nobody beats the wizz,'" said Shepherd. Donnelly laughed; his prediction had come true.

"Gentlemen, this crudity is uncalled for," said Dingmann. "I have a long relationship with Lou Willets. I'm going to start turning the screws to get Locker and those two curb creatures, Donnelly and Collins, off the chair account. Meanwhile, Rhodes, I want you all over this Cox guy. He looks effeminate. Perhaps he has a moral weak spot. Become his new best friend."

Quentin Rhodes should be so goddamn lucky to find Cox's weak spot. I've thought about that spot once or twice myself. For the moment there are bigger bears to dance with. He shut down the surveillance equipment as Dingmann's staff meeting concluded. *Our most important goal, misdirection, achieved.*

Chapter Nineteen

"Hey, did you hear Ilium bought Global Broadcasting?" Collins hung over Donnelly's partition.

Donnelly pushed away from his typewriter. "So? Does it mean anything to us?"

"Good question," Collins said. "They're going to need programs. GBC is dead last in practically every time slot."

Donnelly stared off. "Do we do anything? Develop some program concepts?"

"Yeah, we should."

"How long?"

"In a week?"

"Deal. Do we tell Leeson or Locker?"

"Not now." Collins laughed. "Maybe never; the results could be extracurricular and possibly pseudonym city."

"Escape hatch?"

Collins nodded. "We reveal all in a week."

***

In the back room at McGarry's, Collins sat, a pitcher of beer between him and Donnelly.

"Okay," he said, "I call this *Felon Hunters*. We can either do this news style or as a scripted show. I say scripted." He handed Donnelly a folder.

Donnelly opened it and read. "Opening Shot: a gray, extended cab van waits to be released onto I-94. In addition to its extra length, a section has been added down its middle to stretch and widen it. The sheer size of the vehicle is ominous. It has two large tires on each side of its rear panels. A low whump, whump, whump rumble comes from the big over-bored high-powered V8 engine.

"Narrator: 'This van has been parked at the top of the on-ramp for a half hour. They await word from their spotter shown here changing a tire.'

"'Seventy-five minutes ago *Felon Hunters* spotted the fugitive Twymon Smallwood at the Detroit Metro Airport International Terminal. He picked up a passenger in a black Chrysler Imperial. They are on their way downtown; we have the tag number.'"

Donnelly cocked an eyebrow. "You scripted the whole thing?"

"Yeah. Seemed like a good idea at the time." He finished his beer and poured himself another.

"If you say so," said Donnelly. He continued to read. "Narrator: 'Inside the van, Judge Spencer Chumley drums his fingers. Sixteen people sit facing a modified Ilium Electric Chair. The felon hunting team wear dark blue suits, white shirts, and striped ties.' The two women have on dark, conservative jacket-and-skirt combinations with minimal jewelry."

"Why suits?" Donnelly reached for his glass.

"A TV-ready appearance. The look of *Felon Hunters* has to seem a legal, logical process," Collins said.

"Makes sense," said Donnelly. "Back to the narration. 'Multiple murder warrants have been issued for Smallwood. He is also wanted for dealings with Oriental counterfeiters and drug dealers, including his passenger, who carries bulk bales of hash.'

"'Scan shot of the van passengers: The Judge, the driver, a public defender and a prosecutor, a clerk of the court, two chair wranglers, a support tech, a switchman, and a packaging specialist who handles the remains. Six jurors and a jury alternate can be transported to the team should a problem arise. Two of the jurors are women.'"

"Do these people get named?"

"Not sure," said Collins.

"Now we're getting to the action part," said Donnelly. "The small speaker on the dash of the van crackles to life. 'Target in sight. Black Chrysler Imperial. Approximate speed, eighty miles per hour. Plate number confirmed. He will be the tenth vehicle exiting your bridge overpass; to you.'

"Narrator: 'The driver counts the vehicles squirting out. "Seven, eight, nine," and releases the clutch. Exterior shot of rear tires screeching. The van rockets down the on-ramp and merges with traffic, two cars behind the Imperial.'

"'A chair wrangler sits on a jump seat between the judge and the driver. He targets the Imperial with a spotting scope. 'Two passengers, rear seat. Driver. No shotgun rider. Steel wheels. Oversize tires. Serious car. Pin him on the barrier.'

"'Exterior shot, no narration: The driver accelerates, which puts the passenger side of the van opposite the driver's side of the Imperial. They reach a curve and the van swerves right and forces the Imperial into a concrete road-repair barrier.'

"'Close-up: A special twenty-four-inch-wide pliable rubber convex strip mounted to the van's side grabs the Imperial. In a shower of sparks and screaming sheet metal, it holds the van snug against the barrier.

"Exterior shot: The Imperial rocks back and forth, attempting to escape. The chair wranglers jump out, gas the occupants, and drag Smallwood out through the rear window.

"Pan shot: The rear of the van opens and the judge, lawyers, and clerk step down. The jurors are seated in three rows. The tech hooks up and tests the Ilium chair. He plugs the power cord into the step-up transformer powered by a secondary engine mounted under the modified van's hood.

"Focus shot: Smallwood stands as Judge Chumley reads the charges over the din of traffic. Smallwood's shouts are bleeped obscenities.

"'How do you plead?'

"'Mo [bleep] Fu [bleep],' screams Smallwood.

"Prosecutor and Defense make five-minute presentations.

"The judge nods to the Jurors.

"'We find the defendant guilty as charged, your Honor,' says the woman foreman.

"The judge's sentence is barely audible above the traffic.

"They strap Smallwood into the chair. The judge nods and the Switchman does his job.

"Smallwood's hair stands straight out.

"Narrator: 'Smallwood's eyes pop as if he were in Shotgun Willie's on Totally Nude Night. His fingers wiggle like a card shark before a trick. As suddenly as a spark winking out, it's over.'

"Exterior shot: A workman-like cleaning and repacking. Smallwood's mouth remains open and his ears still smoke. The packaging specialist slides a black plastic bag over him. Whistling, he attaches a hose leading to what resembles a portable pool inflator.

The air goes out of the bag and Twymon Smallwood turns into a lump. The specialist wraps three packaging straps around it.

"Narrator: 'A contract hauler will collect Twymon Smallwood, no longer a threat to society, within thirty minutes.'

"Interior: Looking out the van window, adrift in a sea of cars, Judge Chumley says, 'That went pretty smoothly, if I do say so myself.'

"Narrator: '*Felon Hunters*: making justice triumph and America safe. Next week, Newark.'"

Donnelly clapped his hands. "Jim, this script is outstanding! You've outdone yourself this time. You're right there as things go down. This show will rack up sponsors too. Amoco high-test gas, panel trucks, Firestone tires. Big mass-market guys. Mondo advertising budgets: can you say a gold mine?"

"And Ilium?"

"Find out Nick's take. The angle should move a ton of Comfort Chairs."

***

Another night at McGarry's and another pitcher of beer. "Okay," said Donnelly, "the first episode of *Felon Hunters* is outlined and ready to shoot. How about the biggest market of all?"

Collins rubbed his neck. "Which is?"

"Kids," said Donnelly, "and their parents."

Collins sighed loudly. "Jesus, Frank, that's a good idea."

Donnelly went on. "The kids will have Johnny Volt, crime fighter extraordinaire. Get a designer for the Johnny Volt costume, someone for the comic book, and another for the action figures."

"Action figures?"

"Something I noodled. Kind of a masculine doll…"

"Doll?" Collins's eyebrows arched in mock horror. "What do you want to do to these kids?"

"Trust me here. There's a fortune in the accessories like capes, electric chairs, and bad-guy figures. Bigger than the comic books and the young adult novels. Check out the promo campaign." He slid some loose pages across to him.

Collins read, his brow creasing. "Hey, kids! The newest toy! Johnny Volt! With a complete line of wanted criminals!

"Sit 'em down in your own miniature Portable Electric Chair (battery supplied).

"Strap 'em in!

"Juice 'em!

"Whirr! Buzz! Zap! Zot! Zam!

"Hear his lungs go through their final exhale!

"Smell the acrid flesh! (100 odor packets supplied.)

"Check for a pulse in the bad guy's lifeless wrist!

"Feel the power! You are the man!"

"You're sick, Donnelly," he said. "Anyone seen it?"

"No, I thought we'd fine-tune this, the *Felon Hunter*, and the adult product and decide whether we present to our bosses or get an agent."

"Well," said Collins, "we could add, 'play State Pen. Be the first on your block to own one.' Maybe put fake quotes on the box."

"Like?" said Donnelly.

Collins tried not to smile. "Oh, like, 'A real scorcher: Joan D'Arc'; or, 'Great fun: Caryl Chessman'; or, 'Better than rope: Jessie James.'"

"I'm sick?" Donnelly twisted his face in mock disgust.

"What about the adult product?"

"Kind of a Batman/Superman–type caped guy who pursues the low-lifes that prey on the weak and the poor and commit seriously heinous shit. Johnny Volt brings them to justice and personally throws the switch."

"Anything else?"

"Yeah," said Donnelly. "We televise the real executions. One-hour weekly shows; we'll need a symbol as moderator."

"Who?"

"John Wayne?"

"The Duke?" said Collins. "Never happen." He swirled his beer coaster on the tabletop. "Marshal Dillon on *Gunsmoke?*"

"The Marshal's too busy cleaning up Dodge," said Donnelly. "We need an executioner. The public is expressing resentment and frustration. The Portable Electric Chair shows people justice can be effective without them getting involved.

"Angry enforcers defined not by law but by primal notions of justice and revenge?"

"Ordinary citizens want solutions to society's violent bad actors," said Donnelly.

Collins nodded. "Nothing wrong with toasting these badasses as long as the right ones get toasted." He lit a cigarette.

Donnelly snapped his fingers. "Perfect! The Toaster. Someone who shows neither regret nor doubt."

"Who is this Toaster Man?" Collins exhaled a white curl. "He's cool, slightly aloof. He reveals only satisfaction and withholds everything else. He keeps his head still, at a slight angle. He narrows his eyes, scowls, and curls his lower lip."

149

"Will he have a name?"

Collins thought for a moment. "Job Slaughterthorn." He lowered his voice, "The Toaster." Another drag on the cigarette. "Who will he remind you of?"

"Big and scary, an amalgam of every hard guy you ever knew back in the neighborhood," said Donnelly, "outfitted in black slacks and a black turtleneck."

Collins poured a refill. "Nick should love this guy. The Toaster will stand for law and order and punish the wicked every week in a different major market."

"Live. Original. No reruns," laughed Donnelly.

"We need an agent," said Collins. "This stuff is way above our pay grade. Internally, someone would steal it."

"Yeah," said Donnelly. "The old myths of cooperation dissolve into the messy greed and stupidity of ambition."

"That's way too erudite for a curb creature," said Collins. "Anyway, we'll need a pseudonym. Something innocuous, like Gregory Ellis."

Chapter Twenty

"Dingmann's heading to the new guy's office," Donnelly said, peering into the cubicle where Collins sat amidst his usual pile of debris. "Give me his name again."

"Lou Willets. I'd like to be a fly on the wall to catch the nonverbal signals between those two," said Collins.

"Tape is rolling…?"

Collins studied the mess. "I've got stuff going on. Too iffy to eavesdrop when all the snitches and geniuses are in residence."

"Agreed. We listen over beers at McGarry's tonight," said Donnelly.

***

Bob Dingmann had entered Willets's office and, after some pleasantries, sat in the chair Willets indicated. "I couldn't believe it when they said you were the new GM," Dingmann said. "A lucky break for A&P. Even at Cornwallis I knew you'd go places; you had the style."

Same Dingmann. Smart enough and a would-be politician. Usually takes a while before the boss can find his mole in the organization. Voila! Bob pops his head out of the lawn voluntarily. The best toady is a willing toady. Willets smiled his best press conference smile. "So how are you? It's been a long time. Bring me up to speed."

"Short version," said Dingmann, leaning back and crossing his legs. "After Cornwallis, Harvard. After Harvard, a stint with PSE&G in Newark. Thought I could shake them out of their utility business torpor. Don't know what I was thinking." He sipped his coffee. "After a year I bailed out and joined Ilium. A few assignments. Took a job here in A&P to head the consumer team. I like the ad and publicity business. Exciting like Harvard; think outside the box, off the wall."

"You're married?" asked Willets.

"Yes. Her name's Sue. New York girl; comes from Brooklyn. Met her at a club in Greenwich Village while working at PSE&G and continued to date her when I was in the city on the Ilium Marketing Program. Swept me off my feet; we both like to party. Modeled part time to pay for school, did some lingerie work. We kept in touch while she went to med school in the Midwest and I was on an assignment out there. Moved back to New York. She transferred up here because she's in shouting distance of the city. She's a proctologist, unusual for a female MD, sees a few men but takes care of all the women; makes her own hours at Maqua hospital and we get into the city whenever we need to."

Whoa! A proctologist. I wonder what she thinks of your obvious transparency. Maybe she wanted someone who's easy to read. If she's a partier, though, she and my wife will bond. "I got married myself," Willets offered.

"I guess we both have the ball and chain, Lou," chuckled Dingmann.

Maybe you do, pal, but my dick still swings. "Yes, well anyway, after Princeton I went to work for Hasbro up in Providence. Got married during my year there. Portuguese fisherman's daughter, Elzira, a psychologist. She's a teacher now; I met her after she'd given up her practice. We moved out West shortly after I joined Ilium on the Management Training Program."

Dingmann took another sip of his coffee. "The A&P Department is in many ways like an advertising agency."

"That's part of the challenge," said Willets. His phone rang; he ignored it. "So tell me the real inside dope on this place. I only came to A&P because Nick Jackson told me I should." *I'm going to get up next to Jackson and ride his train. Play your cards right and you'll ride with me.*

Dingmann uncrossed his legs and began, "Our business is mostly industrial, with all of the implied nuts and bolts. A&P is large, most of the people are smart, and our program graduates are recognized as some of the best around. They're recruited into the big ad agencies. It's a dynamic environment and right now we're looking at products way beyond what we normally see." He swallowed. "One is the electric chair."

Willets grimaced.

They didn't brief you? Or are you playing me? Dingmann plowed on. "Sounds stupid, I know; a project code name. We're working on a better one for branding. Basically this chair reclines, warms, and massages the customer. That's only part of the opportunity. Two of our snot-nosed young trainees figured out a strategy to use the chair as a law-and-order-enhancing industrial product to push it out into the upscale consumer market in a big way."

"What do you mean?" said Willets. *Jackson talked about some hotshots. Depends on whose ox is gored, I guess.*

"Right behind the electric chair these same two commuter-college ruffians have an electric toilet in development that performs all sorts of useful and unspeakable functions for its user. Can you imagine the market reach of an electric toilet? Herb Kohler and the guys at American Standard will have heart attacks."

An electric toilet was not in any of my briefings. "Sounds interesting," said Willets. "Get started. Get me involved."

"Will do." Dingmann shifted. "I need a favor."
"That being?"
"The chair is in the control of the Industrial Group. I need to get the account assigned to my group or at least get close enough to manipulate the scenario."

"Who's the industrial account manager?"
Dingmann tried to hide the emotion. "Locker. Joyce Locker."
Oops. Tread lightly. I was told she's tight with Jackson. I don't want to capsize my boat before the race gets under way. "Let me give this part of the plan a little consideration. I'll figure something out."

"Thank you."
Willets nodded and turned to some paperwork.
Dingmann, subtly reminded of the new power structure at A&P, silently rose and left.

***

Donnelly and Collins settled into a back booth at McGarry's, the small tape recorder between them. They toasted each other with an appreciative quaff of Schaefer beer. Setting the volume to level three, he clicked on the machine. Both leaned in to hear the slightly crackly conversation.

"I couldn't believe it when they said it was you, Lou," said Dingmann to Willets. A chair scraped. "Even at Cornwallis I knew you'd go places; you had the style."

154

"I'll bet you couldn't," whispered Donnelly. "Must be like the girl who gets well laid and after everything finds out the guy is her first cousin."

Collins sniggered.

They listened as Willets and Dingmann brought each other up to speed on their careers.

"...PSE&G...don't know what I was thinking..."

"Probably thinking about stealing volts, you stupid grubber," said Collins.

Dingmann described his career climb and his comparison with A&P being as off-the-wall exciting as Harvard.

"Off the wall is right," said Donnelly. "Off the wall with your head up your ass chewing your own bullshit and spitting it out to see what sticks."

"Mother of Christ," said Collins, "don't give yourself a stroke. We've got these guys pinned like a beetle collection."

"I hate this crap. Even more when I hear it firsthand."

"I know. Me too. We'll give them their just desserts in due time."

Dingmann talked about his wife, Sue, and her being from Brooklyn.

"...she's a proctologist; makes her own hours at Maqua hospital..."

"A proctologist? Fitting," said Collins. "Wonder if she sees an asshole every time she looks at his face."

Donnelly snapped upright at Dingmann's description of his wife. *It can't be, he thought. No, impossible.*

"Something wrong?" asked Collins.

"If Dingmann's wife is who she might be, I once paid a quarter to see her tits." Donnelly's eyes were looking into the distant past. He did not look unhappy with his memories either. He laughed. "It can't be her."

"You knew his wife?"

Donnelly shrugged. "The possibility is too remote." He muttered, "She was a classmate of mine at Crucifixion grammar school. For a thirteen-year-old she had great tits, though. I wonder how they look now."

"Get a grip," said Collins. "You want me to pause this?"

"No, no." Donnelly waved to continue.

Willets described his life and the fact that his wife was a former psychologist who was now teaching. He moved on and came to what Donnelly thought was his actual objective. "So tell me, Bob…I only took this A&P job because Nick Jackson…I'm sure there's good stuff…I want to be in on it."

"Do you get the impression Willets is leading Dingmann around by the nose?" said Collins.

"Absolutely," Donnelly said.

"Blah blah blah," they said. Dingmann was speaking. "…right now we're looking…one is the Electric Chair…a project code name…two of our snot-nosed young trainees…"

"Got a tissue?" Collins said. "I feel nasal drip on my upper lip."

"Use your sleeve, you hick trainee."

Dingmann continued on the tape. "…once the Electric Chair is established these same two commuter-college ruffians have an electric toilet in development …"

"Ruffians? He called us ruffians?"

156

"Commuter-college ruffians, no less." Collins said.

"...can you imagine the market reach of an electric toilet...?"

"Sounds fun," said Willets.

"I need a favor, Lou."

"That being?"

"Catch the note of caution in Willets's voice?" said Collins. "Very cautious, our new leader."

They heard Dingmann say the Industrial Group controlled the account and Willets ask who was its manager.

"Locker. Joyce Locker,"

"Sounds like Bond. James Bond," said Donnelly.

Willets said he'd give it some consideration and Dingmann voiced appreciation. Ten seconds later they heard a door close.

"Whoops," said Collins. "Willets's radar is on high and he's treading lightly." They both said "Locker" and laughed.

"Willets reminded Dingmann of the new power structure at A&P," said Donnelly and drained his beer.

Collins refilled Donnelly's glass. "Wonder how Dingmann will play this with his staff?"

"He'll say he sits at the right hand of God, who dotes on his every word and phrase."

"His staff meeting is the day after Willets meets with the managers, right?" said Collins.

"Yeah. We don't have that room wired. But we have Dingmann's. We'll tune in to that. Should be entertaining."

***

As he listened to Dingmann's staff meeting, Donnelly imagined him standing at the head of his conference table, his staff sitting erect in attentive anticipation. "All right, gentlemen," he said, "Lou Willets is convinced the Vibrating Electric Toilet is a product worthy of promotion. Lou, in turn, has convinced Nick Jackson. Jackson wants a presentation in ten days."

No! Fuck! I don't believe it. How the hell did that happen? Willets didn't make those kinds of noises when he and Dingmann met. What the hell happened when Willets met with his direct reports? We made this toilet thing up. Shit, should've listened to what went on in Willets's office the last few days. Better pay attention. Damn, Locker must be going ballistic.

Dingmann's troops aren't saying anything.

Dingmann sounded impatient. "You fellows are supposed to be the best and brightest. This product can be a big money maker for Ilium."

"The toilet, Bob, upgrades the urinary and defecation process. Add in the sexual stimulation features and you have a paradigm shift in the bathroom experience."

"Nicely framed, Mr. Rhodes," said Dingmann, "but how do you all suggest we dramatize that proposition?"

"We divide into groups and come back in two days with campaign proposals."

"Excellent suggestion, Mr. Shepherd. Each group should contain at least two but no more than three. We shall reconvene here Wednesday at one. I'll leave you gentlemen to set up the teams."

Hogg, Shepherd, and Drake were not chosen by anyone and were left to form their own team. *Just like getting picked last in stickball. Those clowns should take the hint. I better check Dingmann and Willets's phones before I leave.*

***

"We created a monster when we made up the Vibrating Electric Toilet." Donnelly and Collins were in the company cafeteria late in the afternoon.

"What's happened?" Collins sipped his coffee.

"Apparently Willets had his first staff meeting this morning and wanted a show-and-tell. Dingmann talked about the Vibrating Electric Toilet. Long story short, Willets loved it." Donnelly took a savage bite from his Snickers bar.

"Asshole. How could Willets let himself get sucked in by something like that?"

Still chewing, Donnelly said, "He wasn't the only one."

Collins stared at him, his mind working on worst-case scenarios. "Bad?"

"The worst." Donnelly wiped his mouth with a napkin. "After the meeting Willets got on the phone to Nick Jackson. I just listened to the tape; Willets can be a very persuasive guy. Jackson wants a presentation on the toilet in ten days."

"Did you speak to Cox?"

"Yeah," said Donnelly. "I told her we'd meet with her tonight."

"Do you know if Locker discussed the Portable Electric Chair?"

"I can only presume she did. I guess Willets knew about it from Jackson."

"So the cat's out of the bag," said Collins.

"I guess. Dingmann may be having the last laugh."

"Let's go up to our office. Care to calculate the odds Locker wants us?"

***

They were back ten minutes when Collins's phone rang. "Jim, Ms. Locker wants you and Donnelly in her office right away," said Pat. "Hold on a sec. Sorry, gotta go."

Pissed off alert; we know what for, don't we? "Hey," he said to Donnelly, "surprise, surprise, we've been summoned to Joyce's office. Pat gave us an early warning."

Donnelly shrugged. "Let's get it over with."

***

"What's up?" asked Collins.

"I just came from Willets's first staff meeting," Locker said in an annoyed tone, "We had to do a show-and-tell on each section's activities." *Sniff.* "Imagine my surprise when Dingmann starts talking about a Vibrating Electric Toilet." The pencil she was holding in her hand snapped. "What, pray tell, is a Vibrating Electric Toilet? And what is Dingmann's involvement?" She swept the pencil off her desk and into the adjacent trashcan. "Do you birdbrains have a hand in this?" *Sniff.*

They were in a box. *Need to be careful about how we spin this. Don't want to reveal the listening devices.* "Cox told us Dingmann asked Rhodes to befriend him."

"We knew Dingmann wanted in on this project," said Collins, "so we talked to Cox and devised the most outlandish product we could think of. And, lo and behold, the concept of the Vibrating Electric Toilet came into being. Dingmann asked Cox for a presentation and Cox made it up."

Locker stared at them. They tried to look sheepish. "So the Vibrating Electric Toilet came out of your fertile minds?"

160

"Cox helped," said Collins. He took a Camel from a pack and lit up.

"A good bit," added Donnelly, who coughed.

"Damn," said Locker and lit a cigarillo.

"Damn?" they both said.

"Dingmann described the concept in such a way Willets bought it."

"He did?" said Collins, and blew smoke. He hoped he looked surprised. "The product doesn't exist."

"It will," said Locker. "Willets was enthusiastic; he called Jackson, and Nick wants a presentation."

"Shit," they both said, again feigning surprise.

Locker puffed. "According to Dingmann that's the least of the functions of this appliance. Apparently you can get yourself off if you get the extra cost features. Dingmann put things more delicately." He stared at them. "Did the three of you come up with this too?"

They nodded.

"Christ on a crutch," she yelled. "Dingmann and his crowd are back in the game."

"The pigeon among the cats again?" said Collins. "Hope he's wearing diapers if he presents to Jackson."

"I want a full report on where you are with the Portable Electric Chair."

They made to rise.

Locker grabbed her pen. "Now." *Sniff.*

"You mean right away?" *She's pissed because we let Dingmann outmaneuver her.* Donnelly waved at the cigarillo smoke. "The local burn 'em laws are getting passed in response to the congressional bill.

The speakers' bureau materials are going out to promote community choice in executions…"

"…we're using sympathetic police officials and prominent citizens," said Collins. "The kits, with the slides and scripts, are delivered through our sales force. People are putting pressure on the authorities to get portable electric chairs as a crime deterrent."

"Some of our most successful efforts have promoted lower-voltage chair kits for the education market." A smile played across Donnelly's lips. He drank. "Catholic schools; I guess that's one way to deal with a high student-teacher ratio…"

"In Washington, the bill passed permitting local executions…"

"Okay, good progress," Locker said after ten minutes. *Sniff.* "Now your priority is to think of a way to fix this vibrating toilet fiasco you two created." She threw up her hands. "Please get out of my sight."

***

"Think she's annoyed?" Donnelly asked.

"I know you're being sarcastic," said Collins, "but we are in deep shit, my man. She put the onus on us to sabotage Dingmann's efforts."

"What can we do?" said Donnelly. "We'd better think of something; our asses are on the line."

Collins lowered his voice. "How about we pick up the pace on our search for an agent for the TV shows? We don't need this crap."

Donnelly motioned for him to come over to his desk. "Speaking of TV shows, I've another idea. I'll meet you in the conference room in ten minutes."

***

Donnelly was seated when Collins came in. "How long do you think this Wild West approach to executions will last?"

"Two to three years at least," Collins replied. "Why?"

"Balance. We're going to need another crime show after this fry 'em stuff taps out and people get scared the country's becoming fascist. Already the *New York Times* is thundering."

Collins lit a cigarette. "The Upper West Side is nervous the inmates are taking over the asylum. What are you suggesting?"

Donnelly stared at his notes. "How about," he said, "a show where, for the first half, the police solve crimes."

Collins interrupted. "And the other half has commercials?"

"No. We depict the pursuit of justice for the victims and the courtroom prosecution of the defendants. A name like *Police Precinct* meets *Mister District Attorney*."

Collins considered. He laid his cigarette in the ashtray. "Where's the locale?"

"Where else but the Upper West Side of Manhattan? We could echo the required political statement du jour, kind of a reverse Johnny Volt that'll appeal to the do-gooders and those self-same Upper West Siders."

"Of course the district attorney will be politically liberal?"

"A wet dream of the editorial board of the *Times*."

Collins laughed. "Who will the bad guys be?"

"New stereotypes to fit the *Times*' worldview," said Donnelly. "Any businessman must be a killer or a creep."

Collins nodded. "Every family with money has a dirty little secret."

"Perfect," said Donnelly, and made a note. "Of course Christians and conservatives are a threat to mankind. Anyone Jewish is the guardian of civilization."

"A person of color who commits a crime," said Collins, "is driven to it by the horrible deeds of white Americans."

Donnelly laughed. "You sound like *The Nation* or *The New York Review of Books.*"

"Exactly," said Collins. "Won't people complain? This isn't Silent Majority fodder."

"No, these will be the new stereotypes," said Donnelly. "We'll give them predictability. It'll be a procedural. Any messages will be sublimated to the formula. After the *Felon Hunters* and *Johnny Volt*–type shows, this'll be a reassuring hour for the lefties. We'll rip stories from the headlines and prosecutors will debate moral subtleties. We'll slam the left's messages home with a vengeance."

"Please elaborate."

Donnelly sniffed. "Whites exploit blacks and never vice versa. Corporations and their executives are usually bad. Drug companies are, without exception, bad. There is no such thing as a bad teacher. Societal threats are typically ignored by blasé and uninterested authorities. Our guys will solve them on the show."

"Jesus, Donnelly, you're a dangerous son of a bitch." He picked up his cigarette and took a puff. "What'll be the title?"

"Not sure. *Public Prosecutors and Law Enforcement?*"

Collins shook his head. "How about *Law and Law Enforcers?*"

"Too long," said Donnelly. "*Cops and Courts?*"

"Bingo," said Collins. "Next up, our presentation to Locker on how we screw up Dingmann."

"We discuss that with Cox tonight."

***

Harriet Cox entered McGarry's to furtive glances from the stolid patrons. She made her way to Collins and Donnelly at their table. Donnelly poured her a beer from the pitcher.

"So, what's new?" she said. "Something, from the tone of your call." They had not told her about Dingmann's presentation, Willets's reaction, and Locker's charge to them. In several sentences Donnelly described the circumstances.

"They took me seriously?" Cox laughed and shook her head. "Good grief, don't they understand the product is next to impossible to produce?"

"No." Collins lit a cigarette. He puffed and put it in the ashtray. "Like Frank said, Nick Jackson apparently doesn't think so and asked for a presentation from Dingmann. Has anyone called you or your boss, Kelso?" He picked up the cigarette.

"No," said Cox. She fidgeted, considering what to say to Kelso.

"Could this be built?" Donnelly reached for his glass.

"I suppose so," Cox said, "but only at huge expense and endless design and testing." She faltered.

"Jackson wants a Dingmann presentation," Collins said, "because of our stunt."

"Apparently," said Cox quietly.

"You know," said Donnelly, "we've forgotten something basic." He nodded to Cox. "You're the client and no one's presented to you."

Cox brightened.

"Correct," said Collins. "But shouldn't we use it as Plan B? Don't we want the Vibrating Electric Toilet to go away, or at least not have Dingmann or Ilium involved?"

"Agreed," they said.

"Locker," said Donnelly after a minute. "Now let's eat." They continued to talk, fine-tuning how they would broach their strategy to Locker.

***

Locker closed the file of expense accounts she'd been scanning. The worn-out puff sound filled the room. Donnelly and Collins pulled up chairs; Collins lit a cigarette, and Donnelly put a foot on the end of Locker's desk. No one spoke.

"First," Locker said, glaring at Donnelly's size thirteen, "get your foot off my desk." Donnelly slid it off. "Now tell me how you two propose to deal with Dingmann promoting the fictitious Vibrating Electric Toilet and get your own asses, and mine, off the hot seat?"

"We do nothing," they both said.

Locker's neck stiffened and her ears reddened. "Nothing? *Nothing?*"

"Correctamundo," said Collins. *Better stop before Joyce bursts a blood vessel.* "We have a plan."

"Nothing is the plan? This better be good."

"Well, maybe nothing is a slight exaggeration," said Donnelly. In a nonchalant tone he added, "By the way, are you aware Shepherd, Drake, and Hogg are working with Dingmann and his crew on this project?" *Prepare for blastoff.*

"I should have known," Locker muttered. Her eyes narrowed. "How did you two become aware of this?"

"Loose lips sink ships," said Collins. *Keep our comments vague.* He waved his hand. "You know L'Fey with the booze and beer flowing…" *If you want, browbeat those guys and learn firsthand what Dingmann is up to and use that. We may not have to do anything*

"We said nothing and we meant we do nothing," said Donnelly. "Let me ask a simple question. Did Dingmann talk about strategy and how they propose to sell the toilet when he presented? Or did he just show ad layouts with 'dot-dot-dot electrically' in the headline?"

Locker chuckled in recognition. "The ads, of course." *Sniff.* "Where are you going with this?" She fiddled with her wristwatch.

"Do you really believe Nick Jackson should see a presentation on this product," said Collins, "and get all enthusiastic when it could be a disaster in the marketplace?"

"Let me tell you something about Nick Jackson," said Locker. "You think warning him will set us free from this disaster? Not happening. All a warning will do is make him angry."

"Why? Why wouldn't Jackson listen?"

"He believes what suits him and right now he believes this toilet is a possible winner."

"He needs to be disabused of that notion," Donnelly said.

"I don't think you two are listening."

"We have a way." Collins sat back and tapped a cigarette out of a pack.

"Somewhat indirect," chimed in Donnelly.

"Enough of the frick-and-frack bullshit, you two. Give it to me."

"We think," said Collins, "someone should do a research study on the concept of Ilium marketing a product that is not only well beyond its scope and usual market channels, but also is blatantly sexual." He took a deep drag on his cigarette. "The net result could be a backlash from Ilium's core customers, who are of a more, shall we say, conservative, bent. I don't think Nick Jackson wants the company seen as encouraging perverts, especially with the silent majority about to ride high."

Locker pondered what they'd said. *Let's find out how far these two wiseasses have thought this through.* "You're saying why would Ilium want to market something so outside its area of expertise and so open to conservative criticism?"

They nodded.

She considered their premise, weighing the angles. "Okay, say for a moment I accept your premise. Who does the study and how does said study get to Jackson? More importantly, the timing?"

Almost home. "Tyler Doremus, who has Jackson's ear, does it." Locker said nothing. "And Dick Leeson, our so-called boss, who used to work with Doremus and is somehow respected by him, suggests it." Donnelly unfolded a piece of paper and looked down. "You can do these studies with a defendable sample in less than a week. Doremus must have the budget, and I'm sure he wants no more incursions from our department and would therefore support it."

Jesus, that might work. They've covered all the angles. Sharp bastards. Wiseasses, but smart. I'll take smart anytime. "Have you mentioned any of this to Leeson?"

"Of course not; we feel it best for you to brief and instruct him on how to present this to Doremus." Donnelly absent-mindedly rubbed his neck. "You know, Leeson calls Doremus and casually mentions this developing situation to him in the course of discussion and drops in one or two ideas on why the toilet is not a good idea. Leaving the names of all present out of the conversation."

They rose. "Oh, and Joyce," said Collins, "you may have to be rather forceful in impressing on Leeson the need for him to control his motor mouth."

Clever. They don't want their fingerprints on it. Nor mine. Good idea. I can talk to Nick about all this as soon as it blows over. Actually, he might be able to license the manufacture of this toilet to a third party for them to make under their own brand name. I'll suggest that afterward. "Could work," she said. "I'll talk to Leeson."

Chapter Twenty-One

Guy Pearson, the most wanted man in the United States, was in a hole, shoveling. He had been on the run since he jumped his $25,000 bail. The press—fueled by leaks from police agencies—painted him as a monster, his actions direct and coarse, without any subtleties. The force of public pressure hit so hard it could have been spring-loaded.

Pearson traveled some fifty miles out of Boston to the quiet cemetery where they had buried Mary Jane Davisson. He obsessed about her, but felt no guilt that the heroin he'd forced on her caused her to go into toxic shock.

The dirt was soft and the digging went quickly. The light of the turned-down Coleman lantern played across his light Armani blazer. His sweat-soaked Sulka pima cotton shirt hung loose, the silk tie halfway down. The blade made a scraping noise as it met resistance. He salivated at the idea of the open coffin and Mary Jane in his arms. He jumped down and popped the casket. Within a minute he had her funeral clothes off. Not a mark on her perfect body. He was ramrod ready.

His fingers lingered briefly at her neck before slithering down to her breast. His hand encircled it, tweaking the nipple. He met no resistance as he found her lips with his; she was in a place he had yet to visit. Her body was a dead weight as he moved lower and tried to spread her legs.

Suddenly the headlights of a police cruiser came on. The cruiser's hand spotlight swung left and right, advancing slowly. A trail of spittle ran down the side of Pearson's mouth. His mind shouted *escape* as he kept out of sight. He boosted himself up and crawled between the graves toward the gate. As he clambered over the wall the spotlight caught him. The siren started up and a radio crackled to life. He ran, gasping, his breath drowning in his throat and smoothing out again. Strange sounds assaulted him. His shoes made a sucking sound as he went through swampy overgrowth.

He came out of the bird-haunted mud flats into a run-down industrial area. The sight of an approaching police car, lights flashing, forced Pearson to stumble into the darkness of an abandoned building. Drops of perspiration slid down his forehead. The dazzle from the outside streetlights faded and the room he entered came into view. Years of pigeon droppings had covered every surface. A doorway with a soft red light above seemed the only exit unless he chose to go back where he had come from. He hid in tinted darkness, deciding.

A sudden rush of noise startled him. A moment later he realized they had called his name over a police loudspeaker. His slim shoulders heaved up and down and his face ballooned with fear. He stared, eyes flickery and disturbed, a sense of frustration building. He crumpled to the floor and lay with his hands over his head. They burst into the room and handcuffed him.

***

The evening news blared Pearson's capture; his arrest, his jumping bail, and the subsequent manhunt repeated endlessly. Late newscasts added details of his assault on Mary Jane Davisson's final resting place. The story, because it had no racial overtones, was the perfect fantasy for the wealth-resenting press.

One newscaster drew himself up and in stentorian tones said, "Guy Pearson was a know-it-all, so they say, born into wealth, who read more books than might have been good for him, which caused him to disagree with everyone. Somehow all this privilege turned Guy Pearson into a stone-cold killer, a serial rapist, and the head of an immense illicit drugs operation. How he fares in a court of law remains to be seen."

Back in a holding cell for the second time in a month, an arrogant Pearson laughed at all of them. He claimed Mary Jane was buried with some valuables and he'd been merely digging for them.

Of course all of this appeared in the press. The magnitude of the monster was being defined. The country was shocked such a twisted freak should be walking among them. His picture appeared in every supermarket tabloid and his deranged face loomed on the cover of *Time* magazine.

***

"How did this animal get liberated?" asked Abe Floss.

"For starters," said Justin Hitchcock, "try your set-'em-free judges. Then throw in his father, the high-powered lawyer. Welcome to the American justice system. If you've the coin or a high-enough profile, you're out."

"You exaggerate." Floss, sitting in one of Hitchcock's high-backed leather chairs, sipped his drink.

"You think so?" an irritated Hitchcock said. "If you're Guy Pearson, you get your high-priced lawyer father. Flaunt the system and cause a riot or set off a bomb that kills innocents, no problem. Find a clone of Pearson senior and hide behind some judge's self-serving interpretation of the Constitution." He gulped his drink. "Or a maze of stupid federal statutes twisted to a reading totally

172

unintended by the authors. The do-gooders will act out their innermost compulsions because they are so oppressed or have been so abused."

"Look at young Pearson," said Floss. "I expect his father will move for a change of venue to get the trial out of Boston. Even with these new laws to decide and act at the local level, we still haven't seen much activity to deal permanent justice." He glanced at Hitchcock. "A natural timidity by officials, I suppose."

"Pearson doesn't deserve humane treatment," said Hitchcock. "Perhaps he can be a platform for the speedy justice we seek."

"Since the graveyard incident Pearson's eyes are beginning to bulge," said Floss. "Maybe from pressure; the small, black-and-white pictures in the news don't communicate the shock of seeing him.

"Suppose," said Hitchcock, "We goose the process? We use the impact of Pearson's crimes to ram what we want through the legal system. That'll give us leverage to shortcut everywhere possible. We'll be in a better position to re-establish order."

Chapter Twenty-Two

Harriet Cox walked out of George Kelso's office, head down, face burning with a mix of embarrassment and annoyance. The conversation had not been pleasant. Kelso had gotten word of the electric toilet and wanted to know what the hell was going on. *That was the pleasantest part,* she thought. He was not satisfied with her admittedly lame answers. *Now I realize the meaning of the phrase "having a new asshole ripped." Crude, but descriptive. Kelso tells me I'd better build the damn thing.*

On her way back to her office she had the feeling the walls were closing in around her. Walls, she realized, partly of her own construction. She'd been caught up in Frank and Jim's lunacy and gone along with this silly toilet idea. Then she got carried away when she presented to that odious man Dingmann and his cadre of fops. They were sure right about them.

A depressed Cox entered her green-linoleum-floored cubicle. The fluorescent lights flickered. Irritating but hard to pinpoint. Cox had called the maintenance office. Two men with a ladder came, removed the egg-crate drop ceiling section, peeked in, nodded, and said they would return and replace the bulbs. *Two weeks passed and no sign of them. Typical. Cripes, what a workplace: a second-hand gray metal desk, recycled file folders, and third world cabinets and worktable.*

She stared at her drawings. Ideas bounced around her head. *I'll be goddamned if the Brooklyn-Bronx yo-yos are going to ruin my life dreaming up some cockamamie scheme and throw me into the middle of the design-build mess.*

Okay, okay, my mess. But they're the cause. Tarnation. Start thinking about the electric toilet, Harriet.

Let's do the easy bit. A half hour later her pencil moved assuredly in the disposal and circuitry section of the sketch. *Gotta do the seat design.* She sighed and pounded the desk with her fist. *You can't build what you can't draw.*

The idea hit her. In a fitness magazine she read regularly she'd seen an article about possible damage to the male ability to deliver sperm as a side effect of too much time on a bicycle seat. The resultant design was a radical departure from the old hang-your-butt-into circles or ellipses. *Marvelous! Use the basic shape of a saddle with an opening in its center. Accommodate male or female, break waste down, and dispose of it. An embedded transformer would launch a charge across small amounts of water to produce ozone within the radical new "flush" cycle. It'd provide the bathroom with a crisp, clean, after-the-thunderstorm smell. Miles away from the stench of the Ilium men's room on Mondays.*

Over the next days she began the design in earnest. She spent a morning at the Maqua library examining anatomy books and took several with her back to the office. Her first enhancement was to render seats or saddles in different sizes to handle varying physiologies. She drew up a thin, medium, and stout version and added one for children. A seemingly insoluble problem was how to fit multiple butts of unusual sizes? She went back and forth between anatomy and waste-disposal circuitry as solutions or enhancements came to mind.

She found the creative process stimulating. Days of teeth-gnashing and frustration followed by euphoria. Ideas flew. Nothing really like it and one of the reasons she loved engineering.

The saddle horn was the final flash of brilliance. It could be added as a purchased accessory and would allow the occupant stability, leverage, and other amenities.

It was eight in the evening. She picked up the phone and punched in an extension of a model-maker in the R&D Department she knew could render her design quickly.

"Gustafson," a gravelly voice answered. Cletus Gustafson, the head model maker at Research and Development, was a genius by nature and not given to social niceties. He was indistinguishable from his work and always toiled in the quiet of night.

"Cletus! Harold Cox. I've a pisser of a product for you to mock up. It'll be a gas!" Gustafson was oblivious to her punning. Cox liked him. They had met at an engineering seminar and had got on well. She appreciated his craftwork skills.

"Bring 'er on over and let's start," he said. "I can't wait."

After Gustafson examined the drawings he came over and shook Cox's hand. "This is the most innovative product that's come out of this nuthouse in the last ten years." He positioned a sheet of aluminum on a shaping horse and began to pound out Cox's design.

"She'll be a little chilly on the tush in mockup," he said. "But mold her in a soft plastic, she'll give you the plushest dump you ever mounted up for." He shaped the metal as he talked.

Cox filled him in on the Nick Jackson presentation while he worked.

"This contraption will give even that bald-headed pervert a start," Gustafson said. He had attended many developmental product pitches to Jackson and wasn't a fan of the CEO but did respect his business acumen. Gustafson had seen his share of idiotic products, and their high IQ designers, deep-sixed at such presentations.

In no time Gustafson had the basic saddle shaped and the work-opening cut out with a welding torch. "Lemme soften this corner," he said to Cox, "'fore you hop on for a test ride and your nuts get cut off." Cox blushed and had to turn away.

"What's this depression here on the front?" Gustafson asked as he hammered.

"An attachment point for an accessory item." She reached into a small brown lunch bag and took out a wooden block carved in a rough, pommel shape. "It's a saddle horn of sorts." She grabbed a screwdriver and screwed an insert that looked like a tiny rubber track into the block. "I made it myself out of an old bulldozer toy. The carved wood block allows the user to hang on. It'll attach with a few screws from the underside."

"Gotcha," Cletus said. "You ginned this up Rube Goldberg-like. I'll have to smooth out the edges for you later."

"The guts are more important than the surface quality," Cox said. "I put in a battery; as part of the manufactured toilet it'll be wired." They worked, with minimal conversation, deep into the night. As they wrapped up, Gustafson drilled the four holes for the strange-looking wooden pommel and attached it from beneath using machine screws.

"You were right; this thing is a pisser. Let's try 'er out." Gustafson swung his leg over the saddle-toilet and settled on. The seat fit him seamlessly. "Damn this is comfortable," Gustafson said, snuggling in, positioning himself over the anatomically shaped opening, the fly on his jeans fitting perfectly against the attached pommel. "What's this?" he asked, his thumb on the black switch on the top of the pommel. Cox swallowed several times. *Oh, God, what do I do?*

"Don't!" Cox yelled. "I wouldn't…I haven't tested…" She was too late. Gustafson had thumbed the switch and the modified toy motor powering the rubber toy caterpillar tread started up. Her modification to the motor, rapidly switching polarity, was audible. Back-forward, back-forward, back-forward.

177

Less than a minute later Gustafson was screaming, "Sweet Jesus!" and hanging on to the pommel with both hands, his face quickly slackening into an orgasmic twist.

"Turn the goddamn thing off!" Cox shouted.

The wet spot was spreading on the front of Cletus's jeans as the model maker slumped forward, whispering "My god..."

She reached in, being careful not to touch Cletus's jeans, and turned off the device. "I warned you."

"You did, oh yes you did," Gustafson whispered hoarsely. He lit a cigarette. "That thing is..." He shook his head, and with an embarrassed laugh said, "Something that'll fit Nick Jackson's worldview, that's for damn sure."

"You can bring some of your many skills to bear in its refinement. I must say it seemed to work pretty quickly on you," Cox said.

"Oh, Lordy, yes." Gustafson agreed. "Wait 'til Nick gets a load of this. If you'll excuse me, Harold, I'm gonna go in the can for a minute and clean myself up. After that I'm out of here."

Cox was aroused. She wanted to jump on the machine herself and get her rocks off. *What a night. I can always use the vibrator. Interesting look at Cletus Gustafson. I like the way he surrendered to the moment. He's an attractive man. And talented. A bit older, but still...* She shook her head.

She went home and slept instead. Her last conscious thoughts were that she wanted Donnelly and Collins involved in this project. They would have to ratchet up the normal eighteen-month new product development cycle. With all the stops pulled out there was no doubt they could cut the cycle way down and get parallel approvals on safety and electrical. Ilium swung big weight in the electrical industry and had the development cash liquidity to back it up.

***

The multiple hues of dusk couldn't beautify the row of nondescript tall and narrow double-decker houses preening themselves along Reid Street. Collins had been unable to find parking on this gloomy evening, so he and Donnelly labored up the steep hill toward McGarry's. "Christ, I'm out of shape," huffed Collins as he stepped inside.

Donnelly followed, panting. "We sit on our ass in that decrepit office with all kinds of noxious poisons around us, what do you expect?"

"We can't stay here much longer, Frank. This place is ruining us. We need to get ourselves an agent." McGarry's was quiet as Collins went to the bar.

He grabbed some beers and they took a table in the rear.

"When's Cox due?" Donnelly finished half the glass and wiped his mouth with the back of his hand. "She said she wanted to talk about the toilet."

Collins glanced at his watch. "Twenty minutes or so." He drank some beer.

"Have you followed the Guy Pearson situation?"

"They caught the dirtbag, didn't they?" said Collins. "I understand Daddy's moving for a change of venue."

"This just in," said Donnelly. "The judge granted it; he's going to be tried in Pittsfield."

"Pittsfield?" Collins looked toward the door, gathering his thoughts. "So Pearson's daddy chucked The Hub and is heading West?" He leaned back. "That's about as far from Boston as you can get in Massachusetts. I hope the yokels will be able to contain Pearson."

"The *Gazette* mentioned a state police barracks near Pittsfield. Presumably they'll beef up the locals."

"Stimulate Electric Chair sales big-time, don't you think?" said Collins.

"Enough to beat projections," said Donnelly. He chuckled. "Amazing to me is the sales of the lower-voltage version chair to grammar schools. All those campus protests are motivating school administrators to keep the little shits in line." A muffled cough caused Donnelly to look up; the bartender loomed over them, a large, thick man with a creased face and dark eyes almost invisible under a maze of eyebrows. Three, perhaps even four. In a gravelly voice he said, "Call for either Donnelly or Collins. You can use the phone by the bar."

"I'll take the call," said Collins. "Finish your beer, Frank." He turned to the bartender. "Thanks, Mitch."

Collins returned, muttering to himself.

"What's up?" said Donnelly.

"That was Cox. She's bushed—too tired to join us. Sends her apologies." He grabbed his beer and finished it. "She was up all night." Collins laughed. "She actually built a working vibrating electric toilet, complete with the extra get-your-rocks-off features. She wants us involved with it. Said she's the client and doesn't want Dingmann's people anywhere near it. Apparently her boss is on her case because he was out of the loop."

Donnelly sighed. "We may have to go back to Locker and tell her to stop everything we suggested."

"Like Leeson talking to Doremus…"

"…and rigging, I mean doing, a study…"

They weighed their options. "You hungry?" Collins said. "I'd like a legitimate meal, not the burgers and fries they serve here. I'm more creative on a full stomach."

"Where?"

"Bonta's," said Collins. "The new place at the corner of Hexamer and Dalquest near the train station."

***

Bonta's occupied the first floor of a remodeled limestone house. A hostess directed them up a flight of granite steps to a snug anteroom and through a wide arch into a half-full dining room. She seated them at a corner table.

"What do you think?" said Collins.

"Seems okay," said Donnelly after they had ordered. "The room looks a little narrow for a restaurant. I guess the length compensates."

"You the Sunday architecture section critic for the Maqua *Gazette*?" Collins sipped his martini.

"No, you retard, I'm the…" Donnelly stopped midsentence. Two couples were in the anteroom about to enter the dining area. *Jesus, is that Sue? Holy mother, of all the restaurants in all the cities in upstate New York…*he laughed to himself over the cliché.

"What's going on?" asked Collins.

"Don't look. Dingmann and Willets are here with their wives; wait 'til they come into the main room."

They watched as a waiter led them to a table opposite from where they sat. The husbands' backs were to them.

"How did Dingmann get a babe like that?" Collins questioned.

"That babe," said Donnelly, "is Sue Costello, and I went to grammar school with her."

"Is she the one who charged a quarter to look at her tits?"

"That was a long time ago," Donnelly replied.

"Think she charges Dingmann?" asked Collins.

"Maybe," said Donnelly, laughing. "What do you think of Willets's wife?"

"Older than I thought she'd be, but not too shabby." Their food arrived and they began to eat. Collins finished chewing and said, "Do we go over and say hello?"

Donnelly put his fork down. "I don't think so. It'd interrupt their meal and might give Sue a heart attack. Let's finish and go to L'Fey. Maybe we can brainstorm the toilet and the chair."

"I've also been thinking," said Collins, wiping his mouth with his napkin, "the original strategy probably holds. Outsource the toilet."

"Will Cox go for outsourcing?" Donnelly signaled for the check. "Will her boss?"

"That is beyond an issue of manufacturing. We may be forced to go around them. If it's a big success Corporate can bring it back in-house or buy whoever's making it," said Collins. "What about the chair?"

"We should propose that the Ilium TV network televise Guy Pearson's trial. Live. If he gets the hot squat as a sentence, the ratings will be so high the GBC corporate suits won't know where they went." Donnelly pushed his plate aside. "Let's go." Donnelly glanced over at Dingmann's table. His wife looked up and stared in confused recognition. He nodded slightly.

She mumbled a few words, rose and walked toward the ladies' room.

***

Donnelly and Collins stood in the anteroom chatting with Ray Bonta, the restaurant's owner.

Donnelly felt the tap on his shoulder. He turned and faced Sue Costello. "Frank? Frank Donnelly?" she said in a soft voice.

"None other," Donnelly said, with a disarming smile. "Hello, Sue, I thought it might be you but I didn't want to interrupt your dinner." He waved his hand. "We're a long way from the neighborhood up here, aren't we?" *Christ, she's attractive. She's a victory lap a putz like Dingmann doesn't deserve.*

"We've traveled a way since then, Frank. It's nice to see a familiar face." She glanced back into the dining room. "Not too many of those around here. Maybe we could get together and catch up."

Whoops. Ball back over the net to me. Do I hit a return or let the shot pass? "Sure, I'd love to."

She reached into her purse and handed him a card. "Give me a call and we'll set something up."

"So you're a doctor," he said, taking the card. "I'll be in touch."

"Look forward," she said and walked away.

***

"She recognized you?" Collins and Donnelly were leaving Bonta's.

"Yep," said Donnelly. He passed her card to Collins.

"Yeah, a proctologist. So I've heard…" Collins smirked.

Donnelly took back the card. "She asked me to give her a call." He went down the last step.

Collins stopped. "Will you?"

"Don't know."

183

"You're playing with fire, you know."

"You think so?" Donnelly asked. He scratched his forehead. "Probably." He winked. "But it'd be worth it."

Collins wagged his finger. "You're thinking impure thoughts and not considering your career."

Donnelly laughed. "You just won the hypocrisy award. Now let's go to L'Fey."

***

"...you're telling me this toilet actually works?" *Sniff.* "With all the extra features?" *Sniff.* "You're now telling me some model builder in R&D sat on it and had an orgasm?" *Sniff.* "With his jeans on?" Joyce Locker sat on a bar stool at the mostly deserted L'Fey.

"Yes to all four," Collins said and sipped his martini.

"Nothing else?" her face reddened.

"Easy, Joyce, easy," said Donnelly. "We recommend we do what we suggested earlier: outsource." The ice tinkled as he picked up his Jameson's. "The toilet has some big sales and marketing requirements and challenges. Adults can share one, perhaps, within a reasonable body shape parameter." He stared at her. "I defer to your, um, superior knowledge, but I would presume a woman in pants can't use one without taking off all her lower garments. Wearing a dress, she'll need to remove her panties. She can't just hike her skirt, drop her panties and sit down. Kids are a whole different story. Do you even want a kid to use one of these? Only a person rich enough for multiple versions may be able to become a customer. This idea begs for a sophisticated market. That market won't be Des Moines."

"What's this really all about? Some foundry guys catch you degenerates dating their daughters?" *Sniff.* She grinned and lifted her glass. "I can't imagine you two rushing over here unless someone screwed up. A foundry foreman's daughter might be the happiest situation."

"Come on, Joyce, we don't only go to you with trouble." Donnelly stole a glance to make sure no one was near. He leaned closer. "We want to discuss Guy Pearson. You know his trial was moved to Pittsfield?"

Locker sipped her martini.

"We think the trial is an event made for television and sure as shit the new Ilium TV network will need both ratings and programming."

She took another sip. "An event made for television? How?"

"The sheer drama of the trial; the strategy, the tactics and how Guy Pearson deports himself. Broadcast from the opening gavel to the judge handing down the sentence."

"If Pearson gets the chair, we televise the execution," added Collins. "With these new laws, that'll happen fast. In an Ilium Electric Chair, of course."

"Good product placement, Joyce," said Donnelly drily.

Not bad, not bad; nobody's ever broadcast trials on network television. It just might work. Wish I had a little less to drink tonight. "Anything else?"

"Yeah," said Collins. "You need to get this to Jackson fast before some other network aces us out."

"You can talk him into outsourcing the toilet while you're at it," said Donnelly. "Box out Dingmann."

"Give me a full proposal tomorrow morning."

"Looks like an all-nighter," Donnelly muttered.

***

"Donnelly and Collins have been waiting ten minutes, Ms. Locker." Joyce smiled wryly and entered her office.

"Glad you could join us, Joyce," Collins said, stubbing out his cigarette and looking at his watch.

She ignored the sarcasm. "You have something for me?" she said, settling into her chair.

Collins held up a binder. "We toilers in the vineyard, hewers of wood and carriers of ashes, have labored mightily these many hours to produce this 'Modest Proposal.' It is yours, oh mighty manager, to have and to hold, from this day forward, to do with as your divine will pleases."

"One's an original. We have extra copies," said Donnelly. "In case you spill something we'll have a replacement." His mouth curled upward.

"We think this is pretty damn creative," said Collins. He put the binder on Locker's desk. A white label on the front cover read Ilium Electric Chair.

Locker picked it up.

Donnelly held up a hand. "We've been following the *Wall Street Journal*'s reports on the progress of Ilium's acquisition of the GBC Network. Like we said last night, the ideas in this proposal will catapult GBC into the number one news and daytime slots overnight. Whether GBC can hold the ranking is for the programming eggheads to figure out, but this baby is a sure launch pad." He turned to Collins.

"Last Wednesday the *Boston Globe* described Guy Pearson as the decade's most odiferous and perverted serial killer, drug dealer, and sexual deviant. His daddy lawyer cited the need for an impartial court and successfully petitioned for his trial to be moved to Pittsfield. The latest victim, Mary Jane Davisson, is the daughter of Captain Ike

Davisson of the Massachusetts State Police. They're headquartered in Framingham, and Pearson argued a Boston trial might be prejudicial."

"See me after lunch and we'll talk," Locker said. "Now get out of here." She opened the binder; her mascaraed eyes flicked back and forth. "Hold my calls," she said to Pat.

***

Locker pursed her lips and let out a breath. *Impressive. Original as hell. These two operate way above their pay grade. Nick Jackson bought himself a sub-performing network, and I don't find this kind of thinking in their current programming.* She riffled the pages. *Their self-proclaimed "Modest Proposal" could send the ratings into orbit. A big-assed opportunity for GBC, Ilium Electric, and all of us.*

I love the logic. The Massachusetts State Troopers caught young Pearson red-handed, in flagrante. Everyone hates him. Won't matter if they move his trial to Mars, the media will be all over it. This will be the hottest broadcast event since sliced bread. Daddy Pearson will try to suppress as much testimony as possible, but the trial will be a grisly sideshow anyway. Like they laid out: everything the viewing public drools for—a fallen rich guy, a big lawyer who's going to get hoisted on his own petard, rampant perversion, money, drugs, and likely a high-profile execution.

They even researched GBC's lack of programming and proposed Nick use Ilium's legal muscle to pry open access to the proceedings and negotiate an exclusive agreement to televise every moment. Do the court sessions in daytime and prepare recaps for prime time. A combination of the trial of the century and the first televised murder trial in the world. Ilium will have all the raw footage, leverage, publicity, and advertising platforms it can handle. She read further. *Even a feature film.*

She turned to the last pages and laughed. *As part of the deal Ilium should negotiate is that Guy Pearson be executed in an Ilium Electric Chair. Pittsfield is the site of Ilium's Residential Wall Receptacle Department, which gives leverage. Not the trial itself, but choreograph the prison, its policies, and its procedures. This kind of outrageous bullshit is the stuff Nick Jackson is made of. He'll love this.*

Nick's also hot for the toilet. Like those two said yesterday we might possess the lever to pry the toilet away from Dingmann and his people. Those shits Shepherd, Drake, and Hogg are involved? Gotta stop. They're Duff's guys; he's been asleep at the switch. "Pat," she hollered, "get Wall in here on the double." *Sniff.* She lit a cigarillo.

***

Though the request from Pat to come to Locker's office had been mildly delivered, Duff Wall sensed trouble.

"Afternoon, Duff," Locker greeted him with no invitation to sit. *Bad sign.* "You wanted me, Joyce?"

"Indeed I do," Locker said. Wall stood, sweat forming on his pudgy neck, unsure whether to take a chair or duck. "Your guys Shepherd, Drake, and Hogg are working on a project for Dingmann."

Wall's pudding-like complexion sped from vanilla to treacle. He tugged at his belt, reaching under the roll of flesh that hung over it. "Er, I didn't, don't know." He turned to go. "I'll, uh, get right on it, Joyce."

"Hold it! What the hell are you going to do?" *Sniff.*

"Um…ask them to not do this?"

"No, Duff. Drake, Shepherd, and Hogg report to you." Locker eyed Wall. "You work for me. Together we are members of a group with a mission. Your three sat in meetings with Dingmann, large portions of which were dedicated to undermining us. His maneuverings are not part of our plan. I don't want your people conspiring with Dingmann. Am I clear?"

"Joyce…" Wall's armpits were soaked and the sweat was beading on his forehead.

"I'm not finished." *Sniff.* "I know I can't do anything overt to Dingmann." *Sniff.* "I can do something with my own people." She lowered her voice. Wall braced himself. "I want you to manage those Benedict Arnolds out of their Dingmann activities. Before they get their mitts on any opportunity, they'll feel our collective foot in their nether regions. I don't care what you do, but make it stick. Understood?" She lit another cigarillo.

"But Joyce…"

"This isn't a debate or a democracy," she said. "You don't have a vote. If they don't stop this crap immediately, their raises will be zip, their reviews will be worse, and they'll find themselves in Technical Publications." She puffed on the cigarillo. "Unless you can figure something more threatening." Another puff. "If they doubt, have them come talk with me."

Wall stared, unmoving.

"Go. Now," Locker said.

Wall scurried out of Locker's office, thankful his ass was still attached, and took refuge behind his own closed door to figure out what he would do about his three troublemakers. He got on the phone and made a bunch of calls to friends and contacts around the company.

***

Shepherd, Drake, and Hogg sat in Wall's office. "Ilium cultivates relationships with a number of energy-related enterprises," Wall said. "One of these initiatives is Big Oil. The Corporate Long Term Strategic Plan indicates energy will be one of the booming businesses of the future. Another is mining and conversion into fuel. Yet a third deals with trash to fuel."

"Duff?"

"Hold your water, Austin. Part of the Big Oil program is a sophisticated Ilium system to both control and monitor the well-drilling process. It is now in beta test. The company is assembling a marketing strike team to sell the system to other Big Oil customers as well as independent drilling companies. One of you will go there."

"But Duff?"

"I said, hold your water." Wall slapped the desk. "The second assignment deals with ore conversion. The third assignment deals with trash to fuel. To train for these assignments you will be immediately relocating to the operational sites. In those four months you will create marketing, advertising, and selling materials. Upon completion you will begin the actual sales portion of the program. These are one-year assignments. How those go for you will affect your careers."

"Where's the well site?" said Drake, lighting a cigarette.

"Eagle Pass, Texas."

"Eagle Pass is South Bumfuck," blurted Hogg.

Drake exhaled. "The ore conversion?"

"Iron Mountain, Michigan. On the Upper Peninsula, in case you don't know."

"The trash to energy?" Drake said in a low angry voice.

"Massena, New York, a little north of here."

"Screw this shit; we decline the opportunity," sputtered Shepherd, looking at Hogg and Drake, who nodded in agreement.

"Not so fast, fellows," Wall said. "Your positions are scheduled to be evaluated and will likely be eliminated next month. Staying here in your present capacity is not an option." He waited for a reaction. None came. "There are some openings of a more junior nature in Technical Publications."

"You can't," began Drake.

"Au contraire," interrupted Wall. "Joyce signed off on this. Go back to your offices. Think about this as an opportunity. Perform well in Eagle Pass, you go to Beaumont. Do well in Massena, you go to Utica. Ditto Iron Mountain, then Flint.

"Or," he said, "review your recent actions and decide where your real loyalties lie." He waved a hand in dismissal. "Find your decision hats. I'll be in Locker's office."

***

Drake, Shepherd, and Hogg proceeded to the Tech Pubs conference room. Its shiny green Formica cast a sickly pallor on their faces. None of them said much. Finally Drake sighed. "Do you get the feeling we've been bagged, tagged, and are already on our way?"

"Bastard," drawled Hogg. He shook a cigarette from a pack and lit it. "We're found out; I'll bet it's the Dingmann stuff. Wonder how?"

"One of Dingmann's guys? Rhodes?" said Shepherd, also lighting up.

"I'm betting Donnelly and Collins," said Drake.

"Y'all think so?" Hogg questioned. "Why? Nothing in it for them."

"Oh yeah, there is," Drake replied. "They're after the toilet business and we're an obstacle. Dingmann looks bad with Willets."

"What y'all care to do?" Hogg puffed on his cigarette. "Not even a hint of a posting. This is pure bullshit. Eagle Pass. That's on the goddamn border; to get into Mexico you wade across the river. Massena puts you in Canada. Iron Mountain has a ten-month winter."

Shepherd looked up at the ceiling. "Tech pubs as the alternative? You think them two New Yorkers did this to us?

"Who knows? With those weasels I wouldn't put it past them," replied Drake.

Shepherd waved his cigarette. "Well, we have two objectives. One, we figure out if the threat of this assignment is real, which appears likely. So we kowtow and return to the Joyce Locker fold. We bust our balls so Donnelly and Collins get it worse."

Drake sat up straight. "Wait." A minute later he returned, holding a thick binder aloft. "Behold the Ilium bible, the Department Employee Manual; revel in its cruelty and simplicity." He smirked. "You know those counterfeit parking passes floating around?"

"Yeah," said Shepherd. "The guys in the Art Department figured out they could be duplicated; I've even used one on occasion."

"Right. We all have." Drake lit up and exhaled. "But we didn't get caught. Donnelly and Collins have two almost perfect duplicates. Rumor is they got them in New York."

"What all does it mean?" asked Hogg.

"The answer is here in the Manual." Drake read, "'Any willfully false representation of departmental permissions, approvals, or perquisites for the purpose of obtaining or enjoying same, when such have not been officially granted, will result in an unpaid suspension up to a maximum of immediate dismissal based upon the decision of the General Manager.'"

"Holy shit," said Hogg.

"Holy shit indeed," said Drake. "I'll mention the passes to Dingmann. It'll be Pavlovian; he's such a rules mongrel." He took a deep pull on his cigarette.

"Those two will think they went to a barbecue dressed as the pig," said Shepherd.

***

"Got a minute, Bob?" Drake caught Dingmann coming out of his office.

"I suppose so." Dingmann glanced at his watch. "What's up?"

Drake looked up and down the empty hallway. He stepped closer and in a low voice said, "Joyce Locker." Dingmann's head snapped up. "You know, Bob, Wall is our manager. He all but told Hogg, Shepherd, and me our next assignments would be in either Eagle Pass, Texas; Iron Mountain, Michigan; or Massena, New York. The alternative is a junior position in Tech Pubs. Cleared with Locker, he said. Obviously they found out we were sitting in on the toilet account." Drake left out the ticket back to Locker's operation.

"How'd Joyce find out?" Dingmann asked.

"The betting's on Donnelly and Collins." Drake stepped aside as a secretary bustled by. "We're not clear how they knew."

"That's unfortunate," Dingmann said and began walking. He motioned for Drake to come along. "I'm not sure what I can do about this."

"Are you aware they own gate passes?" said Drake. "They apparently found a way to forge them."

Forging gate passes is cause for dismissal. This may give me some leverage. "I want to know the next time they are using the counterfeit pass," he said to Drake.

Drake's eyes gleamed. "Their cars are out back, parked against the chain link fence in the rear of the lot with one car between them."

Drake looks ready to burst. Does he want to add something? "Anything else?"

"Neither one of them is attending the training classes." This was a calculated guess by Drake.

Dingmann planted his little finger on his lower lip as Drake finished. *Another no-no. Those two don't like rules. This is getting better. Drake, Hogg, and Shepherd are low-life informers. Not on my team. Eagle Pass might be the place for them.* "Could be useful," Dingmann said by way of dismissal. *There'll be more on the menu than food for my lunch with Willets. First, though, a quick stop at security to find out if Donnelly and Collins registered gate passes and whether in fact their cars were in the back lot.*

***

"You hear from Joyce?" Collins hung over Donnelly's cubicle. "She said she'd see us after lunch. Damn. I wanted to haul out of here and get the weekend going."

"Me too," said Donnelly. He drummed his fingers. "Oh well, back to work."

Collins's phone rang. He listened for a minute, mumbled something, gathered a folder, and went to Donnelly's desk. "We're going to Willets's office. Joyce's with him; they want to meet."

"Do we know what about?"

"Didn't say," said Collins. "We haven't officially met Willets; Locker probably wants to preview the chair program with him. Nothing on the tapes to indicate otherwise." Donnelly grabbed his chair binder.

Collins and Donnelly walked down the hallway to Willets's office; they passed Drake, who winked. "Enjoy yourselves, boys," he said.

They shrugged and continued on their way.

Marsha ushered them into Willets's office, where a stern-faced Joyce Locker and another man sat.

Locker introduced them to Willets, who turned to other man, "This is Gino Pacelli," Willets said, "head of security for the Maqua Works."

They nodded, their minds racing.

Willets indicated they should sit. "An egregious breach of company rules has been brought to my attention." Willets paused, his eyes scanning the room and came to rest on Donnelly and Collins. He turned to Pacelli.

Pacelli, a slight man in a black suit, walked to where they sat. He leaned over them and said in a thin, reedy voice, "Not even senior program employees may use managers' passes without written authorization. You boys used forged gate passes to sail in and out of the main gate unchallenged. That's cause for dismissal. What do you have to say?"

They both rose, towering over Pacelli. "First of all, pal, we're not boys," said Collins. "You may call us Mr. Collins and Mr. Donnelly."

"Second, pal," said Donnelly, "gate passes? Not us." He turned to Collins. "Should we call an attorney before this goes any further?"

Collins turned to Willets. "Should we?"

Joyce Locker suppressed a giggle.

Willets looked stunned. *Lawyers? That's all I need. Dingmann smooth-talked me into this. This is not a career-enhancing moment. Damn, they surely don't act like first-year trainees. I didn't review their files first. Joyce Locker, and by implication her people, are in tight with Nick Jackson. Damn. I can't appear weak.*

Pacelli drew himself up. "Let's deal with facts, shall we? Your cars are registered with the company. Those cars were observed in the parking lot behind this building with gate passes displayed. The gate passes have been determined to be illegal."

"How did you determine they were our cars?" said Donnelly.

"The VIN numbers, Mr. Donnelly," said Pacelli. To forestall the obvious he added, "Your cars were backed in flush against the fence so we couldn't view the license plates."

"Did you break into these cars that are allegedly ours? Did you perform this so-called inspection yourself?"

"My people identified the cars in the lot as yours." Pacelli leaned back and crossed his legs.

"How could you do that?" said Collins. "We both have very cluttered cars; I can't even see my dash, so how could you?"

"Appropriately vague," said Donnelly. "Tells us you don't know. Seems," he turned to Willets, "we have a conclusion in search of a rationale."

"Sloppy police procedure," said Collins.

"What would you know about police procedure?" said Pacelli with a snarl in his voice.

Collins laughed. "I've forgotten more than you'll ever know...pal."

Sniff.

I can't lose control of this situation. "I have to believe Mr. Pacelli," Willets said. "I could dismiss you both out of hand. I'll be lenient and suspend both of you for a week without pay. Collect anything personal you need and leave the building." He rose.

Donnelly and Collins glared at him. "We'll remember this. Our lawyers will be in touch." At the doorway, Donnelly turned back. "Oh, and really nice meeting you, Lou."

"I chose not to bring up the issue of their not attending classes, Joyce," said Willets.

"They haven't had the time, Lou," she said. "You never gave me the courtesy of a warning this was coming down. I've had them working overtime on stuff." She leaned over Willets's desk. "I take all this personally. You've made a serious mistake." *Sniff.* "You'd be well advised not to listen so much to Dingmann. Talk to Len Lovelace about Mr. Donnelly and Mr. Collins. Then to Nick Jackson." She spun on her heel and left.

In the hallway Locker caught up to Pacelli. "Gino, not all trainees are goofballs. Mr. Collins is a former New York City police officer. Mr. Donnelly is a former New York fire marshal."

"Give me a break, Joyce," said Pacelli. "They're nothing but wiseasses. I've seen their like before."

"Whatever you say, Gino," said Locker.

***

Willets buzzed his secretary. "Tell Len Lovelace to please come and bring Donnelly's and Collins's complete personnel files with him."

Lovelace sat while Willets scanned the files. His lengthy conversation with Len Lovelace reinforced what he'd read. Extremely high-potential individuals, who played hardball when crossed. *Normally I wouldn't let trainees be a factor. But there's a wild card…Nick Jackson likes them and they have definitely been crossed. If they do something drastic I will be the one affected. Damn.*

***

"On a scale of one to ten how badly did Pacelli want to handcuff us?" They arrived at their cubicles and began stuffing files into their briefcases.

Donnelly chuckled. "Eleven." He turned serious. "Jentzky. Marvin Jentzky," he said. "Pack all the stuff we've been working on—the chair, the TV shows—everything."

"Why? And who's Marvin Jentzky?" Collins asked.

"Wait 'til we're outside," said Donnelly. "Someone is trying to take us out at the knees. Now it's our turn. Let's get back the proposal we gave Locker. I'll tell Pat we need to update it. We'll talk tonight at McGarry's."

***

Back at his apartment Donnelly took out Sue Costello's card. He dialed Maqua hospital and after a delay of several minutes, was connected. "Hi, Sue, it's Frank. Is this a bad time?"

"No, no," she said. "I have a few minutes."

Now what do I say? Well, I'm free next week, thanks to Willets. "Good. Just touching base as we discussed at Bonta's. Are you around this coming week?" *How lame am I?*

"Oh, I'm sorry, Frank, I'm at a convention in New York next week at the Plaza. If you get to New York, give me a call. Perhaps we can get together the week after?"

Not quite a brushoff. "I'll call you then. Have a good day, Sue." *Better keep this conversation to myself.*

***

In a booth at McGarry's, Donnelly said, while chewing a soggy fry, "No use wasting time agonizing over our predicament. They got us; set us up. We know the architects but we'll deal with them later."

"Agreed," said Collins. "So tell me who Marvin Jentzky is." He put his cigarette in the ashtray.

"Think Hollywood. Marvin Jentzky. He's the producer of a shitload of hit TV shows. His real first name is Shlomo. No one uses it anymore, including his own family. Too ethnic, I guess."

"You know him how?"

"Marvin 'Shlomo' Jentzky is the oldest son of the man who runs the candy store we hung out in my old neighborhood. Mr. Jentzky, the owner, is a good guy. I'll talk to him. He'll speak to me. He'll get in touch with Marvin for me."

"Why should he bother?" Collins puffed his cigarette.

"My friends and I prevented one of the local gangs, the Tigers, from trying to trash the store and rough up his other son, Saul. They wanted to make it their hangout." Donnelly drank his beer. "We took care of things." He wiped his mouth with the back of his hand. "Saul's my age; we were friends. The Tigers never went near him or the place again. Mr. Jentzky was grateful but we didn't ask for anything. It was a neighborhood honor thing. He'll take care of us. The question is, will Marvin be available? If he is, we have the perfect shortcut for a shot at the entertainment business."

"Call him," said Collins, rubbing his hands.

"Can't. Jentzky is Orthodox. I won't be able to reach him until Sunday morning. Let's get our act together and be ready after I do."

"Okay," said Collins. "I guess we need to stay out of sight. We'll meet at the Maqua library tomorrow and go through the screen treatments and plans."

"Do we tell Cox?"

"Maybe we call her tomorrow; find out if we can get access to her office on the weekend," said Collins, yawning. "My ass is grass. We didn't sleep much last night."

"Good idea," said Donnelly. "Why don't you contact her? I'll book tickets for LA tomorrow to fly out Monday. If things don't work out with the Jentzkys we can always cancel the flight and go down to New York for the week. Tell me the gal's name at Maqua Travel?"

"Jeanine Petrucci," said Collins. "She's usually in on Saturdays."

"I'll call and go there in the morning," said Donnelly, "and meet you at the library after."

***

"Okay, Mr. Donnelly, here are the flights for you and Mr. Collins." It was Saturday morning and Donnelly sat in Maqua Travel opposite Teddie Koch. Short and large-headed, she worked with a practiced efficiency. "12:30 p.m., Maqua Airlines 332, to Chicago. American 507, 4:30 p.m. to LA You have a two-and-a-half-hour layover in Chicago. Open return, as you specified. Sunset Towers hotel; you pick up the Hertz car at LAX when you arrive."

"Sounds right," said Donnelly. "Thank you. Jeanine not in today? Jim Collins said I'd see her. Does he know her?"

"She's off this weekend." She smiled shyly. "Jeanine and Mr. Collins dated for a while."

Well, well, a life outside the Works. Tickets in hand, Donnelly headed to the library. After they finished their research, he and Collins spent the afternoon in Cox's office and polished their TV show treatments, pilot show scripts, and tie-in marketing plans.

"Oh yeah," said Collins, "Cox said her sister is in town; wanted to know if we'd be around tomorrow night, meet them for dinner."

Donnelly gathered his stuff. "If we're going to be wining and dining tomorrow night, I'll pack this evening. I'll call Jentzky in the morning and talk to you after." Donnelly winked and said, "When will you pack? Don't you have a date with Jeanine Petrucci?"

"Who told you, that limbo dancer Teddie Koch?" Collins flushed. "I went out with her twice, you bastard, and no, I don't. I'll talk to you tomorrow."

***

On Sunday morning Donnelly dialed a Brooklyn phone number. "Jentzky's," said Sidney Jentzky's tremulous voice. The quavering tone gave Donnelly pause. *He's gotten older; surprise, surprise.*

His memory flashed to his boyhood and Jentzky telling him to "leave the damn Baby Ruths alone."

"It's Frank Donnelly, Mr. Jentzky. How are you?" Donnelly soon found out that his old friend Saul was a lawyer in LA, specializing in entertainment law. *Bingo, there's our agent. Okay, to the business at hand.* "You and the Mrs. must have such noshes for the boys; they've done so well, we at least have to feed them…"

"You're still a mensch, Franky, what can I do for you?"

Donnelly clapped his hands silently. "Mr. Jentzky, is there a way for me to get in touch with Marvin? I'm going to be in LA and a friend and I are involved with something of possible interest to him. I'd also like to see Saul."

"Hold on, boychick, I'll look in my book." A minute later Jentzky was back and read out the numbers. "I'll call Saul and Marvin tonight," he said. "Marvin's in early; around seven his time. I'll tell him to expect your call then. Saul gets in at seven-thirty. I'll make sure they know this is not a social call. When did you say you'd be out there? Give me the other fellow's name."

"We're arriving Monday night, so, Tuesday. His name is Jim Collins. We'll stay at the Sunset Towers."

"Got it. Good luck on your project, Franky," Jentzky said.

After hanging up, Donnelly called Collins. "We're set; Mr. Jentzky came through. We call Marvin tomorrow morning before I leave for the airport. There's a bonus. Saul, my old pal, is now a Hollywood entertainment lawyer." He chuckled. "Can you spell agent, boys and girls?"

"Fantastic. Where do we want to meet up with Cox and her sister?"

"Anywhere but L'Fey," said Donnelly.

"Bonta's?"

"Rather not. Might run across Dingmann or Willets. How about Viola's over on Brzoza near Broc?"

"Deal," said Collins. "I'll call Harriet. We'll meet at seven."

***

"They didn't consult a decorator or art director before they opened this restaurant," Collins said.

"Symmetry was regarded as the only expression of elegance when they originally designed the building," said Donnelly, craning his neck as he took in the surroundings. "Viola went for the sterile look: everything painted white, including the brick exterior. Reminds me of a hospital wing." He sipped his beer. "Food's supposed to be good, though."

"So I hear." Collins stared at his martini and lit a cigarette. "Typical crappy night here in wonderful Maqua."

They looked out the glazed bay window at the rain-swept street. Several minutes later two women alighted from a cab. "That should be the Cox sisters," said Collins, snuffing his cigarette butt.

"Let's do the polite number and meet them at the coat check," said Donnelly, tossing a bill on the bar. They walked to the doorway.

"This is my sister, Emily," said Harriet. "She's my twin." She smiled. "Obviously. I'm a half hour older." Her green sheath dress set off her lithe figure.

"Nice to meet you," they said, extending their hands and receiving a firm handshake.

"I've heard so much about both of you," Emily said. Tall and slim like her sister, she wore a lavender sweater with a dark skirt. Her thick pink lips glowed with the lightest touch of lipstick. Her bright smile revealed a beautiful blue-eyed face crowned with soft flaxen hair. Two large dimples punctuated her peach-blossom cheeks.

Donnelly stopped himself from gaping. *Good looking. I hope she has a brain. Well, maybe not too much of a brain.*

Collins considered Emily. She's cute, but Harriet's nicer.

***

They sat at the cloth-covered table, eating, drinking, and talking their way through the courses. Emily Cox was in Maqua to consider a position she was being offered at Maqua University as an associate professor of history with a guaranteed tenure track.

The sisters learned how Donnelly and Collins had been hired on the A&P program and their recent suspension for allegedly forging parking passes. Harriet explained the parking problems at the vast Maqua Works.

"But this Mr. Pacelli didn't identify your cars?" asked Emily, her sky blue eyes roaming over Donnelly's face.

I'm melting. "He did not. As I said to our boss, it was a conclusion—get us—in search of a rationale." He shrugged. "When I was in grammar school my motto was 'He who laughs last laughs best.' Still is."

The Cox sisters chuckled appreciatively. Collins beamed at Harriet. She smiled shyly in response.

The bill settled; no one made to leave. "You came by cab," Collins said. "Can we give you a lift home? I presume Emily is staying with you?"

"Yes, she is and we'd like that," Harriet said. "Did you arrive in one car?"

"No," Donnelly replied.

"Well," said Harriet, "I'll go with Jim; and Emily, you go with Frank." She put her hand on Collins's thigh and rubbed it back and forth.

Emily did likewise to Donnelly.

They both had immediate erections and made small talk until they subsided. The girls kept straight faces.

With Donnelly following Collins and Harriet, the rides home consisted of in-route groping. By the time they arrived at Harriet's flat both Donnelly and Emily were aroused. Harriet and Collins slowly made their way into her apartment, locked in a passionate embrace.

"Looks like they're playing tonsil hockey," Donnelly said, French-kissing Emily.

She returned his kiss and pulled back. "Let's continue this inside," she said. "There are two bedrooms." She stroked the bump in his trousers. "Steady, big fellow, your time will come." Emily took his hand and led him inside where a door was closing. "Door number two wins the prize," she said, pulling Donnelly into the empty bedroom. She stopped and stared at him. "I've never done anything like this before," she whispered, rubbing her hands under his shirt. "Please help me."

"Only if you want me to," said Donnelly, running his hand through her hair and stroking her buttocks with the other.

"Oh yes," Emily said, rocking against him. "Yes, yes, yes…"

***

The next morning two slack-jawed, suspended A&P trainees staggered out of the Cox sisters' bedrooms. "What time is it?" Collins croaked.

"Do you care?" asked Donnelly.

"No," replied Collins, "but I need to take a piss."

"Me too," said Donnelly. He glanced at a wall clock. "There's time."

"Wonder if the sisters ever did this before?"

"Emily said no," said Donnelly.

"So did Harriet." Collins went to open his car.

"What do you think?" Donnelly mumbled.

Collins hesitated. "Are you kidding? They grew up in farm country. They were probably doing it when they were twelve."

"I'd like to think I was first," said Donnelly. "But I know I'm not."

"I'm glad you survived the reality check," said Collins.

Chapter Twenty-Three

At a quarter past eight o'clock on Monday morning Joyce Locker chuffed into her office as the phone rang. "Ms. Locker, Mr. Jackson is on the line for you."

"Pat, where is the presentation Donnelly and Collins gave me Friday morning? I can't find it on my desk."

"Mr. Donnelly took the binder when he left the office Friday. He said they had changes."

Oh shit, this is not good. She stared into the little holes on the telephone mouthpiece hoping for an answer. "Nick, what's up?"

"I'm up to my ass with this new TV network with shit to show on it, Joyce," Jackson said. "Anything new with my chair?"

Time to kill a bunch of birds with one salvo. "Not only an update on the chair, Nick, but a potential solution to your TV issues."

"Give it to me, Joyce. What've you got?"

In five minutes she described the plan to televise the Guy Pearson trial, the possible execution, and the use of an Ilium chair in the proceeding. *Might as well throw this in.* "They also presented some ideas on the toilet at variance with what was presented to you."

Jackson was bowled over, as Locker figured he would be, by the audaciousness of the Pearson concept. He grasped the originality, opportunity, and profitability of the plan. The conversation was intense, raucous, vulgar, and hilarious. "I want the three of you down here so we can personally go over this. You maniacs get your shit together; take a day. You'll get time to tell me more about the toilet. All right?"

"A day may be difficult, Nick," she said. "They're suspended." She repeated Donnelly and Collins's comments to Willets and Pacelli. "They're off to places unknown." *Better confess everything.* "You've seen their files. I got to tell you, they were very angry. They took my copy of their plan; I told you this from memory. Their version contains an enormous amount of detail."

Jackson immediately understood the implications of Locker's revelation. "Do whatever it takes to get them, Joyce," Jackson said. "Guys like them are the future of the company. I want the three of you here tomorrow, Wednesday at the very latest." The click told Locker that Nick Jackson was one pissed-off CEO. Joyce knew she was not the object of Jackson's wrath.

She hollered to Pat. "Call their apartments. If they don't answer, ask around the group if anyone knows where they might be. Also check corporate travel; find out if they purchased any tickets on a bus, train, anything. Hire a detective if you have to." *She's a damn good assistant and she's relentless. She'll run them down. I hope.*

***

Marsha buzzed Lou Willets. "Mr. Jackson for you."

"Hello, Nick—"

"I understand you're now in charge of parking up in Maqua, Willets…"

Willets's bowels loosened. "I, uh…" His customary smoothness and aplomb headed south.

"…I guess you'd rather do that than the job I gave you, which was running the damn A&P Department."

Willets tried to recover. "Forging gate passes is a matter of company policy as laid out in the employee manual."

Jackson cut him dead. "Bullshit! You got played. Get those two back on the payroll retroactively and in New York tomorrow. Or you'll be lucky to be running even a fucking parking lot!" The phone slammed in Willets's ear.

Willets buzzed Marsha. "Get me Joyce Locker."
The conversation was brief. Locker told Willets she was unable to locate them. Willets told her to find them.

***

A bedraggled Donnelly arrived at his apartment. Most of the single guys on the Ilium program lived like they did in their college frat houses: apartments strewn with empty beer cans, scattered socks and underwear, and half-finished food containers. Many refrigerators were would-be breeding grounds for new life forms.

Donnelly operated differently. He had gone directly from the military to become a fire marshal in the New York Fire Department and frequently bunked with the NYFD engine companies. Both services demanded personal neatness.

Rolled-up socks, boxer shorts, and T-shirts went into the luggage along with his toiletries. An additional pair of socks and undershorts provided an emergency cushion. He began to zip the bag when in the corner of his underwear drawer the black rubberized grip of his Smith & Wesson .38 in the Beretta speed-draw holster rig caught his eye. The carry permit was stuck in the spring clip he normally shoved into the back of his trouser waistband.

What the hell; LA isn't Maqua, but LA has enough crazies. I wonder if Marv will suspect we're packing. Goes without saying Collins will bring his. I'm waiting for him to do a surprise show-and-tell at an Ilium staff meeting. He chuckled. *Would Nick Jackson be less crazy knowing we were both armed? He's most likely no more respectful of guns than he is of other people.* He put the gun and holster under his shirts and zipped up the suitcase, picked up the phone, and dialed Marvin Jentzky's number. He was connected in short order. "Franky, been a long time," said Jentzky. "Pop told me you'd be calling. What've you been up to? Bring me up to speed."

Donnelly gave him a quick recap.

"So you're with Ilium," said Jentzky. "Run into Nick Jackson?"

"Oh yeah. In fact, he's related to my call. We've been working on some products and situations with broadcast..." He trailed off.

Jentzky's antennae quivered. "What can I do for you?"

"Have you done anything with the new GBC?"

"No. But honestly we'd like to," said Jentzky. "Let's set up a time to meet. You and your colleague, what's his name...?"

"Collins." Donnelly decided to not get into their disciplinary issues.

"...are coming in tonight, I understand. Give me your flight and where you are staying." Donnelly told him. "A car will be at your disposal as long as you're out here. We'll meet at noon and do lunch." They talked some more with Donnelly knowing he and Collins had a meeting with one of the top guns in Hollywood.

Next he called Saul Jentzky. They spoke for twenty minutes and Donnelly briefed him fully on the chair and their TV proposal and the scripts he and Collins had developed.

"Holy shit, Franky, this is ninety percent sure to be huge. How much did you tell Marvin?"

"I'll do that tomorrow when we meet with him. We've got some Ilium stuff to deal with," said Donnelly. "We'd like you to represent us; you're the man who can handle it so we all win."

"We go back a long way, Franky. Pop always liked you. I take it you have some internal political issues?"

"Yeah. We'll discuss setting up a front company. I'll fill you in when we're together." He made an appointment to meet Saul late Tuesday with dinner afterward.

He hung up, grabbed his bags, and headed for the airport. A minute after he left his phone rang. Donnelly was out of earshot.

***

Pat dialed most of the morning trying to track down Donnelly and Collins. She'd tried everywhere she could think of, including several times, their apartments, corporate travel, their parents' homes, and a bunch of New York hotels. She was commiserating with Marsha, Lou Willets's secretary, on her lack of success. "Did you try Maqua Travel, the new place down on Dumas?"

Pat reached Jeanine Petrucci. "I've met Jim Collins but not Frank Donnelly," she said. "Let me look." A file drawer opened. "Why yes, Mr. Collins and Mr. Donnelly purchased two tickets for Los Angeles via Chicago on Saturday. Teddie Koch gave them the corporate rate. I hope that's all right?"

"It's fine," Pat assured her. "When are they flying out?"

"Today. Their flight leaves in a little more than an hour at twelve-thirty."

Pat wrote down the information, got off the phone, and ran into Locker's office.

"Chicago and then on to Los Angeles?" said Locker. *Sniff. I should have suspected. They were screwed and they're returning the favor. They've got the material and the moxie. What about the contacts?* She ran her fingers through her hair.

"They're Leeson's guys; get him in here pronto," she said to Pat.

211

"Mr. Leeson's not in today, Ms. Locker," said Pat. "He's having a colonoscopy."

Locker bit back a comment on the appropriateness of the procedure. "Find Duff, then."

***

She met Wall in the outer office. "Duff, we've got a situation. Donnelly and Collins are booked on a plane to Chicago leaving at twelve-thirty because of everything that went down Friday. I lay part of this at your feet. Go and get them. This is serious, Duff. Don't come back without them."

Wall left Locker's office and sped to the airport, leaving his car at the curb. Maqua Airport was sparsely populated at twelve-ten in the afternoon. It took precious minutes to determine the gate for the Chicago flight. He ran to the concourse. *Endless, identical boarding areas on each side. Damn, the Chicago flight's at the far end.* He jogged down to the waiting area. *Shit, they're boarding! Where are those clowns?* Finally he spotted them in the line. Sweat poured from him as he put a hand on Collins's shoulder.

Collins turned so quickly Wall was caught off-guard. "Duff!" Collins pulled to a halt. "Why aren't you back in the rabbit warren?"

Donnelly regarded Wall. "You must be on a mission."

"I am..."—Wall tried to catch his breath—"... on a mission. Joyce needs to see you right away."

"Why?"

Wall realized Locker had not told him why. "She said it's important, that's all."

"Tell Joyce," said Donnelly, "we are on our own unpaid time, compliments of Lou Willets. Mr. Willets made it rather clear we were persona non grata on company property during this week. We'll talk to Joyce when we get back to the office next Monday. Perhaps Hogg or Drake or Shepherd could fill in for whatever she needs. Why are you here and not Leeson?"

Wall told them.

"Fitting," Collins said. "Sorry, Duff, we're boarding. Nice talking to you and thanks for seeing us off." They moved toward the gate attendant collecting tickets.

Wall followed. "Look, I...look, I know what happened and why it happened and who made it happen. Joyce is desperate to talk to you. She's bullshit but she's on your side. Come back with me."

Donnelly stopped. "Once again, why?"

"Joyce didn't tell me but she'll rip me a new asshole if I come back without you."

"I'm sorry for your troubles, Duff," said Collins, "but we're on unpaid leave and we'd prefer not to be inside the Maqua Works for the next week." He handed his ticket to the attendant and boarded the plane.

"If ever," mumbled Donnelly and did likewise.

Wall stood, helpless, visions of his career in flames. The boarding area closed and Wall walked down the concourse. At a phone kiosk he called the office. He reported his failure and their comments to Locker.

"Tell me again why they wouldn't come back?" Locker said.

"One, they said Willets told them they were persona non grata on company property this week. Two, I couldn't give them a specific reason to talk to you."

Locker realized she hadn't told Wall why. "My fault, Duff." *Sniff.* "I was in too much of a hurry. Get back here and we'll activate

213

plan B." He clicked off. *Shit. Haste makes waste comes down on my head; details, details, details. I can't blame Duff, or those two; I'd do the same damn thing they did. That whole parking system is a fiasco. It may cost us big-time and wreck the Lou Willets Express. In every cloud a silver lining lurks.*

Wall went out of the terminal and saw two tickets on his windshield and a tow truck approaching. With a muttered curse he jumped in his car and sped off.

***

"Pat spoke with Jane Ronan at Corporate Travel. She'll arrange for them to be intercepted in O'Hare at the gate for their LA flight. They will see I talk to them." *Sniff.* "Their plane lands in about an hour, and the LA flight leaves two hours later."

Wall, chest still heaving and sweat-stained shirt sticking to his arms, did not respond.

Locker felt a twinge of unaccustomed guilt for sending him on such a fruitless errand. "Go cool off, Duff, and get something to eat. Come back at two-thirty."

***

"Why the hell didn't we check our bags?" Donnelly said, as he and Collins struggled with their luggage and threaded through hordes of travelers at O'Hare for their connecting flight to LAX.

"We didn't want them lost by some half-drunk baggage handler," said Collins. "No one told us we had to change terminals to get the LA flight. O'Hare is huge." He turned sideways as a phalanx of passengers streamed off a plane. "What a mob. We'll check them through on the way back."

"Are we going back?"

"Eventually. If for no other reason than to get our stuff." Collins adjusted the strap on his garment bag. "Somewhere in this endless corridor is our gate."

"At the ass end of the terminal," said Donnelly. "We're not due to leave for ninety minutes but let's make sure everything's copacetic."

***

The agent looked up, checked a piece of paper, and said, stuck-out teeth flashing, "Mr. Donnelly? Mr. Collins?" She spoke with a slight lisp.

They dropped their bags. "Yes?" they asked.

"We've been waiting for you. I've been instructed to ask you to call your office. A Joyce Locker. The message says, and I quote, 'Nick Jackson wants us in New York.'" She moved to the side. "The phone's right here; I can dial the number."

"Do we?" Donnelly asked.

"Might as well," said Collins, "or she'll put Leeson or Wall on a plane to LA and mess up our fun."

***

"...so tell me again why we should haul our asses to New York?" Collins paused. "While those same asses are suspended without pay?" Donnelly, sharing the phone, nodded in agreement.

Good question. "Any meeting with Nick Jackson is an opportunity. I outlined what I could remember of your idea of televising the Pearson trial and he loved the concept."

215

"So?" questioned Donnelly.

"He wants you guys in New York to explain it."

We've got all the copies of that proposal, don't we Joyce? "We need to discuss this, Joyce. We'll call you right back." Collins held on to the phone.

Donnelly considered the still-empty gate and turned to Collins. "Do you think we meet Jackson? He goes for this and we make ourselves a powerhouse ally and give entrée for Marvin Jentzky repping our other stuff."

"Makes sense," said Collins. He dialed Locker's number.

"We'll do it," they both said when Locker answered.

Sniff. "Okay. Can you come directly to New York?"

A quick glance and a nod. "We guess so," they said.

"Okay." *Sniff.* "I'll meet you at the Waldorf tomorrow; we'll make the reservations. I'll be in around eleven. Let's get you on a New York flight. Can you put the agent on?"

They handed the phone to her. "Woman wants to talk to you," Donnelly said.

The agent was on the line for several minutes, taking notes. "Okay," she said to them with a cheery smile. "You're booked in First Class on the New York flight," she gestured. "Leaves from that gate in forty-five minutes," she said as she tapped on the console. A minute later she handed them their tickets. "Your hotel is the Waldorf Astoria. Someone will bring your bags onboard. Can we do anything else?"

"I need to make a call to Los Angeles," Donnelly said.

"Why don't you do that in the First Class lounge?" the agent said. "Make your calls and enjoy refreshments in the process." In five minutes they were in the lounge, with drinks, snacks, and a phone.

***

"I could get used to this," Collins said.

"Me too," agreed Donnelly. "Let me call Marvin Jentzky."

"What'll you say to him?" Collins munched on a pastry. "Lead with our highest card, the Nick Jackson summons?"

"I will. Jackson has indeed summoned us to New York to discuss one of our projects, which will benefit him." He dialed.

***

"Marvin's onboard," Donnelly said, putting the phone on the cradle. "We trust each other." He caught Collins's grimace. "He'd be fucking over not just me but his father, and that he will not do. Besides, he wants in with Jackson and the network." He lifted the receiver again. "Time to call Saul."

The conversation with Saul Jentzky was longer. "I asked Saul," Donnelly said afterward to Collins, "to go ahead on setting up a front company for *Johnny Volt*, *Felon Hunters*, and our other stuff. I said he'd get the proposals in a few days. He's with us on all the rest."

The toothsome agent reappeared. "Your flight is boarding, gentlemen. Your bags are at the gate, if you'll please follow me."

Chapter Twenty-Four

The cab from LaGuardia dropped them at the Park Avenue entrance to the Waldorf. They looked up at the hundreds of windows looming over them, speculating which room would be theirs. A doorman hustled their bags and walked up a broad flight of stairs. They threaded a gauntlet of tourists gawking at the nine-foot-high clock with the eight faces of its base having likenesses of seven American presidents and Queen Victoria. "Why show the fat Brit?" asked Donnelly.

"The clock was built in London, which enhances the hotel's snooty reputation," said Collins.

The doorman set their bags by the front desk. "Stiff necks in the morning," Collins said, handing a bill to him.

The desk clerk gave them the once-over. "Do you gentlemen have a reservation?"

Donnelly leaned in and fingered his name badge. "Well...Allen...or do I call you Mr. James? Reservations? Believe it or not, we do."

The clerk's eyebrow flicked up.

"If the man says so, they do."

Donnelly felt a hand on his shoulder and a "Hello, Frank, how are you?" in a husky voice.

Donnelly turned, surprised. A beefy middle-aged man with thinning hair and deep-sunk eyes stood, smiling broadly. Recognition dawned on Donnelly—the man was once his father's apprentice, now

218

chief of security at the hotel.

"Mr. Bradley, how are you?"

"Great, Frank, how's your dad?" He turned to the clerk. "Allen, give them each a bedroom suite. Mr. Donnelly and…?"

"Mr. Collins," supplied Donnelly. "And dad is fine."

"Yes, Mr. Bradley." The clerk pushed two room keys forward and snapped his fingers.

Bradley frowned. "Make sure the rooms are next to each other." The clerk withdrew one of the keys and substituted another.

"Any messages for them, Allen?"

Thirty seconds later the clerk handed an envelope to Donnelly, who opened it. "Message from Joyce to send the Pearson TV proposal to Nick Jackson's office ASAP in preparation for a meeting. She'll meet us tomorrow at eleven here in the lobby."

"Nick Jackson? Ilium?" asked Bradley. They nodded.

"You've done well, Frank. Your dad must be pleased. You'd better go. I'll arrange for your luggage to be delivered to your rooms."

Donnelly reached into his briefcase. "Can I ask a favor?"

"Anything," Bradley replied.

He pulled out a thick envelope. "I need this sent by the fastest way possible to this man, Saul Jentzky, in Los Angeles."

Bradley took the envelope. "Consider it done."

They talked for several minutes, said their goodbyes, and headed over to Ilium headquarters to drop off the proposal for Jackson.

"*Felony Hunters* and the other stuff to Saul Jentzky?" said Collins as they walked.

"Right," said Donnelly. "Time to stop goofing around. Should we leave a copy of the Pearson proposal for Doremus? Nick'll probably roll him in on this."

"Doremus? Yeah, not a bad political move either." They stopped at a corner. "So your father helped Bradley?"

"He was a hard guy when we lived in Crown Heights. Dad took him under his wing and made sure he stayed straight. He went on the job, did well, and now he's apparently chief of security here."

***

At seven-thirty Donnelly's phone rang. "Let's get something to eat," Collins said. "Bull and Bear okay with you?"

"Yeah," said Donnelly. "What do you think of the rooms?"

"This is how the other half lives. Old World elegance: high ceilings, rich brocades, marble bathrooms, and designer bath products, formal window treatments, crystal-and-brass lamps, and triple-sheeted bedding." He paused. "I'll meet you in the hallway in ten minutes. Don't forget the dress code."

***

The maître d' seated them at a white-clothed table near the rich mahogany bar. The electronic stock ticker running across the back wall set the theme. Donnelly noted Collins casing the bar patrons. "What's going on, Jim?"

Collins lit a cigarette. "A room of expense-account high rollers and rich people playing pretend. Check out that woman. Wrinkled, bleach-blond curly hair and well dressed. Pearls and a flash of gold. No diamonds, but I bet her purse is Chanel. I figure late fifties or early sixties." He exhaled a stream of smoke. "The one next to her? Flush-faced, expensive cigar, shaved head, eyes sporting horn-rimmed glasses fixated on the stock ticker. Has had a few pops tonight. He's younger, early to mid-fifties. Listen to her."

The woman lifted her martini and said to the man, "So have you ever been in a threesome?"

The man, concentration broken, stammered incoherently.

The woman chuckled, "Oh, come on...I'm sixty-one and I've seen it all and done it all. Let's not play games, okay?"

The man muttered and took a swig of his bourbon and returned to the stock ticker.

"Did you do two women? Or were you with another guy?" the woman said, a little more loudly.

Heads turned furtively.

The woman finished her drink and pushed her glass forward. "I found I prefer multiple partners. One guy just doesn't do it for me. I've had three guys at a time."

The man threw some bills on the bar and stumbled out, cigar clamped between his teeth. A man in his late sixties slid into the newly vacated seat and began a conversation with the woman.

She signaled for another drink and inclined her head toward her seatmate. The man pushed some bills forward and brought his chair closer.

"Better than a soap opera," said Donnelly. "Upper-echelon life in New York; so this is how our betters behave." He leaned back. "We've been sitting here for at least ten minutes and the clown who seated us failed to provide menus. Not even a junior woodchuck to fill our water glasses."

"They've been too busy listening to the morality play." Collins took a drag on the cigarette. "I'll give you a morality play. Harriet says her boss, Kelso, had an electric toilet shipped to Jackson today. They were going to install it in his executive washroom."

"Does it have the extra features?"

"Absolutely." Collins sniggered. "Nick will get a serious workout." He looked up as the waiter approached.

In a series of rushed and uncoordinated visits, water glasses were placed on their table, with a trail of ice on the floor. The waiter quickly reviewed the specials of the night and handed them menus. Within two minutes the captain arrived and hovered, waiting to take their orders.

"This place is noted for service? Unbelievable." Donnelly drank half his water. "Did you tell Harriet about our day?"

Collins tapped an ash. "Yeah. I filled her in on all the back and forth. Did you call Emily?"

"Uh huh." He looked up. "Suppose we wind up on the coast?"

"Too soon to tell." Collins sat back as their drinks arrived. "What happened Sunday night seems like an exception to their behavior."

"Our charm won them over," Donnelly said.

Collins chuckled. "More likely it was a combination of alcohol, loneliness, and I don't know what else." He sipped his martini.

"We need to figure out whether we want to maintain a relationship with them," said Donnelly .

"Indeed we do."

***

"Oof!" A dull thump resounded as the Ilium shipping crate caught a hallway corner in Nick Jackson's executive suite.

"What is this goddamn thing, Rocco?"

"A new kind of toilet. Jesus, Leroy, watch your step. This is the

222

CEO's office, not some transfer warehouse..."

"It's you, Rocco. You're moving too goddamn fast. I can't see back here."

"I know, I know," Rocco said, "always my fault; never yours. You didn't feel the step, the floor was too slippery, fill in the blank. Be careful where the hell you're going. You ever met the broad who runs this office? My oh my, is she ever a piece of ass. Some advice? Avoid her. If you don't, the conversation will not be pleasant. You won't want to be in earshot if this shipping crate dents her damn wall. Let's set this up in the bathroom suite and get out." Rocco shivered as he recalled how horny Florence could be when presented with a sweaty deliveryman and how sharp her fingernails were.

He stared out a window. "I hate driving a truck to the city, especially on a Monday; like trying to stuff a rat into an aspirin bottle. Stuck on the damn bridge approach for two hours, no fun. You'd think if HQ could be anywhere in the world, they'd choose someplace other than New York City. Like Connecticut."

"Yeah, yeah, okay, almost there." They tilted the dolly and the crate slid off. Rocco pulled the nails and staples, snipped the packing straps, and cut the tape holding the toilet to its shipping pallet. Leroy stripped off the protective framing, stacked the debris on the dolly, and centered the crate next to the traditional toilet.

"Whoa, shit! No plumbing?" said Leroy.

"The plumbing, as I can tell, is self-contained, but not so visible," said Rocco, stepping back. "Look," he reached toward a pipe, "we plug in, hook up the water and waste, and get out of here before the suits storm in."

After twenty minutes the Ilium Electric Toilet gleamed, waiting.

***

Florence entered the office suite, fresh from her morning workout. Her strong business fashion sense dictated clothing tailored and purchased in matching ensembles of jackets, skirts, blouses, and passingly feminine neckwear. She kept jewelry to a minimum. At home a small mahogany box held a number of magnificent pieces given to her by Jackson or others who either appreciated her assistance or support while they worked with him.

Today she would complete arrangements for Thursday's board meeting and Jackson's end-of-the week trip to Dubai. A plethora of board presentation materials remained to prepare as well as getting those materials and Jackson's golf clubs to the corporate jet. The sultan of Dubai had arranged a series of meetings in the sultanate. Jackson would probably reside in accommodations provided by the sultan but, just in case, she had reserved a suite at the Dubai Hilton.

Jackson seemed sanguine about the board meeting, but for Florence it was a nightmare of egos and demands. She didn't speculate about what else Jackson might be doing with the people he met in Dubai. It was enough just trying to keep him semi-sated and focused when he was in New York.

Florence considered it part of her job description to relieve Jackson's sexual tension if such became obvious to her while he was working on a project and was within her reach. They had never mentioned a word like love. For Florence, he was a duty. For Jackson, Florence was a perquisite. They were both comfortable with their bargains and, if they'd stopped to think, would have concluded their affection for each other fortuitous.

Her skill as an executive assistant allowed Nick Jackson to exercise his prodigious business talents as he circulated throughout the corporate world. Her brains were Florence's ticket to success.

She'd read and committed to memory the carnal arts of the *Kama Sutra*, giving her a skill that only added to the enormous bonuses he paid her.

She did a quick sweep of the office. Everything was in order. She stepped into the bathroom suite, flicked on the lights, and stopped short. *They delivered the electric toilet last night. Was it that hunky Rocco?* She felt herself stirring. *Enough!* Nick was deciding how to bring this wild concept to market. She checked the wall connection. The sleek metal shape struck her as an amalgamation of Brancusi's modern art designs and Tutankhamen's mask with its elegant animalism. She sensed a strong feminine hand in the appearance and the craftsmanship of a master metalsmith in the details.

I wonder how this works. An industrial-looking Arabian stallion at rest, begging to be mounted. Hmmm, doesn't seem to be any actual piping. What the hell, must be part of the functionality? She came closer. *I don't think I should pee, though. Why not? No one's around. I ought to be able to figure this out. An anatomically correct receptacle of some sort.* She slipped off her panties, hiked her dress, and mounted up. Her first sensation was one of warmth and relaxation. *This is sooo relaxing.* A minute later she was peeing like a racehorse. No urine smell, no muss, no fuss. Soft warm air flowed with just a hint of disinfectant. *Nothing beats a whiz.* She sat contented, a child on its first hobbyhorse, carefully manicured hands resting affectionately on the pommel, idly stroking the protuberant section of the toilet. *What's this?* She flicked the switch. The overwhelming pleasure was immediate. In a matter of minutes she came and came and came.

***

"Flo, Flo...Florence, wake up!" Jackson shook her. She was still shuddering in the saddle in the grip of orgasmic spasm. "What the fuck's going on? What's wrong? Are you okay? What are you doing?" Amazingly, Jackson did not stutter during this burst of excited interrogation. Anything that brought Florence to her knees so quickly had intense interest for him. "Are you all right?" he repeated, almost laughing as he realized Florence's problem was most likely clitoral. Then he spotted her lust-filled eyes. "Sh-should I cancel this morning's meetings?"

"Your call," she said, a bit out of breath, reaching for his ballooning trousers.

He started to shuck his clothes. She stepped out of the bathroom suite, made three calls, and locked his office door. As she turned he swung up on the saddle, ramrod-ready. She got on behind him and thumbed the switch on the pommel. She fondled him while he thundered on his first ride. Then he rode her from behind. For a good part of the morning they shouted across the plains of pleasure, until their voices were lost in the winds of release. Exhausted, they finally staggered into the shower together, too tired to do anything but clean themselves off.

Jackson murmured afterward, "I've banged women who people told me were machines but I never banged a machine so much like ten women." The ice cubes in Jackson's scotch rattled as he sat back.

Florence sipped some honeyed tea, trying to restore her voice. "If Ilium markets this product, we're going to need corporate legal warnings pasted all over."

Jackson laughed. "Willets and his boy Dingmann want to come down and give us a presentation."

"Do those two from the advertising and promotion department work for Dingmann? Seems they have out-of-the-box ideas." *They're also attractive.* "Or do they work for Joyce Locker? You're seeing her this afternoon, aren't you? A binder with proposals regarding the chair is on your desk."

Jackson snapped his fingers. "Move them to tomorrow morning, will you? Joyce's team is smart. Those guys work for her. I'll review the chair proposal tonight. I'd be interested in their take on the toilet."

She made a note.

"We're way behind schedule." He scratched his groin.

She smiled. "Anything else?"

"Go out and research upscale bathroom fixtures while I'm in Dubai next week. Get a feel for how many opportunities we might be looking at."

Florence made another note.

"A little outside your normal job description," he chuckled, "whatever that is. Pick out a new bathroom for your place, and have one of those toilets installed. Sort out the details with the gang in Maqua and the tax people."

***

"Jentzky's onboard." Donnelly smiled and hung up, "I'll call him when we're leaving New York. I briefed him on what we're presenting to Jackson."

"What'd he say?" Collins surveyed the skyline out the window.

"Enthusiastic. Gives him an in with Ilium and Nick Jackson."

"Saul?"

"Yeah. He won't get our package for a day or two but he's put some wheels in motion. He wants to meet with us when we come out."

"How soon?" Collins punched out a cigarette.

"Depends on Nick Jackson," said Donnelly, sipping some dregs of tea.

"Not Joyce?" Collins blew smoke.

"Not Joyce." Donnelly put the cup down, rose, and went into the bathroom. "When's she due to arrive?"

"In about half an hour," Collins replied. "I'm heading back to my room to pack in case we get out of here quickly tomorrow. I'll let you know when she calls."

"Ditto," said Donnelly. "I left a copy of the Pearson TV proposal for her."

"That's like sticking a finger in her eye," said Collins.

"I'm sure Joyce'll share her feelings on the matter," Donnelly said.

***

"Joyce is finally here," said Collins. "We meet her in twenty minutes by the front desk. Flight was late."

"She should've taken the train," said Donnelly. "Pick me up on the way down."

Locker was waiting for them at the elevator. *Sniff.* "Got word from Nick Jackson our meeting is off until tomorrow morning. Oh, and I have the Pearson proposal." *Sniff.* "Glad you decided to finally share."

"I'm hungry," said Collins.

"And I'm thirsty," Donnelly quipped.

Her face reddened. *Sniff. Didn't rise to the bait.*

"How about McSorley's?" asked Collins.

"Sounds like a plan," Donnelly replied.

"Where is McSorley's?" muttered Locker.

"Downtown. You'll love the place," said Collins. "Help you stave off the coronary you look like you're going to have. Good beer, too. And they've just begun admitting women. Think of the glory."

"Mildly amusing, Jim," said Locker.

"Food's not haute cuisine," said Donnelly, "but you'll be so full of ale you won't give a shit."

She headed toward the Park Avenue exit.

"No, Joyce. No cabs; we go by subway. Much quicker when you're going downtown. Put the subway down as a cab on your expense account. We'll go out the Lexington Avenue exit and take the train to Astor Place." Donnelly laughed. "You can mix with the proletariat."

Sniff.

Hanging on overhead straps as the Lexington Avenue local rocked downtown, "Here's the deal on McSorley's," Donnelly said. "Mugs of house-brand ale. Tasty little devils. Check out the burgers or the cheese and onion plate on the chalkboard menu: big slices of raw onion, hunks of sharp cheddar and mustard laced with horseradish. The sawdust neutralizes the bouquet of a hundred years of spilt ale soaked into the floor."

McSorley's was not crowded during the early afternoon interim before the tourists and the local workers piled in. They sat at one of the empty tables, top scarred with decades of abuse. Donnelly rose and went to the bar at the right of the door. He returned and plunked down six mugs of ale.

"This is a pretty good place," Locker said, putting down her ale. She leaned back in the chair, which squeaked every time she moved. "Kind of nineteenth century."

"Well," said Collins, "been here since 1860 or so. Every time

I'm here some new photograph or article drapes the walls." He put down his mug. "Time for food."

"And more ale," said Donnelly.

On the battered table sat a platter of cheddar chunks, onion, and saltines. Locker chewed a burger, the juices dripping down the side of her mouth.

Collins ate a hunk of cheddar. "Simple fare, but filling." He reached for a saltine.

"Appropriate for us simple folk," said Donnelly.

She finished her mug. Its replacement stood in front of her. "Why were you two flying to Los Angeles?"

So we begin. "We wanted to enjoy our suspension in style," Donnelly replied. "Getting the hell out of Maqua and the perpetually shitty weather seemed like a really good idea."

"Not that our travels should matter to anyone other than us," added Collins and lit a cigarette.

Donnelly sipped as Locker digested their answer. The low buzz of conversation and the clanking of mugs served as a backdrop. *What's next—an eruption or an attempt to engage?* He glanced at Collins, who winked.

The chair squeaked as she hunched forward. *Sniff.* "Did your travel involve business? Stuff you two developed?" *Christ, I sound like a prosecutor.*

"Whatever could you mean, Joyce?" Collins slowly blew a stream of smoke toward the ceiling, lifted his mug, and took a large gulp.

"You know damn well." She smiled, a charming grin hiding a hard-nosed attitude. She picked at a piece of cheddar. The chair squeaked once more.

Donnelly and Collins said nothing.

"Well?"

Collins leaned forward. His chair did not squeak. "By Willets's definition we were suspended without pay. Which made us, technically, unemployed." He sat back.

"And free to do whatever you want?" *Let it ride. Damn it, I can't.*

"Did we say that?" said Collins.

Locker rolled her eyes and sighed deeply. "No, you didn't. But you inferred it."

"You're implying I inferred it, you mean?" said a straight-faced Collins. Donnelly snickered.

Locker looked toward the ceiling, fists clenched, face reddening. She swallowed and stared at them, a thin smile on his lips. "Remember when you joined the company, all the documents you had to sign?"

They nodded.

"I don't know what you two think you have in your back pocket, but it isn't yours."

"Oh?" said Donnelly.

"Oh yourself," she said. "You both signed documents giving any and all work you perform while in the employ of Ilium to be the property of Ilium." She grabbed her mug.

Donnelly glanced at Collins, who smiled. "You think?" asked Donnelly. "I'm not sure, Joyce, what got into your head about our trip to Los Angeles. We signed a lot of documents—Len Lovelace watched us doing so. Right, Jim?" Collins nodded. "But I have no memory of signing a document such as you describe." He turned to Collins. "Do you, Jim?"

"Not at all," said Collins in a flat tone. He ate a hunk of cheddar.

Damn. They never signed those documents. Lovelace and everyone else missed this. If they've developed anything they're free and clear. I underestimated them.

"Will the real Joyce Locker please stand up?" Donnelly waited a beat. "Or perhaps Lou Willets in disguise?"

She said nothing, her mind racing. *In a matter of minutes I've lost their trust with my officious prig routine. Double damn.*

The sounds from the bar filled in the lack of conversation.

Collins coughed lightly. "Your round, Joyce."

She rose.

"Unless," interrupted Donnelly, "you want a good dinner in a different place and you can tell us about tomorrow with Jackson."

Sniff. "Let's do that," Locker said. "What's the place?" Change the scene, change the mood. You know, Jim is kind of attractive. Where did that come from? Dancing with him at the Christmas party? A few minutes later Burt was dead.

"Gage and Tollner, been around for ninety years," said Donnelly. "Ten minutes by subway to Brooklyn. Excellent food, gas-lit elegance, historic décor. You'll be comfortable and relaxed." He extended his hands, palms out. "Should appeal to your newly found upper-management mindset."

Whoosh, right across my bow, "Sure. Let me visit the ladies'. I'll be back in a minute."

"A line was crossed, don't you think?" said Collins.

"Oh yeah," said Donnelly. "There may be no going back. That said, we need to keep our options open."

"Agreed," said Collins. "By the way, you didn't sign those pages, did you?"

"Of course not," said Donnelly. "Distracted Lovelace and pretended to sign and moved on to the next page. What did you do?"

Collins shook his head. "Same deal. Great minds, et cetera." He took a deep breath. "Here comes Joyce. What's said is said. We concentrate on a home run with Jackson tomorrow."

Donnelly emptied his mug. "Let's not forget to let Joyce know Doremus has a copy of the Pearson trial TV pitch. We'll tell her it was her idea."

"Wasn't it?" Collins laughed.

Chapter Twenty-Five

Florence observed Locker, Donnelly, and Collins straggle into Jackson's outer office. *None of them particularly chipper.* She picked up the phone and spoke in low tones to the executive kitchen. "A pot of coffee will be here directly. Cream and sugar? No? Fine. Pastries and bagels? Anything else? Tomato juice?"

"Might I get a small bottle of Angostura bitters with the juice?" said Locker.

"Most certainly," said Florence. *Confirms my suspicion you partied last night.*

"The bitters," said Locker, "will aid our swift recovery."

Florence smiled. *Your recovery? You'd better take them before Mr. Jackson gets here.*

Sniff. "These two"—she jabbed a finger—"run efficiently on multiple beers."

"Let's hope so," said Florence, taking the bitters and pastries from the steward. She led them into Jackson's office and seated them before a large coffee table. An English wing chair with a high seat cushion and another armchair remained vacant.

"You know, Joyce," said Collins, "you mentioned the TV strategy might be a little touchy. We followed your suggestion to cover the bases and got Doremus a copy of the Pearson TV trial pitch."

Dealing with these two was never an issue of subtlety. Did I suggest any possible legal entanglement during discussions of the Pearson trial? I hope the coffee, tomato juice, bitters, and food help me remember whether I should be uppity with the two of them. I sure bollixed things with my attitude last night. At least they gave me a heads up before we got nailed in a conversation with Nick. No sense getting annoyed. I'll go gracious. "Thanks for reminding me."

"Good timing too," Donnelly whispered to Collins as Jackson and Doremus said hello to Florence outside the office.

"Morning, people," Jackson said, moving briskly. Doremus, Jackson, and another man entered. Florence wheeled in the coffee cart from the outer office and poured a hefty cup for each. She put down two sets of sugar and creamer and withdrew.

Jackson began. "This is Ken Abeel from our legal operation." He paused a moment as greetings were exchanged. "Let's get moving," he said, rubbing his hands together. "I've other commitments later this morning."

Donnelly took notice. Hmmm, no stuttering. What's going on?

"No charts and graphs?" Jackson said. "Good for you. You have suggestions about this Pearson trial?"

"We do," said Collins. "We'll highlight our proposal." He gestured to the copy Tyler Doremus held. "We began this electric chair project and then Ilium bought the GBC network. GBC is dead last in the ratings. What we propose is a turbo-charge boost, utilizing a high-profile badass like Guy Pearson. Impossible, everyone said." He stared at Jackson and said softly, "Until they announced the trial would move to Pittsfield." He turned to Donnelly.

Jackson and Doremus sat straighter. Donnelly stood. "Pittsfield is over the mountains and through the woods," he said, "and can be a tightly controlled location." He knocked on his copy of the proposal. "Live coverage of a major trial has never been done on television. Any network doing so would reap a ratings landslide. Pearson gets the chair? Go live with the event. The ratings will blow the competition away. We're not even discussing the promotional opportunity for a broad spectrum of Ilium products. Internally, something for everyone."

Sniff.

"I'm assuming, Joyce," said Jackson, "your sinuses approve?"

She nodded. *Sniff.*

"Good." Jackson picked up his coffee cup. "I love crisp decision making. Thanks for getting this proposal to us, Joyce. Tyler briefed me on the major parts. No doubt the shit hits the fan when we advance this concept. Fortunately, we have leverage in Pittsfield. Ken will cover all the legal bases to push this through quickly. We don't want anyone cutting our legs out from under us. Ken?"

Abeel consulted his notes. "We believe the senior Pearson will file a motion to dismiss the trial." Collins and Donnelly raised their hands. He ignored them and plowed on. "We'll file a request to extend media coverage before Pearson even knows." Jackson stirred and Abeel plowed on. "We researched precedents establishing the public's right to be involved in the process. Our arguments are overwhelming." Donnelly and Collins continued to wave their hands. "Receiving a little advance warning," Doremus said, "is invaluable to us as we get positioned. I appreciate your heads up on this, Joyce. Smart way to go."

Her head bobbed in appreciation.

"Ken...?" Doremus turned to Abeel.

Both Collins and Donnelly noisily cleared their throats. Abeel paused, annoyance flitting across his features. "Yesss?"

"Clinton Pearson won't be the one filing the motion," said Collins. Jackson's head snapped up. "The prosecution will."

"Pearson wants to play to a larger audience," Donnelly said. Abeel went to respond but Collins cut in. "He's theatrical to

236

begin with, and a strong presentation will help restore his reputation regardless of how this turns out." To Abeel's glare he added, "He knows his son is a dirtbag, but if he plays this right he can attack the government's case and the witnesses they put up. Pearson will figure the prosecution will react differently if they're on public display."

"Is this a federal case?" asked Jackson.

"No," said Abeel. "We think the federal government dumped the case on the state. The feds think this is an accident waiting to happen because of the likely theatrical aspects. One factor of which you would not necessarily be aware is that the sitting judge, George Robertson, is a constitutional stickler and will likely lean heavily in favor of our arguments. I happen to know George from law school. We were on Law Review at Columbia."

No one commented. Abeel reddened.

"Okay," Jackson said. "Time to talk about some other considerations. Ken, thank you for sitting in." They rose as Abeel picked up his notes and glowered at Collins and Donnelly. They smiled at him as he passed.

"Tyler, anything to add?" said Jackson, settling back.

"This idea of broadcasting the trial on live television is unprecedented," Doremus said. "I expect with our legal muscle and the profile of the perpetrator we can make a strong case in our favor." He turned to Donnelly and Collins. "I agree with your view the state will try to block this eventuality, but we can do this. I don't expect Judge Robertson to give us any special consideration, but according to Ken, he will listen carefully."

"Yeah! Y-you bet your ass they'll listen," said Jackson. "W-we've got a lock on Pittsfield—the whole county, for that matter. We're the biggest company in the area."

"Hardball won't be needed, Nick," Doremus said quietly. "Everyone concerned will be aware of our leverage. We'll never have to say a word."

Locker nodded.

"Are the GBC guys on board with this? It'll be a big adjustment for them," said Donnelly.

"They'd better embrace change," snapped Jackson, "unless they want irrelevance." Doremus bowed his head. Locker pursed her lips.

Jackson waited a moment. "Good, okay, get all the paperwork moving and tell Abeel to finish whatever else the legal guys need. Remind him I don't pay the legal department to tell me what I can do. I pay the legal department to tell me how to do what I want." He sat back.

"This will upset the status quo in the broadcasting business," said Collins. "You needn't search hard to see the downstream profit for the new Ilium network."

Christ, Jim, I'm excited too, but don't give up too much for these sharks to smell in the water. They aren't stupid; they may stumble on some of our other ideas. He took a sip of his coffee.

"L-lets not get all scattered here," Jackson said. "We need to execute what we've got and n-not step into our own brainstorming bullshit."

"Right," said Doremus. "Just getting the concept approved is a major project. The other networks will be in shock when we execute this strategy. We want them to be fighting the previous battle while we're on to the next engagement. Joyce's team produced a great plan."

Jackson put down his cup. "Okay. Let's move on. First, I appreciate the suggestion of network coverage." He nodded to Locker. "Second, I love the notion of frying this scumball in the Ilium chair. My vision is this creep's hair on end and lightning shooting out of his eye sockets. My wheels are spinning."

"Next is the toilet project." He shifted in his chair. "I want to bring the engineer in to discuss the pieces, parts, and manufacturing process. It's an impressive engineering job." Jackson's tone told Donnelly and Collins he had not only taken a ride but also pushed the pommel button.

Donnelly repressed a laugh. Jackson, intent, continued, oblivious. "The sleek design suggests a cost outside the mainstream residential and commercial markets. The engineer might suggest cost savings for the product."

God help Cox. She's a big girl. Jackson thought he had fun on the toilet? Take a ride on Harriet Cox. Collins was immediately ashamed but half sniggered. He disguised it as a sneeze-cough.

Donnelly jumped in. "We're not sure the toilet should bear the Ilium brand. Given social trends and the likelihood for personal injury lawsuits, it might be good to take some legal and trademark shelter and license the product to offshore manufacturing partners who would brand on their own. This toilet has European, Scandinavian, and upscale promise. We could start in Europe, the Mediterranean yacht havens, and the Middle East and migrate back into the states through word of mouth."

"G-great fucking idea, guys!" Jackson banged his hand on the coffee table. "I've taken steps to explore other manufacturers but that's the whole answer. I'll talk to the engineer, get a feel for the product, and we'll get moving." Locker observed Collins and Donnelly acting cool during a Jackson compliment onslaught. Doremus pressed his lips together in silent amusement.

"You and your guys came through again, big time, Joyce," Jackson said turning to Locker.

Sniff.

Donnelly smiled. *Even tough gals need a little hug. It was a good tactic to be as upfront with her as possible. Get some breathing room. At the same time play things close. Joyce is a good boss but she is a good boss loyal to Ilium, full stop.* He and Collins had come to understand that anyone who wore a suit in Ilium would stick the knife into you. *Just like the police and fire brass did.*

Everyone stood. "Joyce, stay a minute, will you?" Jackson said.

"We need to go over some additional details," Doremus said to Donnelly and Collins. "Why don't we pop into my office?"

***

After his office door closed, Jackson said, "Okay, Joyce, why don't you tell me what the hell is going on up in Maqua."

She pressed her lips together. *I've always leveled with him but some of this, like my mouthing to Donnelly and Collins, could put me in a bad light. Time for some light editing.* "Our new general manager, Lou Willets, listens to the wrong people."

"Like who?"

Willets is Nick's guy; at least he hired him. But how much is that a factor? "Like his former prep school classmate, Bob Dingmann."

"Wasn't he the guy who pissed his pants?"

"He was. He submarined Donnelly and Collins. Convinced Willets they should be suspended because of the parking lot crap. Dingmann probably read him half the personnel manual and prodded him. Willets, as you know, suspended them for a week."

Jackson nodded, recalling his phone call to Willets. "How did they react?"

"Not well." She toyed with the dregs of her coffee. "They're tough-minded; they don't take shit from anyone. The Works' chief cop, Gino Pacelli, a Fearless Fosdick type, couldn't prove their cars were the one with the phony passes. Pacelli lied his ass off and, being former investigators, they called him out on it. Made him look like a fool, which Willets ignored." *Sniff.* "They felt they got sandbagged. They were changing planes in Chicago on their way to Los Angeles when we caught up with them and convinced them to come in for this meeting."

"LA?"

"On a scale of one to ten, it was a ten they were on their way to leaving the company, if you want to know the truth, Nick."

"They were that angry?"

"More like they realized the chicken shit and the bureaucracy didn't match their own vision. They'd had enough of that in their prior jobs."

Jackson grunted. "Yeah, their files made for some of the more interesting reading I've had for a while. They think and act way outside the box and could do really well at today's Ilium. I wonder how successful they would have been in our day?"

Was there some kind of ethnic dismissal in his comment? Or was Nick tooting his own horn? Probably the latter; Nick feels he's responsible for this shift in Ilium's ways of thinking. "Not very, I'd venture," she said. Joyce was seemingly against the system, but up in Maqua, the system was unchanged. For all her bluster and femininity she was an integral part of the old guard with the ingrained prejudices and loyalties of the insider. Jackson knew this, and used it.

He stood by way of dismissal. "Make certain those two don't fly the coop, Joyce. We don't want to lose them."

She understood all too well. *That's one I can't guarantee.*

241

***

"Mr. Willets would like you and Mr. Collins to call him as soon as you're free." Florence handed Donnelly a pink message slip.

"Could you let Tyler Doremus know we'll be on this call?"

"Will do, Mr. Donnelly," Florence said. "You can use the visitor's office next door. The phone can be used as a speaker phone."

Whenever Collins encountered Florence he couldn't help but wonder. *She's a walking occasion of sin, a guaranteed boner prompter.* She was definitely hot under all her designer business suit. Buff and tight. Collins shook his head.

Donnelly punched the speakerphone button and dialed Willets's number.

After a minute they were connected.

"Willets."

"Frank Donnelly and Jim Collins, here. Mr. Jackson's secretary gave us a message to call you."

Willets began with no preamble. "We've been looking at the parking pass issue and decided there were mitigating circumstances. Without going into a long explanation, we are lifting your suspension until we sort out the details. You both can return to Maqua with Joyce Locker when you finish your business in New York. This episode got out of hand, unfortunately."

Unfortunately. Right. You would no more apologize to us than to an ant you squashed on your way to a meeting. Someone reamed your ass, and I can guess who. "Thank you," said Donnelly. "Unfortunately, *back at you, pal;* we expected to be on suspension for an entire week and Jim and I made family commitments to visit parents and siblings. We cannot be back in Maqua until Monday."

242

Donnelly and Collins knew Willets seethed. "Very well, if it must be," Willets said, and disconnected.

"Up yours," said Collins to the dead phone. "Yank our chain and think we'll return slobbering with gratitude?"

"Make certain we get paid for all this shit since we're no longer suspended," said Donnelly.

Locker was at the doorway. "Paid for what shit?" she said.

"We just talked to Willets," said Collins, "and surprise, surprise, he gave us a reprieve. Glory be, we can return to Maqua in good standing. He said what happened was, quote 'unfortunate', quote, and we'll sort out the details later. Which means, to our ears, this isn't over."

Donnelly cleared the desk. "We told him we wouldn't be able to get back until Monday since we had made all sorts of family commitments."

Willets isn't letting this go; he's keeping them on the hook. Mistake. Sniff. "I assume, since we had to drag you two out of the Chicago airport, you were flying somewhere on a quick in and out." *Sniff.* "And get back in time for your family dinner." She laughed harshly. "I'm not going to get my panties in a twist over you guys and what you are or aren't up to." Her tone hardened. "The more you play a dangerous game the more apt you are to get your butt kicked."

"Thank you for the obvious input, Joyce," said Collins. Her face reddened. *This is better than bear baiting.* Donnelly shook his head. *Okay, be conciliatory.* "We appreciate you're an Ilium lifer and value your advice. You understand, we try to give Ilium value for what we get paid for. We're not the typical college frat guys goofing around on the Ilium program; we have adult goals and objectives."

"A lot of people respect you on a personal level," added Donnelly. "We think we can have some fun along the way."

"You two don't mince words, do you?" In her gut she

243

experienced something rare: a sense of fun and anticipation.

"Doremus wants to see us," said Collins. "Are you also meeting with him?"

"No. I need to make some calls. You can bring me up to speed on Doremus before I fly back to Maqua."

***

Tyler Doremus motioned for them to sit. His office was spacious, befitting his place in the corporate pecking order. No suffocating pictures or artwork clogged the wall; the windows and the view made up for the lack of decoration. Doremus chuckled. "So how do you guys like working in Maqua?"

"The truth?" said Collins. *Why should I tell him? For one, Frank and I no longer give a crap. He looks like standard preppy issue in a Brooks Brothers suit, button-down shirt, conservative pattern tie, and black wing-tip shoes. Of course this will find its way back to Jackson.*

Doremus waved a hand.

"How about we start with hamster-brained sociopaths in leadership roles?"

"Including Joyce Locker?"

Incoming! Collins paused deliberately. "No." *Actually, when you really think about her, she's a great catch for someone. What about Harriet? Hell, variety is the spice of life.*

"Maqua," said Donnelly quickly, "is like being the last human in Vampireville and trying to buy groceries at sundown."

"That bad?" The smile was reluctant, as if in conflict with a corporate dictum.

"What Maqua does," said Collins, "is kill any hope staying in your current job will work out for you." He sat back and pulled out

244

his cigarettes. "How's the GBC merger working out for you?" He lit up.

Doremus glanced at Collins. *Oh my, they're clever. Now they're grilling me. They've earned the right.* "Not well. I've never been involved in an acquisition where the acquired company wants nothing to do with the parent company." He ran a hand across his cheek.

"They don't want to listen to the wisdom of the headquarters people from their industrial giant parent?" Donnelly smiled.

Doremus grimaced at the truth; two large dimples appeared in his flushed cheeks.

"Not only that," added Collins, "but I bet they'll think the idea of televising the Pearson trial is nuts and will ignore any entreaties." He took a puff. "In other words, you're pretty sure they'll tell you to buzz off and stay in your playpen." He blew a smoke ring. "This from people whose ratings are dead last in every survey."

"Exactly," said Doremus.

"Does Jackson know this?" Collins held his cigarette aloft.

"Not yet." *He's looking to me to get this network integration done and I'm not about to admit I'm persona non grata with the GBC people.*

"So how are you going to present the trial concept?" asked Donnelly. "Any ideas?"

"None that make any sense. We'll sort this out in quick time, I'm sure," Doremus said, clenching his fists.

Donnelly watched the fist slide out of view. "Maybe we can help," he said. Collins glanced at him but said nothing.

Doremus blinked. His dark eyes darted back and forth between his two guests. *I don't know much about either one of you other than you are brash. Not corporate, mind you, but Nick Jackson appears quite taken with you.* "How?" he said.

"Let me make a phone call," Donnelly said, standing. "Is there a phone we can use?"

Doremus took the hint. "Use mine. I have some business down the hall. Tell my assistant when you're finished." He hauled himself out of his chair and headed out of his office.

"Jentzky?" Donnelly nodded while Collins stubbed out his cigarette and lit another. "Will he do it?"

"Yeah, he gets in good at the highest levels of Ilium. We throw a life preserver to Doremus, convince him to let Jentzky present the idea to the GBC clowns. GBC will listen because he's Marvin Jentzky and their ratings are in the toilet. They have a new owner and they'll realize self-preservation is a potent incentive. Doremus will like it because Jentzky's long-term bread is buttered with him."

"What about us?" The smoke curled up from Collins's cigarette.

"One, we gain a powerful ally in the upper echelon of Ilium no matter what we decide to do. Two, Jentzky's gratitude, and favors are like gold in Hollywood. Three, no matter what we do, owesies are coming to us."

"I love your logic," said Collins. "Make the call."

Donnelly dialed, spoke to a secretary, and after a brief delay Marvin Jentzky came on the line. Using the speakerphone he described the situation.

"Televise the Pearson trial? Brilliant, Franky. Televising the execution? Outta sight. Jackson loves the idea, you said?"

"Big time," said Donnelly.

"Tell me the problem."

"GBC wants nothing to do with Ilium." Donnelly outlined Doremus's charge from Jackson and his lack of success. "This is a little bit out of his experience, Marv. You have the credibility in the industry; they'd listen to you."

"Yes, GBC will listen to me. They've ignored me at their peril in the past. Any suggestions regarding Doremus?"

"Speak to him," said Donnelly. "Are you heading to New York anytime soon?"

"For this," said Jentzky, "I can be on tonight's redeye and in his office tomorrow morning."

"Play this opportunity any way you wish," said Donnelly. "Can he call you in the next half hour? He's poster-boy WASP, probably majored in Caucasian studies."

Jentzky laughed. "Ask him to call me; I can't wait. And Franky? I owe you. I'll get Saul to send over your stuff and we can talk when I get to the city. Where are you staying?"

Good question. "The Waldorf."

"Gillian will make the reservation. You and I and your colleague Collins can have dinner tomorrow night."

"Look forward to it," said Donnelly. He turned to Collins. "Let me get Doremus, tell him Jentzky's waiting for his call and will fly in on the redeye and meet with him tomorrow morning. He ran his hand over the telephone. He saw a card sticking out from under it. On impulse he dialed the number labeled "stimulus." The phone rang twice on the other end. "Hello," answered a throaty voice. "You have reached the stimulus hotline. Do you want oral, anal, screamers...?" Collins laughed and Donnelly quickly hung up.

"What a place," said Collins. "Between the phone and the vibe between Florence and Jackson, we're in a sex-saturated palace."

***

"Marvin Jentzky? *The* Marvin Jentzky?" Tyler Doremus had

returned to his office and slid into his seat. "How'd you line him up?"

"Unimportant," said Donnelly. "Bring him in and GBC listens." He and Collins made to leave. "Better call him now if you want to do this. He's a busy man." Doremus waved them back to their seats.

Doremus dialed. After fifteen minutes of conversation he hung up, face beaming. "Jentzky will be here tomorrow morning and we can strategize favorable outcomes regarding GBC. Let's break, catch up on phone messages, then I'd like you guys to come back after lunch and sit down again with Ken Abeel. I want the legal angles covered."

"What about Joyce Locker?" Collins said.

Doremus ran through a mental political checklist. "Good idea, I'll tell her." He made a note. "We'll get together at two." He thought for a moment. "Can you two stay for the rest of the week?"

"We were about to check out of the Waldorf; we'd been upgraded to suites."

"Keep them," said Doremus. *I think you guys saved my ass. I'll throw them another bone.* "Stay the weekend." He rose.

"You're very generous. Thank you," said Collins. He and Donnelly stood in the doorway. "If you see Locker before we do, would you tell her you asked us to stay over?"

"No problem." Doremus gathered some papers.

Donnelly called the Waldorf and extended their stay through Sunday evening in the same rooms.

***

When they returned to the visitor's office, Florence told them Locker had left.

248

"Did she say whether she was going back to Maqua?" Donnelly said.

"She said she was going back to the hotel."

"She's probably picking up her luggage," said Collins. He turned to Florence. "Did Doremus talk to her?" Florence nodded. "Okay." He said to Donnelly, "I'd better call Pat and tell her we'll speak to Joyce tomorrow."

"Ask her to call Willets and tell him Doremus wants us here," said Donnelly.

Collins finished his call with Pat. "We're staying the weekend, right?"

"Thanks to Doremus, yeah," said Donnelly. "We're with Jentzky tomorrow night. Our stuff is different; nothing remotely like it on television. I feel in my bones we've got a winner."

"Well, while you're feeling your bones give a call to your buddy Saul to keep him in the loop and let him know his brother will be calling."

"Right," said Donnelly. "We don't want to lose control before we get anything in writing. You know the drill, being as how you're another one of the guys who never signed the non-compete up in Maqua."

Collins chuckled. "True enough, true enough. Listen, I've been thinking. Your weaseling around about phony family get-togethers gave me an idea. Why don't we take a shot at calling up the Cox sisters and ask them to come down here for the weekend? Revisit the scene of our recent crimes?"

"Not a bad idea. Always thinking, always with the creative approach. I like your style. Go ahead."

Collins dialed.

"Cox, product engineering,"

"Yes sir, Jim Collins calling from advertising and promotion. Mr. Donnelly and I are at corporate headquarters in New York reviewing progress for our Electric Chair product development project. It might be advantageous for you to come down to the city for a meeting. I won't suggest you come immediately but perhaps in light of the importance of this activity, you could give up a weekend to go over the details?"

"I'll check my testing schedule for some reliability programs I'm running, but your suggestion sounds possible." *She doesn't miss a beat. Clever girl. One worthy of inclusion.* He heard papers rustling. "I believe I can get under way by Friday afternoon," Cox continued. "I may bring someone to take minutes."

"Good," said Collins. "As usual, you anticipated the requirements. Call me back at this number," he recited the number of the Waldorf, "and leave the details of your arrival. A suite awaits you and your assistant. Try to fly into LaGuardia. It's the most convenient all around. Thanks for your quick response and we'll talk soon."

"Good job," Donnelly said. "Kudos."

"You did hear she'll be bringing Emily. This could be another wild one if we play our cards right."

"This won't do much for our Catholic chastity program."

Collins chuckled. "We all stumble occasionally."

Donnelly phoned Saul Jentzky and told him his brother would be calling.

"Should we discuss with Doremus our idea of having a weekly show televising executions?" Collins asked.

"Saul will give him the materials so Marv Jentzky can make the proposal." He turned to Collins. "Let's grab a bite, after which we hear what Doremus and Abeel have to say."

"Happy, happy, joy, joy," said Donnelly. "Put on your bullshit protectors."

***

"You were right, Frank," Collins said as they walked into the hotel lobby. "I think we heard more doubletalk and corpspeak this afternoon than all the time we've been up in Maqua."

"Nothing like talking past each other to score points."

"Made me thirsty," said Collins. "I'm going to have a drink. Join me?"

"I've got some calls to make." *Sue's in town for her convention; maybe she can shake free.* "I'll see you tomorrow morning."

Donnelly went to the elevator bank and Collins stood, deciding which of the three Waldorf bars he would go to. He was leaning to Sir Harry's when out of the corner of his eye he spotted Joyce Locker coming up the steps from the Park Avenue entrance trailed by a doorman carrying several packages with a Bergdorf Goodman label.

Whoa, Bergdorf's! Toto, she's not up in Maqua anymore. Do I do the gallant thing and ask her for a drink and see that the packages go to her room? Or do I head to Sir Harry's and get started? Decisions, decisions. Collins walked over to the doorman, slipped him some bills, and said, "I'll take those." He grabbed the packages and turned to Joyce. "I thought you were going back to Maqua today."

"I'm going back tomorrow morning."

"Great, join me for a drink at Sir Harry's?"

"Well, well," Locker said, "a display of manners. What a pleasant surprise." She smiled. "Seriously, Jim, I'd rather get this stuff up to my room. Why don't you join me?"

Now I'm a schlepper, a bag carrier. We go up there and she'll start digging about what Frank and I are up to. No good deed goes unpunished. "I suppose so," he said.

They got on the elevator. "Fifteenth floor," she said to the operator.

"What room are you in?" he asked. "Frank and I are on this floor."

The doors opened and they stepped out. "I'm down the corridor," she said.

As Collins brought the packages into the suite Joyce said, "Put them over by the wall, please. Take off your tie and drape your jacket on the chair"

"Yes, sir."

"Don't be a smartass," Locker said, but a crinkle of a smile showed around her eyes as she appraised him. *His brashness and self-assurance are attractive. I've never really thought of him outside work. Maybe I should. To me, he's more intriguing than Frank.*

"Would you like a drink? I've a Macallan stashed in my luggage."

"Yes, please." *Beats sitting in Sir Harry's for ten bucks a drink.*

Joyce tossed her suit jacket on a chair, went into the bedroom, rummaged in her carry-on, and came back with the bottle of Macallan. She turned up two hotel glasses, rinsed them in the sink, added some ice, and poured two fingers of the single malt into each. "Savor this," she said as she joined Collins on the couch.

"Is there any other way?" The short-sleeved silk blouse Locker wore when she took off her suit jacket revealed a shapely woman.

They made small talk, avoiding the topics of the evening before at McSorley's. Collins sipped his drink, turned to her, and said, "How many people know that half the martinis you drink in L'Fey are water?"

"You're the first to notice," she laughed. "I'll need to have a word with Tappy; he's getting careless behind the bar." She raised her glass in a mock toast.

Nice throaty laugh, kind of sexy. "We both did. Remember, Frank and I were investigators; we tend to notice things." He returned the mock toast. "Not to worry; your secret's safe."

All she ever wears to work are business suits. Good posture but the suits make her appear boxy and plain. The blouse defines her breasts. Nice, very nice. With her jacket on I couldn't even tell she had them. Her arms have soft but visible muscle definition. Great legs, shapely rear chassis. She's the whole package. "You look like you work out," he said.

"I do 10ks. I run all the time to train, but only to train for the 10ks. Fartleks, intervals, like that. Speed play, you know?

"Fartleks?"

"It's Swedish. Means varying your pace throughout your run, alternating between fast segments and slow jogs."

Christ on a crutch. Did I hit her hot button?

"What do you do, Jim?"

"Do?"

"Outside of work, I mean. What lights your burners?"

"Well, I work out. A habit left over from my days on the job in New York City. I drink, although sometimes not responsibly, but I appreciate this Macallan. I read, I write, I chase a few women." *Okay, let's get something on the table here.* In a soft voice he asked, "Do you chase any men?"

Do I chase any men? Inwardly she sighed. *How to answer that question? There are no men and there haven't been for a while. The only thing I chase these days is my job.* "Not much opportunity; it's the low end of the pool up in Maqua." *Do I chase Jim Collins? I feel the attraction.*

How do I respond? Is a signal being sent? I have to proceed with caution. After all, she is my boss. But oh, my, is she a looker. With brains to boot. One false move and I'm in serious trouble. "Maybe it's the lovely weather Maqua has."

Again the throaty laugh. She sensed Jim's attention was fully focused on her. She tried to imagine the physical side of this man. She put her arms up along the back of the sofa to enhance his view of her jutting breasts. "I never thought of it that way. Perhaps I should take advantage of the warmer weather down here." She finished her drink.

"Perhaps you should." *She's aiming those torpedoes at me. Is this a come-on or a trap?*

"Freshen your drink?" At his nod, she went to the minibar.

As she filled the glasses an ice cube spilled onto the coffee table. Collins reached for a napkin to wipe the moisture. Joyce's hand, reaching for the same napkin, brushed across his. The effect was electric. She slowly pulled her hand away. The only sound was the faint hum of traffic from the street. A moment later she placed her hand back on his.

This must be what it's like when the lion meets his lioness: a recognition, respect, the giving and the taking. They sat, not speaking, her hand on his, Collins debating what he should do.

She took her hand from his and moved it slowly up his sleeve and to his face.

Taking her cue, he lightly stroked her neck and cheek.

Their eyes met and they kissed, slowly at first and then with growing passion. She pushed him back into the cushions while her tongue made the first invasion. He responded with vigor. She fumbled at his trousers; his hand slid into her panties. Soon their clothes were off and they were in the bedroom.

***

"I think I knew this the first time I saw you," said Jim, leaning on his elbow, running his fingers through her hair. "I shouldn't have let those frumpy business suits fool me for so long."

"Well," said Joyce, "I'm glad you finally figured things out." She started to stroke his member. "There are going to be some stipulations concerning this relationship."

"I'm more than happy to discuss them with you," said Collins, moving his hand to her breast. "Shall we do it again? I sense a certain receptivity."

"Oh yes," said Locker, tightening her grip. "Let's."

Never felt this way about a woman and I clearly feel it being given back to me.

Joyce was asleep when Collins went back to his room after

leaving a note. No noise or light came from Frank's suite. He lay down on his bed and in the moments before he slept he thought, *I've been around the block, slept with a few women, talked to more, had fun with some, had eye-opening experiences with others, but this is something more sharply defined, different than with Harriet. Joyce must have known this when I couldn't yet see it. I'm not exactly Mr. Sensitivity.* All of these thoughts were strangely soothing and he drifted off. At 3 a.m. he jerked awake. *Holy shit, Harriet will be here Friday. What do I do?* He stared off, eyes still closed. *Nothing! Let the good times roll!* He turned over and slipped back into what his mother called "the sleep of the just."

***

When Donnelly parted from Collins he took the elevator to the fifteenth floor and walked down the hallway to his room. Inside, he found a phone book and called the Plaza hotel. "Dr. Susan Costello, please."

The phone rang several times until a breathless voice answered, "Hello?"

"Sue?"

"Yes, yes, who is this, please?"

"Sorry, it's Frank Donnelly. I got called down to New York. When we talked the other day you said if I was here to give you a call. " *How weak does that sound?*

"Yes, I did…didn't I?" She was still trying to catch her breath.

Enthusiasm not present. This is a big mistake. Get off the line and join Collins at the bar. "Well, I guess you're busy with the convention: I'll give you call sometime up in Maqua." *Hang up now and preserve your dignity.*

"Sorry, Frank, I had to run to catch the phone. I'd love to get together. When were you thinking?"

"Tonight? I'm right down the street at the Waldorf." *Do I sound needy?*

"That'd be great," she said. "Where?"

"How about dinner at the Edwardian Room? It's in your hotel." He looked at his watch. "Meet you at seven in the lobby?"

"Look forward to catching up, Frank. See you in the lobby at seven."

Donnelly hung up and dialed the restaurant.

***

Sue Costello came off the elevator in a white sheath dress, a matching handbag, a string of pearls and three-inch heels. Her black hair was cut in a swept-back short crop. Her eyes swept the lobby and alighted on Donnelly. Her smile went full wattage as he walked toward her.

"You look great, Sue," said Donnelly as he grasped her hands. In her heels she was eye level with him. "Thanks for joining me. Are you hungry?

"Famished, actually. You don't look so bad yourself, Frank."

"A table awaits us at the Edwardian Room."

"I peeked in earlier. Very elegant; a far cry from where we grew up."

As they sipped their wine, they caught up on the doings of old friends and schoolmates from the neighborhood. They laughed as they recounted the times.

"What did you do after Crucifixion, Sue? I think you were around for about a year and then you went off the radar."

She swirled her wine glass, put it down and said, "I went to St. Agatha's for freshman year and then went to Non Sum Dignus for two years."

"You were studying to be a nun?" Frank considered. *On a scale of one to ten it's less than one I would've come up with this.*

"It seemed like a good idea at the time." She picked up her glass and sipped.

"Your mother." Donnelly recalled her: pleasant, but like many moms in the neighborhood, could be formidable.

"Yes, I was acting out," she winked, "as you may remember. My parents thought it would help my soul to pretend a vocation. I went along with it to get out of the house."

"Wow." Donnelly shook his head at the absurdity. "Really?"

"Really. Two years was all I could take. I came back and finished at St. Agatha's. I'd learned how to behave." She scanned the menu.

The waiter approached and they gave their orders.

They made small talk while they ate. Donnelly put his utensils on the plate, wiped his mouth with a napkin, and asked, "So, how long have you been married?"

"About two years."

"Where'd you get married? At Crucifixion?"

"No, at City Hall," Sue said. To Donnelly's raised eyebrow, she added, "He's not Catholic and if it didn't work out I could get a divorce a lot more easily than an annulment." Tight-lipped, she added, "As things are turning out, a good decision."

Step away from the trouble in River City. "How unhappy were your parents at the City Hall idea?"

"Very, until I explained why." She toyed with her vegetables. "That eased the steam coming out of their ears and allowed my mother to reduce the frequency of her rosaries to save my soul." She sipped her wine.

"How'd they take to your husband?"

"They thought he was a condescending ponce." She paused. "My paraphrase."

258

Donnelly grinned, recalling Collins had called him the same thing.

"Do you know my husband, Bob?"

"We work in the same department," Donnelly said.

"So you like him?" Sue said, and laughed.

"I refuse to answer on the grounds it might incriminate me," he said, straight-faced.

"I take it you've crossed him? Or vice versa?" Her eyes twinkled in amusement. "You were a cop; why didn't you just shoot him?"

Donnelly, snorting, almost spat out his wine. "I've been tempted." He leaned forward. "If this is not too personal, I have to ask, how long did you know him before you got married?"

"It's a fair question." She looked down. "Two months. I'd finished my residency and I was exhausted, physically and mentally. I met Bob through an acquaintance from the hospital. We clicked. He was very gallant and acted like a Catholic schoolboy during our, for want of a better word, courtship."

His mouth flew open. *Jesus Christ, what does she mean? He never touched her?*

"Some other time, Frank," Sue said.

Donnelly lifted his hand toward her, then lowered it. *Nothing to say.*

"What about you; have you come across any appropriate females in the vast Maqua tundra?"

"I've gone out a few times with the sister of an engineer I know." He crossed his arms and leaned back. "It's not serious."

"Glad to hear it," she said and smiled.

How should I take that? He nodded.

They continued to talk until Donnelly looked around and realized the room was almost empty. He signaled for the check and they walked to the elevator bank.

As the elevator doors slid open, Sue said, "Thanks for one of the best evenings I've had in a long time." She pulled him close and kissed him, her tongue slipping between his teeth. Donnelly felt the sensation go down to his feet. He responded and they stood for a minute in an embrace. A muffled cough from the elevator operator caused them to separate. "Frank, it's best you stay here. Please call me when we're back in Maqua. Goodnight." She stepped in and the doors closed.

Chapter Twenty-Six

Marvin Jentzky met them in the lobby of the Waldorf. He wore the LA travel uniform: jeans and casual shirt. Donnelly introduced him to Collins. "Glad to meet you, Jim," said Jentzky. "You do good work." He turned to Donnelly. "We'll talk about that tonight."

"Right," said Donnelly. They discussed Doremus and Nick Jackson and the corporate setup at Ilium. "We'll get together in Doremus's office?"

"Sounds good." Jentzky was a bear of a man in his early forties, broad chested and deeply tanned. His clean-shaven face framed a jaw line that might someday morph into jowls. His nose, Donnelly knew, was broken years ago in a street fight. His tight-cut black curly hair crowned a wide forehead.

"Okay," said Donnelly, "Doremus said he wants us there, at least for the introductions."

At two minutes before eleven Jentzky was ushered into Doremus's office, where Donnelly and Collins sat. Jentzky strode across the carpet, holding out a hand. "I've been looking forward," he said.

Jentzky's gleaming black shoes caught Doremus's eye. *Extra points.* He gestured for him to take a seat. *Impeccably turned out. Dark blue suit, expertly cut to fit his frame. Bespoke? The enamel cuff links match the red silk tie. Hermès? Goes well with the striped blue shirt. Turnbull and Asser? For a Hebrew he makes a good first impression.* "As have I," Doremus said. They made small talk for several minutes. "To the matter at hand, if you don't mind," said Doremus. "Ken Abeel, our lawyer, has obtained permission for GBC to televise the Pearson trial. The prosecution protested, but the judge batted the prosecution's arguments aside."

"Might be useful to hear what the judge ruled," said Jentzky.

Doremus reached for a memo. "The judge said, 'he was granted bail and jumped it, didn't he? The police caught him digging in a young woman's grave, for god's sake. We're going to protect his rights as best we can but I'm not going to be seen as coddling him.' He told them to stop wasting their time and prepare their case."

"I suspect," said Jentzky, "the prosecution doesn't want Clint Pearson having a national stage to mount his defense." He waited a beat. "We, however, do. Clint Pearson will make for compelling television." He turned to Doremus. "Is GBC aware of this?"

"Er, no." With a muffled cough Doremus began to sketch the situation with GBC, their ratings, and Nick Jackson's sense of urgency. "I know you are aware of this situation…"

"Always good to recap," said Jentzky.

Diplomatic, Donnelly observed.

Jentzky sat quietly while Doremus continued to talk. "The GBC people want no interference from us. They've made that quite clear in any number of ways. Nothing blatantly obvious, mind you, but they believe they can straighten out the mess they're in. We don't. Their finances are a disaster area. We don't want to blitz them but soon we may be forced to exert our will."

"They'll listen to me," said Jentzky, standing. "Believe me, Tyler," Jentzky put both hands on Doremus's desk, "the GBC people know the handwriting's on the wall. They're looking for a way to acquiesce." He sat and sipped his coffee and rattled off a slew of top-tier GBC executives who owed him favors of one sort or another.

Collins observed Jentzky's movements. His hands, footwork,

shoulders, and eyes suggested unbridled potency. *Christ, he just came off the redeye and he's on like Johnny Carson. He's got the salesman's knack: you're my new best friend; I have something you really want. For an introvert like Doremus this is a free pass to camaraderie, good times, and acceptance. Well, not exactly free; someone has to pay Jentzky. But Ilium'll pay, not Tyler Doremus. Win win.*

"Will you do it?" Doremus said. He couldn't keep the eagerness out of his voice.

Donnelly laughed to himself. *You just lost any negotiating leverage you might have had, pal.*

Jentzky leaned back in his chair. "You want my firm to help you develop this program for airing on the GBC network?"

"Yes," said Doremus.

Jentzky thrust his hand to Doremus. "Glad to be working with you."

Doremus swallowed, realizing he had backed himself into a corner.

"Let's get to work," said Jentzky. "My people will send some papers formalizing the arrangement. You can judge us by our results."

"Fair enough," said Doremus. *If the contract is too odious, the lawyers can let me wiggle out of it.*

"Right." Jentzky lit a cigarette and began pacing. "These new laws the states are passing are moving the country into an age of reproval. The Pearson trial will illustrate the sleaze-packed scandal-scented dysfunctional lives of the criminal class who live in a sort of suspended adolescence and prey on common, everyday folk. Set the stage, if you will."

"Set the stage?"

"Of course," said Jentzky. "Choreograph this event in the right way and the Pearson trial could be the first of a series, wherein GBC televises the trial and execution of selected criminals who will get rounded up as a result of the 'try and fry 'em' laws." He puffed on his cigarette. "Or we could televise only the executions."

Straight out of our plan. Collins glanced at Donnelly. 'What next?' he mouthed.

Doremus scribbled some notes.

We should be what's next. I suspect our usefulness has ended. "We need to return some calls," Donnelly said. "We'll connect later, Tyler." They shook hands and began to leave.

"Thanks for all your help," Doremus said. "Marvin and I will be with Nick Jackson after lunch. We'll talk."

Meaning you've served your purpose. "Look forward to it," Donnelly said, winking at Jentzky.

"Joyce sounded unusually chipper, didn't she?" asked Donnelly.

I hope I aided her in achieving that state. "She's back at the Ilium mothership in Maqua."

"Cold," said Donnelly.

"Maybe," said Collins. "At least she took our staying here in good spirit. Getting an in with the corporate guys never hurts the department. No doubt she spoke to Lou Willets." They entered the hotel lobby.

"I'll leave a message for Jentzky to call me in my room," said Donnelly. "Any preference as to where we eat?"

"Not really. I'll call my folks and maybe see them tomorrow before we greet the girls at LaGuardia."

"Yeah, I should visit my folks too. What time does the girls' flight get in?"

"Four-thirty," said Collins. "Let me know when Jentzky calls."

***

"Nick Jackson is a piece of work," said Jentzky, lighting a cigarette. He, Donnelly, and Collins were sitting in the Bull and Bear. "Dynamic son of a bitch." He took a puff. "Said good things about you two."

Donnelly shrugged and drank half his beer.

They sat in silence, watching the procession of woulda-coulda-shouldas slide into the bar.

Jentzky put down his drink and lit another cigarette. "Saul gave me your stuff and I looked it over on the plane." Puff. "Great concepts. Love the ideas." Puff. "Different and original, in tune with what's going on." He stubbed the cigarette. "But to sell it, especially since this is so different, I'll need sample scripts for each of these concepts and an outline for the next several episodes."

"So, Frank," said Collins, "it's back to the Siberia of Maqua on Monday."

Jentzky smiled wryly and sipped his drink. "Where will you be this weekend?"

"Here," said Donnelly. "Some twins, friends of ours, will join us Friday," he added. "The girls are from Iowa; never been to the city."

"Iowa, eh?" Jentzky chuckled. "Blonds?" They nodded. He finished his drink. "Blond, blue-eyed prairie beauties, right?" They nodded. "Stunning, right?" They nodded. "A word of advice." He sighed and slowly lowered the glass. "Here's the deal. They can age at warp speed into stringy-haired shrews in ankle-length dresses that hide their boxcar shapes. Sorry."

Collins chuckled. *An argument for Joyce, as if I needed one.*

"Pretty powerful image," said Donnelly, grinning. "Is this personal experience expressed as folk wisdom?" *Sue's better looking than both of them, even if she is out of my reach. There are some lines you don't cross.*

"Unfortunately." Jentzky laughed. "I didn't marry her; I saw what her mother looked like." He stretched. "I'm ticketed for the late flight back to the coast. Where do we want to eat dinner?"

"How about Donohue's Steak House?" suggested Collins. "The name's a bit of a misnomer. Donohue is a traditional Irish bar with a small dining room in the rear on Lexington near 63rd. The food's great. Steak doesn't play the dominant role as it does at most beef temples. Calf's liver, ham, various seafood dishes, and burgers are also on the menu. You can pop across the 59th Street Bridge and to the Van Wyck and JFK. "

"Sounds good to me; let's go." Jentzky threw down a wad of bills. "Wait for me in the lobby and I'll get my bag. I'll fill you in on everything that went on with Doremus and Jackson while we eat."

***

Collins pushed his empty plate aside and lit up. "What's your take on Doremus?"

Jentzky sipped his martini. "As you guys said, WASP poster boy." Puff. "Corporate political player." Puff. "Covers his flanks before he'll take any risk." Puff. "Watch your ass with this guy." Puff. "Right now you two are on his good-guy list." Puff. "Don't get so good you'll be a threat." Puff. "Deep down, he's a prick." Puff. He stubbed his cigarette. "Wouldn't be the first time you dealt with pricks, Franky."

"No, it wouldn't," said Donnelly, putting his fork down. He turned to Collins. "We've both been down that road."

"I can believe that," said Jentzky. He cut a last piece of steak and chewed. "I was serious when I said I thought all of your ideas were really good. What you propose is way different from anything on the air. The networks want continuity, which is why we need scripts. Like you did with the one version of *Felon Hunters*."

Donnelly nodded. "We return to Maqua because we like getting paid."

Jentzky wiped his mouth with his napkin. "I'm afraid so." He finished the martini.

"Would Jackson screw us if we left Ilium?"

"Good question, Jim," said Jentzky. "It's a possibility unless you consider giving GBC first shot at anything you develop."

"On a related matter, we may have a slight snag, Marv," Donnelly said. He described their conversation with Locker and them not signing the non-compete agreements when they joined Ilium. "If they find out, they may force us to sign one."

"Non-competes aren't worth the paper they're written on." He waved his hand dismissively and rose. "I'd better get a move on if I'm to catch my plane. I'll settle this bill up front." They shook hands and Jentzky left.

"What do you think?" Donnelly said.

"I like him," said Collins. "He's probably right about the need for treatments."

"You know," said Donnelly, "after Marv's little anecdote about morphing from prairie beauties into boxcar shapes, I'm not sure we can look at the Cox sisters in the same way."

"At least not until we see a picture of their mother," said Collins. *Although Joyce is in my head right now.*

267

"Yeah," said Donnelly, "Imagine them bloating in the coming years and testing the tensile strength of spandex."

"The mind boggles," said Collins. "You're ruining my anticipation of the weekend with these sordid projections." He finished his drink. "If Jentzky were smart enough to know what the Cox sisters were going to look like in ten years, he'd have more box office smashes under his belt. For all we know they could look like old Mae West, a few extra pounds and a lot more voltage. Remember what Yogi said, 'The future ain't what it used to be.'"

"Point taken," said Donnelly. "We're in the here and now. I drew down my checking account to zero so we'd have enough walking-around money.

"Lighten up. I'll go halfsies," said Collins. "Anyway, given our current relationship with Ilium, I suggest we hang out at the Waldorf and charge everything to our rooms. We'll tell Doremus we entertained some of Jentzky's cronies."

"Of course," said Donnelly. "Never was any doubt."

Collins was lighting a cigarette when he stopped short. "Wait a minute! Jentzky used our ideas in yesterday's meeting. Shouldn't we be due something from him?"

Donnelly looked up, exhaling loudly. "Yeah, we should. Let's call Saul from the hotel."

***

Back at the hotel…

Donnelly hung up. "So, do we get paid or not?" Collins puffed.

"The short answer is yes," said Donnelly, standing. "We get a check for the work we did on the Pearson trial and the concept of televising the subsequent executions. Could be big bucks; Saul needs

268

to work out some details but he's sending us each a check for ten thousand to our Maqua addresses to tide us over. The ten big ones'll come in handy. The checks will act as contracts to legitimize his representation of us. A no-brainer for us to sign, don't you think?"

"Indubitably." Collins blew a stream of smoke. "As usual, Frank, you've clutched the straw as the road rose up to meet you. Tomorrow we visit our folks and go on to LaGuardia?"

"Right. Now we find a bar for a celebratory drink."

"Or two," said Collins.

***

A troubled Joyce Locker was at her desk Friday afternoon. Her slim fingers beat a staccato rhythm on the desktop. She had done some hard thinking on the morning flight from New York. *I never thought the attraction would be so powerful and so immediate. Jim is five or six years younger than I am. Can that work? Am I thinking like a schoolgirl? Maybe, but my oh my... I thought I was up here for the long haul; maybe it's my hormones in overdrive—he's smart, ambitious, handsome, witty—What can happen with us? On the other side of the ledger, I can't forget my professional duty. Those two didn't sign the non-competes. Who's acting here, Joyce the boss or Joyce the starry-eyed?*

She picked up the phone and placed it in the cradle. She repeated the process several times. *What to do? What to do?*

Most people thought Joyce Locker was a company lifer. Now, she wasn't sure, but thanks to her McSorley monologue, so were Donnelly and, possibly, Collins.

Those two deftly turned aside my gambit about the non-compete agreement. They didn't sign the damn thing. How could Lovelace be so stupid? Len's been around a long time. You don't work for Ilium without a non-compete and patent rights release. How had those two slick bastards managed to get hired without

269

those forms on file? No time to worry now. Do I alert Lovelace? If I do, he'll be all over them. Damn. And I'd lose Jim.

My family was Ilium. Dad and grandad had worked, struggled, served, and helped build the place. They weren't nutty engineers, manufacturing or marketing hotshots on the way to a career somewhere else. They were Ilium men, with a duty to serve the shareholders and increase the dividends. Didn't do too much for me; they were never home. And I'm following the same path.

She calculated the risks. *Those guys have options. They aren't tug-the-collar college trainees you browbeat into some program or company plan. Lovelace goes after them, they walk. They got kudos from Jackson. Nick warned me to not let them leave. Doremus admitted Donnelly saved his bacon with Nick. Donnelly makes one phone call and shazam, none other than Marvin Jentzky hops a redeye from LA and meets with Doremus and then with Nick, whom he wows. Not only that, Doremus said those two knew when to leave after they introduced Jentzky and they'd gotten comfortable. He gave them high marks for tact. So Doremus is their ally also. Hell, so am I. Time to put my heart ahead of my head. I've become too comfortable living to work. No more. Thanks, Jim, for that.* She felt herself stir.

I better get going on squelching the parking pass crap, warn Willets to back off, and neutralize Hogg, Shepherd, and Drake to avoid a storm over sending them to Siberia.

She picked up her phone once again. This time she dialed Dick Leeson. Leeson, technically their boss, needed to steer Donnelly and Collins back into the routine of brochures, flyers, and ads with pictures of unknowable industrial equipment.

270

Chapter Twenty-Seven

Pilots call LaGuardia a black star airport, which is a designation for airports with water approaches, possible fog, and short runways. Even a slight mistake can cause you to debark, depending on the runway, in the middle of the Grand Central Parkway or an unreserved plot in St. Michael's Cemetery.

The Cox sisters knew nothing about LaGuardia. Their flight squirted out of the queue, its lights sparkling as the plane settled on the north-south runway with a bit of squeak, tire smoke, and taxiing, a landing rather like their relationship with Donnelly and Collins. The sisters were among the first through the gate, carrying small overnight and garment bags.

The men greeted them with smiles and pecks on the cheek. "We're glad you could make it," Collins said. They walked to the taxi ranks.

"Yeah, we'll have a great time," said Donnelly, mentally disrobing Emily. "We'll do the town," he added, with a chuckle. "New York isn't called Fun City for nothing."

The sisters swiveled their heads back and forth. "Golly," said Harriet, "This airport is like a beehive, planes everywhere. I swore I could see people through the windows of some of them."

"I don't doubt it for a minute," said Collins. "LaGuardia's a busy place, especially on Friday evenings. Keeps the air traffic controllers hopping." He went to the taxi rank and they piled into a Checker cab.

***

"My goodness," said Harriet, "the lights here are spectacular. Can you imagine the size of the power bill?"

"A large percentage of which is powered and transmitted with Ilium products," said Collins.

"Magical," breathed Emily. "So many colors and shapes."

"Welcome to Manhattan," said Donnelly. "The lights are for shoppers, tourists, and gawkers. You two are on a guided tour with local forensic experts and representatives of the constabulary."

Harriet turned from the fogged window. "And where might you be guiding us?"

"First, to the Waldorf Astoria hotel," said Collins, "a Manhattan landmark in which we have secured for you both a suite worthy of your station. It has bars and restaurants famous for cocktails and cuisine. We plan to introduce you to all."

"We should be at the hotel in a jiff as long as our driver maintains an economic course," said Donnelly. The cabbie glanced at him through the rearview mirror. "That means the Fifty-ninth Street Bridge, not the Triboro, pal." The cab driver had fleeced his share of first-time visitors to the city; this fare would not join their ranks.

Donnelly fell silent as the girls drank in the sights. *Hmm, they appear relieved to be in the same room. I guess they want at least the appearance of propriety. I hope they're up for something less modest.*

They came off the bridge and began the trek through crosstown traffic. Their driver cursed at another driver in Farsi, made an illegal turn, and pulled up at the Waldorf. "We're here," said Collins, as the cab jerked to an uncomfortable halt.

Everyone piled out. The doorman retrieved the luggage from the trunk and carried the bags up the steps to the desk. He waited impatiently until Collins tipped him. The clerk, judging from the dark circles under his eyes, was at the end of his shift. In a bored voice he asked, "Checking in?"

"Not exactly," said Collins. "'These two young ladies will be occupying the former Donnelly suite. The billing arrangements remain the same. I would like them to have keys for the room."

"Thank you," said the clerk. "Now perhaps these ladies have a valid credit card in their possession and we can welcome them as guests of means."

Harriet dug in her purse, her face flushing. Collins turned her away with a gentle hand in the small of her back. He leaned forward and said softly, "You don't hear well, do you, putz?" The clerk's eyes shifted to him, widening. "What part of 'the billing arrangements remain the same' didn't you understand? Ilium pays the bill, in case you can't read. A company where this young lady is a senior executive. Do we need the hotel manager or Mr. Bradley to settle this matter?"

The clerk swallowed several times as Collins invoked the two people in the hotel he wanted no trouble with. "That won't be necessary," he said, sliding two keys and snapping his fingers for a bellhop. "I'm sorry for any confusion."

"Take time and freshen up," Donnelly said, "then we should go downstairs and have a drink and decide about dinner. The Bull and Bear is one of the best hotel bars in New York."

"We'll meet you in the lobby," added Collins. "You can have us paged, if you wish."

∗∗∗

The doors to the elevator opened and Harriet and Emily Cox, healthy as only Midwest girls can be, stepped out, carrying their coats,

273

Little Red Riding Hoods on their first trip through the forest. Harriet wore a black cocktail dress; Emily the same dress in hunter green.

Collins and Donnelly, prodded by matriarchal training, jumped to their feet and went to meet them. The girls came toward them past the lust-ridden gaze of businessmen and staff. The happy quartet hustled toward the Bull and Bear.

They had a drink and walked across the lobby to Peacock Alley for a relaxed dinner washed down with two bottles of a pleasant pinot grigio. "Where to now?" said Harriet.

"Charley Drew at the Village Room of the Hotel Taft," said Collins. "He plays the piano and sings songs the music teacher never taught."

"Risqué?" ventured Emily.

"Quite," said Collins, "but within the bounds of taste. Even for Iowa girls."

"What about Oskaloosa girls?" said Emily. "That's where we're from, well not really, but Oskaloosa's the place most people recognize since it's at the intersection of 63rd and 163rd Streets, I just say Oskaloosa; we're actually from Moon Lane out in the county, south of town. The mailing address is Oskaloosa so everyone says they're from Oskaloosa. I do prattle on, don't I?"

They assured her she did not.

***

They were escorted to at an open table less than ten feet from Charley Drew's piano. "Good evening, ladies." Drew paused mid-song to greet the Cox sisters. He took a healthy swallow of his ever-present Jameson. "Always a pleasure to have pretty young ladies in the audience." He immediately launched into "The Virgin on the

Verge," to the delight of the crowd. Emily responded by slowly taking off her coat to reveal her dress.

Drew tipped his head in appreciation and sang about the mailman with the longest route in town followed by the woman who had triplets named Tim, Tom, and Tat, so she had no tit for Tat. Emily and Harriet were singing where they could, scatting where they couldn't, and showing lots of skin in the process. After his finale of "Have You Ever Heard the Story of How Falsies Got Their Name?" he gave his signature exit line of "God bless the Irish," bowed to their table, and went off on break.

They realized the time had come to go back to the Waldorf. The long day and alcohol consumption had caught up with the Cox sisters.

***

"The name of the snake is temptation," said Collins, leaning against the doorway to the Coxes' suite with one arm around a slumping Harriet. He inserted the key and pushed. The door huffed open over the thick carpet.

Donnelly needed a moment to digest Collins's meaning as he guided Emily into the room. They stood by the twin beds. "Well, we got them where we wanted them," he said. "Do we undress them?"

"I don't think that would be wise, do you?" said Collins, gently placing Harriet on her bed. "Bad enough us being here and them zonked. If we undress them...well." He smiled wryly.

Collins sighed. "Yeah, but their flesh is sure distracting." *But not near as distracting as Joyce's.*

"Do you want to deal with the consequences if Emily and Harriet knew we'd taken advantage of their condition?"

"Let's exit smiling," said Collins.

"And blue-balled," added Donnelly. *Same as with Sue.*

They found blankets, covered the sisters, and quietly let themselves out.

***

"I know we behaved ourselves," said Collins, "but what a waste of an evening."

"You think?" said Donnelly. "We had a good time; we just didn't get laid."

Collins snorted.

"Okay, okay." Collins shook his head in agreement. "The hell with it."

Donnelly walked over to the minibar. "Drink?"

"Anything that'll numb me," said Collins.

"Couldn't have put it better," said Donnelly, tossing a bottle to Collins.

"Good, Jack Daniels'll help," he said.

"Indeed," said Donnelly, cracking open a Jameson's and swallowing half.

"Glad we have double beds," said Collins. "With our drink intake tonight we're bound to snore. I don't feel like being up all night."

"Just aim your farts the other way," said Donnelly. "I don't want to be asphyxiated."

***

Saturday morning dawned sunny and bright. Donnelly dialed the Cox sisters' room and Emily answered, "Yesh?" Donnelly supposed they were still sprawled on the bed in cocktail attire: an arousing thought. "Brunch and a Bloody Mary will straighten you out. It's a fine day for sight-seeing."

"God," groaned Emily, followed by muffled conversation. "Okay. Give us forty-five minutes and we'll meet you...?"

"In Peacock Alley," supplied Donnelly.

***

They sat in Peacock Alley and Donnelly called for a round of the promised Bloody Marys. Harriet and Emily still looked a bit hammered around the eyes, but only under close scrutiny.

"That was quite a performance at the Taft," said Collins with a friendly smile.

"We had fun," said Emily, sipping her drink. "Can I get another one of these?"

"You're not finished with that one," said Donnelly.

"But I could use another one."

Is that petulance I hear? Or immaturity? Or a hangover looking for a cure? Collins signaled for another round.

The horses are at the starting gate. Aaaand we're off. The waiter delivered the drinks.

***

They did the Empire State building; walked around Saks and Bergdorf's. Entered Tiffany's and cruised the jewelry cases, receiving the attentions of several salesmen until it was established they weren't buying.

They found an Irish bar a few steps below street level and had a quick meal and another drink.

"What say we take the subway to Coney Island?" Donnelly said. "Get a Nathan's hot dog, wander along the boardwalk, go on the Cyclone, ride the bumper cars."

"Sounds fun," said Harriet.

Collins lit a cigarette. "Afterward we'll figure out some place to go for dinner. Not the Taft, though. I don't know if we could stand another night in the Taft."

"That would be a natural fact," said Emily.

"Well," said Donnelly, "let's get started."

For the girls, the noise was one of the overwhelming aspects of the subway. Coney Island, with all of its attractions, had been a blast, they agreed. But most amazing to them was the ocean and the beach, something they had never seen.

They returned on the Brighton line. At the Newkirk Avenue station the doors of their car hissed open and, to Donnelly's and Collins's experienced eyes, trouble entered. It wore boots, tight jeans, and black motorcycle jackets with Tigers emblazoned on the backs, Donnelly knew this gang well; he had tangled with their predecessors when he was younger.

Collins's attention also focused on the group.

Donnelly glanced at him. *At least we're on the same wavelength.*

278

The Cox sisters were oblivious to the unfolding drama. They got a dose of Brooklyn big city reality. Four of the Tigers crowded the aisle and made their way to them.

"Hello, ladies," said the greasiest warrior. "Need some help getting rid of these clowns? We'd be glad to assist you." He had a cruel twist to his smile.

Donnelly stood. "We're coming to the Cortelyou Road station. We think you should get off."

Collins leaned over and released the catches on the subway window. He slid it open. "Here's the deal; the first one steps any closer goes out this window."

"Say we don't want to go?" said the burliest Tiger.

"Guess I'll be forced to shoot." Collins matter-of-factly pulled a small black revolver from his jacket pocket.

Donnelly produced his own pistol. "And I wouldn't miss out on all the fun."

The only noise was the whirring of the fans and clickety-clack of the train lurching to the next station.

"You're getting off here," said Collins.

The biggest of the Tigers gave the hard guy stare. Donnelly and Collins laughed and waved their pistols. The Tigers backed away and, as the doors opened, got off.

The car burst into applause.

The sisters hadn't spoken during the confrontation. The doors hissed shut. "Where did you get those guns?" Harriet blurted

"I was a policeman. Remember I told you?" said Collins. "I've always had this gun, and I have a concealed carry permit. Good item to have in the city. Came in handy."

"And you, Frank?" said Emily in a tremulous voice.

"In my old job I also carried a gun," he said, "for which I have a permit."

"Oh," said Emily, face reddening. "I mean, I guess after all is said and done, I'm glad you had them with you." Harriet shook her head vigorously in agreement. The Cox sisters comprehended that New York, while a city of fun, wonder, and delight, could be a dangerous place.

Several stops later the subway went over the Manhattan Bridge and after a change of lines at Union Square, they reached midtown. "Been a long day," said Donnelly when they had returned to the Waldorf.

"Today was enough excitement to cover a year in Oskaloosa," Emily said. "I loved every minute."

"Let's take a little time to get cleaned up and then meet in Oscar's bar. It's more casual," said Collins.

Once in their room Emily and Harriet waxed enthusiastic about the day's excitement and the places they'd seen. Applying fresh makeup, Emily asked, "Suppose we have a repeat of what happened at our place?"

"I don't know," said Harriet. "I'd kind of like it if we did." She laughed. "Let's see if anything comes up."

"I agree," Emily giggled.

***

Conversation trailed off at their entrance. They wore snug red dresses that enhanced their identical twin features. Collins and Donnelly walked over and welcomed them. Once seated, Harriet promptly ordered a Blue Heaven martini.

"Please use Stolichnaya vodka," said Harriet.

"No gin, no vermouth, it's not a martini," said Collins.

"Pish posh," said Harriet. "Give my sister a Golden Cadillac." Emily rolled her eyes and smiled.

Later, after drinks and a light supper they walked around the lobby. They passed a ballroom and the sound of music caught their attention.

"Can we go inside?" asked Harriet.

"Sure," said Collins and the four of them slipped in.

A wedding reception was in full swing. "Let's dance," said Harriet, taking Collins's hand and leading him into the swirl of dancing couples. Donnelly and Emily joined them.

The band was playing a slow romantic song. Harriet and Collins began to dance and Collins found himself getting hard. She ground herself into him. "Is that your gun or are you excited to be with me?" *I'd rather be with Joyce, but right now you'll do.* He drew her tight.

"Do you have a boner to prick me with?" Emily said, pulling Donnelly close.

It didn't take long before both couples were in their separate suites, clothes flying off.

***

At ten o'clock the next morning the phone rang in Frank Donnelly's face. On the third head-shattering ring he answered. "Yeah?"

Emily grunted and rolled over.

"My, my, Frank, aren't we sounding grumpy? Hurry up and get out of bed. We're going to eleven o'clock mass at St. Patrick's."

"Wha?"

"St Patrick's Cathedral. Eleven o'clock mass."

"Say hello to Cardinal Cooke for me…"

"Please put my sister on the line, Frank. He passed the phone over to Emily.

Emily answered with a groggy, "Hello…"

"Em, get your fanny out of bed," Harriet hissed. "Get over here. We're going to Mass at St. Patrick's. Tell Frank I'm sending Jim back to his room. We'll meet them at ten forty-five in the lobby."

In stark contrast to the night before, the Cox sisters wore longer, more conservative dresses and demure little hats. Before Donnelly had gotten across the lobby Harriet said, "Did you honestly think we would spend a weekend in New York without Mass at St. Patrick's Cathedral?" Emily looked a bit green around the gills.

"Going to St. Patrick's doesn't have to include the eleven o'clock High Mass," said Donnelly.

"It does if you're Catholic," said Harriet.

"I'm Catholic and I don't like the musicals," said Collins. "I prefer the Low Mass quickies." He stopped himself. "You're Catholic?"

"Erin go bragh," said Harriet. "When our ancestors came to America the name was Coughlin. Apparently Coughlin was too complicated for the clerk at Ellis Island who promptly named us Cox. Our great grandfather was a New Yorker before he got tired of the traffic and moved out to Iowa. Small world, huh?"

"I'll say," said Donnelly.

St. Patrick's was packed. High Mass was, as always, interminable with much clanking of incense burners and the choir singing endless hymns. None of the four received communion. Not in the state of grace, all were obedient to Catholic teaching on the subject. The sisters' relationship with God was as unchartable as their relationship with Donnelly and Collins. For their part, the sisters were still plotting the route.

"So, the Met today?" Donnelly asked after Mass. "We can do the exhibit of nudes through the ages. Should be fun. Other stuff is hanging there."

"A good idea, Frank," said Harriet, "but I can't say I care about a bunch of barely clothed fat women lounging around on daybeds. It might be best if we take an afternoon flight to Maqua. We won't roll in on Monday morning and scramble to work with people getting hints of our activities in the city."

"Your wish is our…wish," said Collins.

Emily shrugged. "Is this okay with you, Frank?"

"Much as I'd like the time together," said Donnelly, *and much as I'd like more nookie*, "I won't disagree with the logic." *We don't need any more bullshit than we've already got up in Maqua.*

"There should be room on the 3:30 flight," said Collins morosely.

"3:30? In that case," she slid a finger lightly along the inside of Collins' shirt collar, "you'll see him in an hour." She unlocked the door and they slid inside.

"Ahem," Emily said. She stroked his hand. "Why don't you open your door and we'll, well, you know…" Donnelly fumbled with the key and they tumbled inside.

∗∗∗

It was common practice for senior Ilium executives to bump lesser managers and employees from flights out of LaGuardia to Maqua. The year before a cadre of Ilium managers had perished when a combination of wind shear and pilot error caused their

283

Seneca Airlines plane to crash five hundred yards short of the runway. Those who were bumped arrived home safely two hours later on the next flight.

This tragedy did not penetrate the God-speaks-to-me-alone persuasion of senior management. This mindset was a cornerstone of the culture Nick Jackson had created. Jackson himself always flew on the company jet, not tempting fate.

A sated Donnelly and Collins sat together on the flight from LaGuardia to Maqua. "We go into the office and listen to the tapes after we land, right?" said Donnelly.

"I guess so," said Collins. "Let's get some shut-eye." The aircraft was half-full of Ilium people. The sales types were not ashamed to use rumors and gossip in their relationship building. Neither pair wanted any hint of two guys from advertising and promotion cavorting in New York with unidentified Maqua women.

Seven rows behind them sat Harriet and Emily. The plane's engine droned. "Well?" asked Harriet.

"Well what?" Emily replied, containing a laugh.

"Did you get enough? Are you satisfied?"

"Truth be told," said Emily, "I'm a bit sore." She giggled.

"Me too," said Harriet. She stared out the window at the white clouds off in the distance. Her face became more serious. She turned toward Emily. "Em, what are we going to do with these two? Much as I enjoyed the pleasure parts, I don't think I was ever so afraid as when the hoodlums approached us on the train."

"I was too," Emily admitted. "But Frank and Jim kicked them off."

"With guns," Harriet said. "They were so casual about it. That disturbed me almost as much as the hoodlums. They skate along the edge. They had risky jobs before they joined Ilium. They lived in an

284

unsafe city."

"You take risks," said Emily. "You dress like a man at work; you're really smart and in your way you're street smart."

"Pleasant as they are, they're dangerous," said Harriet. "They're not afraid to do anything. I'm not sure I want to live that way."

"I don't disagree with you," said Emily quietly. "Things have progressed quickly with them, too. Neither of us have much of a social life." She kneaded her hands. "Are we moving too fast?"

Harriet sighed. "Their unpredictability could hamper my career," she said.

Emily sat back and after a minute she murmured, "I had a great time and they're a bucket of fun." Harriet made to reply but Emily waved her away. "I know, I know, you want your career. For me, we're the country mice and they're the city mice. Not a good match."

Chapter Twenty-Eight

Tape hiss momentarily filled the earphones before Willets's voice came on. "Nick Jackson gave me a colossal ream job over that parking pass fiasco. I can't afford another confrontation with him. You better get those yahoos of yours and yourself under control. I'm not going to let some interdepartmental game ruin my career. Are we clear?"

"Clear," Dingmann said. "I apologize. I thought we'd put those two on a short leash with such a blatant violation of regulations. Guess I was wrong."

"Well, Bob," said Willets, ice in his voice, "perhaps Donnelly and Collins weren't even parked illegally. I had only your word and Pacelli's on that. Those 'hotshots', as you call them, caught Pacelli in a bald-faced lie about whether he actually saw their cars or their license plates or their vehicle identification numbers. Sounds to me like you've been up in Maqua so long this kind of nickel-dime stuff is the way the game is played."

"Whoops, show of strength to former schoolmate," said Donnelly. They restarted the tape.

"News flash, my friend; your games may play well here in the sticks but aren't appropriate for the executive suite. Perhaps that's why you haven't moved on. Career-wise, you can't afford this kind of chicken shit; makes you look petty."

"Message received," said Dingmann in a chastened voice. "No more moves without you in the loop first. You can be our guide."

"I already am. And in the future don't forget it." Willets's line went dead.

Dingmann disconnected and muttered, "Damn you, Lou, and the high horse you rode in on."

Collins slapped the desk. "Whoa! Dingmann got the corncob up his ass. He doesn't like it."

"Would you? He got the one with all the kernels eaten off and the cob dried in the sun," Donnelly said, with a nasty sounding chuckle. "From Dingmann's comment I suspect he envisions his career trailing flames and heading for the ground."

"Willets didn't tell Dingmann the parking-pass issue remains open. I wonder how he'll handle it?"

"Whatever he does," said Donnelly, "we'll know first. He's going to be extra careful. He can't afford another run-in with Jackson. I hear it never takes much before Nick figures he made a wrong selection."

"Willets will have to work hard to stay one step ahead."

"So will we," said Donnelly. "Let's listen and see if anything else pops up."

More tape hiss and the sound of Locker talking to Dick Leeson. Ten minutes later Collins slammed the headphones down. "Shitfuck, we're back to doing scutwork."

"Did you expect a promotion?" said Donnelly.

Collins angrily stubbed his cigarette. "We know Locker told Leeson to have us do brochures and shit for all the crap industrial stuff. She's putting us back to where we were before the Electric Chair project." He lit another cigarette.

"We flummoxed her in New York and she's making sure we don't get too uppity."

I did more than flummox her, Frank. She didn't mention any of that, but we didn't really talk business.

Donnelly put his headphones aside. "Look at the bright side. Getting around Leeson is as easy as hunting dairy cows with a high-powered rifle and scope. We'd better get working on those scripts."

Donnelly's phone rang, "Frank Donnelly."

"Hi, Frank, it's Sue."

"Hi, mom," he said. Collins waved as he left.

"Someone there?"

"Not anymore. How are you doing? Where are you?"

"I'm okay," she said. "I'm at the hospital. "I just wanted to thank you for a great evening the other night."

"My pleasure," said Donnelly. "You said to give you a call when we were back in Maqua." He swallowed. "Would you like to get together again? Maybe for a drink or lunch or a dinner?"

"That would be nice," she said softly. "What have you in mind?"

What I have in mind puts me in the confessional. "I know a casual out-of-the-way place. Good burgers, well-tapped beer."

"Sounds ideal," she said. "Something like Grote's in the old neighborhood?"

"Very much so," he said. *Which, come to think of it, is why I like the place.* "How does your schedule look?"

"Wait a sec, please. I can't do anything until next week. Wednesday for an early dinner?"

"Sure," said Donnelly. "The name of the place is McGarry's; here's the address or do you want me to pick you up at the hospital?"

"I'll meet you there. Say six?"

"Great, see you then." Donnelly put the phone down and sat back. Be honest with yourself, Franky, you're in a high-risk situation. How honorable are my intentions? She's great to talk to, and she's not like one of those scatterbrained broads I've encountered before, but she's married for Christ's sake, to Dingmann, no less. How the hell could she have done that? Yeah, yeah, yeah, but you want to do more than talk to her, but it's the Catholic thing holding you back.

***

Smoke and noise saturated the Monday night happy hour air at L'Fey. Now was the time of the red-cheeked loose-tie braggart; preening and self-aggrandizement were in full swing to the tinkle of ice cubes and the sloppy gurgles of drunks. Soon, this might become the night of the DUI. Yet few L'Fey customers were ever arrested, a possible outcome of some unknown financial agreement between Ilium and the city of Maqua.

Rufus Hogg sucked on his beer. "Duff told me we don't need to go to Eagle Pass; I can stay here. But they're changing accounts around and I'll be doing limit switch brochures until they sort everything out." He sounded a bit relieved.

"Explains my catching time in technical publications," mused Drake. "Can't say I'm happy. Better than Iron Mountain, Michigan, though. I couldn't picture my prodigious talent being dumped in

Nowhereville. I doubt the place has a cocktail bar within fifty miles."

"Everything's getting squirrelly this past week," said Hogg. "Stuff must've happened somewhere. Our luck could turn up."

"In your dreams, old son. I'd be careful not to push it, either. Donnelly and Collins were at a meeting in New York. Don't make a commotion before the chips finish falling."

"Guess you're right," said Hogg. "We hide and stay alert, get a feeling for who's on top this month. Go with the winners. I always say."

"Should we squeeze some subliminal suggestions into Dingmann's tiny brain?" Shepherd said. "Something he'll think he thought of that'll snap back on those assholes. I want to get promoted and get the hell out of here. I'm sick of the cold weather and the dirt and the Ilium lifers. I'm ready for an opening in San Diego."

"Working light bulbs or washing machines?" said Hogg.

"No," said Drake. "Diesel truck and train engines and a division making heavy-duty logging equipment. We don't do brochures for the log guys because those enviro lynch mobs would get their address."

"Donnelly and Collins are off traveling on account work. Guess we ought to sit and talk about next actions. The battle for truth, justice, and the American way."

"I don't think so, pal," said Shepherd. "For the time being we just hide and watch. Hide and watch." His mind strayed to Anna Mae Hogg's tits.

Chapter Twenty-Nine

Abe Floss hung up and sat back. *So Nick Jackson wants to televise the Guy Pearson trial on his new network.* He looked up at the ceiling, calculating. *The idea is brilliant. The question is, will the FCC let him do it? What if Pearson is electrocuted? They want to televise it, too. What'll the country do? Answer: be glued to their TV sets.*

He leaned back in his chair and stared out the window. He ran a hand across his cheek. *The war is the administration's Achilles' heel but right now civil disorder is rampant. The political center of this country feels threatened; things are getting out of control. Do we take steps to restore the rule of law?*

He sipped his coffee. *Yes, before the election so we can swing attention back to our strength, the war, where the country agrees with us. First things first.* He picked up the phone and dialed.

"Hello," said Justin Hitchcock on the fifth ring.

Jeffrey must be elsewhere. "Justin, Abe Floss here." After a few pleasantries Floss said, "Jackson and his newly acquired TV network want to televise the upcoming Guy Pearson trial and any possible electrocution."

"With one of those Ilium Electric Chairs, I suppose," said Hitchcock.

Floss chuckled at the drollery. "I would expect no less from Nick."

"It winds up at the FCC," said Hitchcock.

Let's get to it. "And what do we want to happen?"

"People realize steps are being taken. I have three Republican

291

Commissioners and at least two will do what they are told. You?'

"We have two," said Floss. "I can vouch for both."

"So, done deal," said Hitchcock. "After things get back to a semblance of normality, game on."

Not much gets by him. "Be interesting to see how this plays out; I suspect this might take a while."

"Probably will," said Hitchcock. "Ilium stock should be a good buy right now."

Ever the capitalist and a good idea. "Indeed," said Floss. They said their good-byes and disconnected.

Within half a day they had briefed their respective commissioners and contacted their brokers.

Chapter Thirty

Spectators lined up behind the barricades outside the Pittsfield, Massachusetts, Superior Courthouse. They braved the wet and windy weather, eager to witness the circus the Guy Pearson trial would offer. Dozens of state and local police stood guard.

A makeup girl worked feverishly to keep Donald Quite's fashionably long hair in place. After she finished her efforts, Quite, recently hired as the lead GBC correspondent, motioned to the cameraman. "Let's do the setup. We can slot in when we do the arrival of Clint Pearson and his retinue."

After some additional primping on Quite, the director pointed.

"Today," Quite began on cue, gesturing to the courthouse behind him, "under a dull gray sky and almost one hundred and forty miles from Boston, the historic trial of Guy Pearson is ready to begin. Guy Pearson is described as a serial killer, drug dealer, and sexual deviant. His father, the well-known lawyer and activist Clint Pearson, says he will prove his son innocent of all charges.

"The latest victim of record, Mary Jane Davisson, was the daughter of Captain Ike Davisson of the Massachusetts State Police. Pearson said a Boston trial would be prejudicial since the state police are headquartered in nearby Framingham. He cited the need for an impartial court and successfully petitioned to move the proceedings here to Pittsfield."

Quite summarized Pearson's alleged offenses and the charges brought forward by the state of Massachusetts. Finished, he handed the microphone to an assistant and walked over to the director.

"What now?" he said.

"We wait for Clinton Pearson and obtain reaction shots," said the director. "Get him to answer some questions."

The media converged on a pinstripe-suited Clinton Pearson as he rounded a corner, surrounded by assistants and clutching his leather lawyer bag. He moved down the sidewalk to muttered catcalls and muted cheers, staring impersonally at people through wide, brooding eyes.

"The guy perceives almost everything," said Quite, a Pearson admirer.

"And comprehends practically nothing," said the director, who was not. "He floats in shitstorms like a butterfly in an earthquake."

"So you say," said Quite. "He also dislikes the establishment with a cordial and eloquent loathing. Admirable, that." He shifted to intercept. "Mr. Pearson," Quite yelled, elbowing several competitors as he and his cameraman moved in. "Any comments before the trial? Judge George Robertson is presiding. He is a well-known hard-line jurist. Any qualms?"

Pearson recognized Quite's friendly face. He waved at the throng and turned directly toward the camera. "We talk about justice in America. We strive for justice brought about by the people, not by judges who are tools of the establishment or prosecutors who are equally tools of the establishment." He flashed another smile. "Don't forget the wardens and the police officers." He began to walk toward the court building. After a moment he turned. "I am unaware of any law against being annoying."

Quite spoke directly to the camera. "So the proceedings begin, possibly the trial of the century." The camera panned the congested street and the front façade of the court building. He spoke over the camera images. "Jury selection is first, followed by the judge's opening of the court. The jury will be sworn in and the prosecution

294

and defense will make their opening statements. This process alone could take weeks. The prosecution and the defense then call witnesses. These witnesses are examined and cross-examined. The judge will instruct the jury, closing arguments will be made, the jury deliberates, and a verdict is rendered."

He waited as the camera panned upward to the American flag flying over the court. "The prosecution seeks the death penalty. The recent passage in the Congress of the law popularly known as the 'Barbecue Bill' has enormous implications for Guy Pearson since additional appeals for a felony conviction are blocked and the state wherein the crime was committed may impose the maximum penalty. Pearson may be the first high-profile victim of the controversial portable electric chair."

The director tightened on Quite. "The United States remains in the minority of nations in the world using death as a penalty for certain crimes. Many view this practice, and the new law in particular, as barbaric and against American values. Others see it as a very important tool in fighting violent premeditated murder. The Pearson trial once again brings the issue front and center." The director signaled wrap-up. "Stay tuned to GBC for gavel-to-gavel coverage. This is Don Quite. Back to our studios in New York and Doug Upton."

The red light on the camera winked out and Quite handed his microphone to an assistant. "I need a stiff drink before this travesty begins," he said.

***

Donnelly and Collins traded looks. "Quite torpedoed the chair," said Donnelly, "and the law-and-order program in general. Jesus, he sounds like the editorial page of *The Nation*."

295

"Well they are the flagship of the left." Collins puffed on his cigarette. "Quite's just like them. A story preconceived in his head; in his case one sympathetic to Pearson and son. So, political, yes, what else is new? At least he answered the producer's need for drama."

"Not our problem, kemosabe. We're fully engaged in doing spec sheets for obscure industrial products. Do we call Locker and alert the corporate interest to Quite's deviant anti-Iliumism?

Donnelly thought for a minute. "Nah, we do ourselves some good and go to Doremus. He can have the privilege of watching Jackson erupt. I'm sure they're taping this. GBC hired Quite before Ilium bought them."

Collins stubbed his cigarette. "Didn't Quite go to 'Nam and do standups dressed like a peasant?"

Donnelly laughed. "Yeah, there he was, standing in some jungle dissing our guys, surrounded and protected by those same guys. A wonder someone didn't frag him. One TV critic wrote he looked like he was going to an antiwar costume party on the Upper West Side. Another said he resembled an extra out of *Doctor Zhivago*." He picked up the phone. "I wonder if Jackson will shitcan Quite?" He began to dial. "Let me get Doremus."

"Call Jentzky," Collins said, "and suggest Ilium may need his expertise."

***

Tyler Doremus stuck his head in Nick Jackson's office. "GBC's hotshot reporter, Don Quite, is at the Pearson trial. He just said, and I quote, 'The United States remains in the minority of nations in the world using death as a penalty for certain crimes. Many view this practice as barbaric and against American values.' Not exactly a rousing endorsement of the Ilium Electric Chair."

Jackson bolted from his seat. "Goddamn it! What's the deal with Quite?"

Doremus stepped inside. "He was hired before we took them over. Quite is a well-known lefty and an admirer of Clinton Pearson. He threw softball questions at Pearson as he walked into the court building. You can watch Quite on our new videotape system if you want."

Jackson's face turned red. "What are these bozos at GBC doing? Call them and tell them to fix this or they'll all be fired."

Doremus began to leave. "Wait a minute," Jackson said, "what's going on with the Burt Rawley murder up in Maqua? We don't need some showboat like Quite to get hold of the Ilium Electric Chair part of Rawley's untimely exit. The shit would hit the fan. Ilium department heads can't be killed during a company function."

"Nothing so far," said Doremus. Anticipating a Jackson outburst he quickly added, "I'll get on it." *Dodged the bullet. Who to call? I'll check with Locker and find out what's really going on.*

***

"The police don't have doodly, Tyler," said Locker. "Their prime suspects are the dwarfs who were distributing the favors at the party. According to my information, Rawley was killed by someone with a pretty fair knowledge of electrical engineering." *Sniff.* "Do you know Gino Pacelli?"

"Refresh my memory, Joyce."

"Right now, he's the head of security for Ilium in Maqua." *I hope he won't be for long. Let's find out if he can deliver.* "He should be up to speed on this but I suspect he's not. If I were you, I'd use Nick's name and put the heat on him."

Doremus chuckled. "So you like the guy, Joyce?"

Locker had the grace to laugh. "He's a snake, Tyler, but he has connections inside the Works and with the Maqua Police Department. They're the ones who are supposed to be looking for the dwarfs. We can't figure out what those weasels did or did not witness, which may be critical. Hold his feet to the fire."

"Will do. Thanks, Joyce." After he hung up, the light bulb went on. *Pacelli's the one who lied about Donnelly and Collins and caused them to get suspended.* He asked his secretary to reach the man.

***

"Gino Pacelli on the line, Mr. Doremus."

"Mr. Pacelli, this is Tyler Doremus in New York. Nick Jackson asked me to get an update on the Burt Rawley homicide."

Pacelli made no response.

Gotcha, thought Doremus. *To you, Burt Rawley is yesterday's news. You have no political instinct whatsoever, you fool.*

"We are conducting an ongoing investigation, Tyler," Pacelli finally said, "in close cooperation with the Maqua Police Department."

Okay, he goes with my first name in an act of simulated friendliness and then feeds me pure clichés, which tells me he's also clueless. "Thank you, Mr. Pacelli, I'll report that to Mr. Jackson." He hung up before Pacelli belatedly tried to add details.

***

"Marvin, Frank Donnelly here. You watch the first day of the Pearson trial?"

"No," Jentzky said. "Something not good, I can only presume."

Donnelly described the scene at the Pittsfield courthouse and Quite's role. "I alerted Doremus. I suspect he's talked to Jackson, who more than likely bounced off the wall."

"Tell me again, Franky. Spare no details."

Jentzky was in business mode. Donnelly felt as if the Grand Inquisitor had interviewed him. "Got a question, Marv," he said. "What's the status of your relationship with Ilium and GBC?"

"Done deal," said Jentzky. "We're accepted by the GBC people and are working with them on a variety of projects. Haven't had many dealings with Ilium corporate other than Doremus. What's going on in your fertile, devious brain, Franky?"

"Well," said Donnelly, "you might want to call Doremus and tell him you saw the disaster in Pittsfield and you and your organization can help."

"And if I do?" *Okay, Franky, show me you're as astute as I always thought you were.*

"Doremus will feel he's got an oar in the water with GBC; he gets Quite off his soapbox and into a more neutral mode. Doremus'll look good in Jackson's eyes. Quite's still a top reporter and draws viewers." Donnelly sat back and sipped a Coke. "Of course" he added, putting the can down, "he'll owe you his ass for pulling his chestnut out of the fire."

"Good assessment, Franky," said Jentzky. "Anything else?"

"Nick Jackson may get on his case about the murder of Burt Rawley." Donnelly quickly summarized the event. "Radio silence from the police, of course. I don't think Ilium is applying pressure.

299

The cops are probably chasing the dwarfs, who I think had nothing to do with it, although they may have seen who did. The engineer, Harold Cox, said whoever wired the chair was an expert."

"Interesting. There's a movie in this, either a farce or a drama. Talk to you later." *We'll see if I owe you for this.*

***

Tyler Doremus was thinking about the Burt Rawley murder, the situation with GBC, the Pearson trial, and Donald Quite, the prima donna. He knew Nick Jackson wanted things remedied quickly.

He sat back and lit a menthol cigarette. The smoke wound coolly down his throat; he puffed it out in a thin stream that climbed upward, dispersing softly. The casual action belied his mood. *I can't be frozen by indecision here. This GBC situation is new territory with different kinds of players. I almost wish Donnelly hadn't called, then Nick wouldn't be tasking...*his extension flashed.

A moment later his intercom beeped and his secretary said, "Mr. Jentzky."

Could be the answer to my quandary. "I'll take it." He picked up the receiver. "Marvin," he said, his bonhomie causing him to wince. "What can I do for you?"

"Don Quite put on some performance at the courthouse today," said Jentzky. "What was Jackson's reaction?"

The crux of the matter. Do I use Jentzky? It's hit the fan; we're paying him so why not utilize the resources at hand? He took a deep breath. "I'd like whatever assistance you can lend, Marvin. We need to rein in Quite or everything goes up in flames. I haven't met Quite, but I suspect this'll be tough to do."

"Well, in this particular situation he can't afford to screw up," said Jentzky. "This is his third network in three years."

300

I should have been aware. "Go on," he said.

"I'll persuade him," said Jentzky. "I've known Don for ages. His greed is bigger than his ego. The trial will be such a groundbreaking event he could be the hottest property in news broadcasting."

Doremus lit another cigarette. "You think so?"

"Maybe, maybe not," said Jentzky. "The important factor is as long as the trial goes on he thinks so."

"Whatever you can do," said Doremus, blowing a stream of smoke, a feeling of relief welling up inside him. "We want our coverage fair and balanced. That's the rule for all his work."

"Fair and balanced?" Jentzky chuckled. "I'll make sure he gets the message."

Do I ask him about the Rawley murder? "Do you have another minute?" Jentzky assured him he did. Doremus explained the Rawley situation.

"The Maqua cops let Rawley go to the back of the queue," Jentzky said. "I presume you're the largest taxpayer in Maqua?"

Doremus grunted assent.

"Put a blowtorch to them," Jentzky continued. "Suggest they interview the engineer who designed the chair about who in the room was capable of the wiring."

Doremus was scribbling notes. "Great. Let me know how it works with Quite. Talk to you later, Marv."

***

A light rain fell as Sue approached McGarry's. Donnelly—spare umbrella in hand—stared down the other end of the street. "Hi, Frank," she said.

"Sue!" he whirled around. "Sorry, you took me by surprise." He smiled sheepishly. "Let's go inside." He offered his arm. *Keep it formal.*

***

"I didn't think a place like this existed in Maqua," Sue said, lifting her beer in a silent toast. "How'd you come across it?"

"Jim Collins, a friend of mine from work," Donnelly said, acknowledging her gesture. "He found it." He sipped his beer. "McGarry, the owner, was a cop in the Bronx who worked with Jim's father. He won the place in a poker game."

"Marvelous. Almost Damon Runyon, except it's up here." Sue's laugh was musical, a pleasing note to Donnelly's ear.

"Points for the Runyon reference, Sue. And yeah, we are up here; you're a doctor and I'm an Ilium employee working in the same department as your erstwhile husband."

***

"I'm on call tonight," Sue said, waving away a refill. "It's doubtful, but you never know." She munched from a bowl of pretzels Donnelly had grabbed from the bar. She looked down, a flush creeping across her cheeks. "I almost invited you to my prom at St. Agnes, but I chickened out at the end."

"I didn't go to my prom," said Donnelly, nodding. "As a matter of fact, I didn't go to any proms." He moistened his lips and lowered his voice. "But I would have gone to yours."

Sue's eyes widened. "You didn't go to any proms?" The flush remained.

"I didn't date much; I was pretty wrapped up in sports…"

"Didn't you play baseball?"

302

"Yeah." He rubbed his face. "I had a bunch of teams looking at me; a couple wanted to sign me. The money was pretty good, but my parents said get the education first."

"So you didn't sign?"

"Right." He sighed. "I hurt my shoulder that summer body surfing at Riis Park while I was half in the bag. Got flipped out of a wave on a stormy day. I was lucky I didn't break my neck or get paralyzed."

He swirled his coaster along the damp surface of the table. "Tell me, how'd you become a doctor?"

"I was lucky, Frank." She stared off. "My folks didn't have the money to send me to college. I was going to go to Brooklyn College at night, but I got some scholarship offers."

Donnelly smiled. "You were the smartest girl in our class at Crucifixion; I guess you did as well at St. Agnes. Where'd you go?"

"Davidson."

"Davidson?" Donnelly scratched his head. "North Carolina. Right?" She nodded. "Great school, the Wesleyan of the South, if I remember."

"Yes, I took science and biology courses as well as bunch of liberal arts. Extra credits and all that. I had a full scholarship. I was then accepted into Johns Hopkins Medical School, where I had a very generous aid package. With a couple of jobs and lean living I got out almost debt-free."

Sounds like no social life whatsoever. "Impressive. And it conforms to the Irish view that if things come easy they don't count."

"How very true," she laughed

"I guess you didn't get out much," Donnelly said.

"The longest I went out with anyone was with Bob and, as I said in New York, it was a two-month whirlwind. He acted the true gentleman. Too good to be true…" She reached into her purse. "My pager. I have to go." She leaned forward and ran her hand up his thigh. "I'm sorry, Frank, next time we'll really get together." The hand traveled farther. "Your place?"

"You're a married woman," Donnelly said, covering her hand. *God, I'm attracted to this woman. I'm as stiff as a board. If she doesn't stop I may explode.*

"But not a happily married woman," she said, leaning forward and moving her hand upward. "And I don't intend to stay married much longer. If I'd known what Bob really is..." She stood.

Reflexively, he rose. She came into his arms and there was no hiding his condition. Their kiss was long and deep. They broke and she took his hand and they walked out, Donnelly signaling he'd be back.

As she climbed into her car, she said, "Next time I'll tell you why I'm not really married. Good night, Frank."

Donnelly returned and had a double Jameson with a beer chaser.

Chapter Thirty-One

The sun speckled through Lou Willets's office window as he looked down on the front gate of Maqua Works. *They haven't washed these windows since the building was built. Almost seventy years of smoke, grime, and particulate matter. Even with my power and position, I can't get a clean window. Well, it was a manufacturing facility. I should hang that prevaricating shit Pacelli out the window and make him clean them. Dingmann?* He laughed. *Probably not. I'll bet Jackson's are washed in New York and he's on the 50th floor. He'd throw the maintenance manager off the roof if they got dirty. Positions me in the food chain, I guess.*

A voice interrupted his daydream. "Good afternoon, Mr. Willets's office, Clare speaking, how may I help you?" *Husky, unlike Marsha's squawk.* "Marsha's on vacation for the next three weeks. I'll make a note you called her."

A minute later Clare Duckett appeared in the doorway. "Mr. Willets? I completed the paperwork for your meeting with Mr. Lovelace. Would you like to review it one more time?"

"Yes, I meet him in a half hour. Come in." Willets walked over to his couch. "Take a seat. We can spread this on the coffee table. You understand this is highly confidential information?" *Confidential is an understatement. We're rating and ranking all the hi-pots, the comers, in the department.*

"Yes, Mr. Willets." She inched a little closer.

He read the document carefully. "Looks good," he said, gathering the papers together. "Tell me about yourself, Clare. Are you married?" As she began her answer Willets's mind wandered.

Pouty lips; they appear wet. Gloss?

"...and my husband recently returned from Vietnam. He's the chief electrician for the Exhibits operation." She looked down.

The hell? "You must be happy to have him back."

"Oh, yes...it's just..." A tear leaked down her cheek.

Who am I, Dear Abby? Okay. Nice body. Nicer tits. Was Burt having a taste? I'm not sure I want to get into a honey trap with this girl. Better find out why she's crying. "Just what?" he said, on her cue.

The words spilled out rapidly. "We-we're having problems."

Hell, I can be of some help. What am I thinking? Do I get a little before she goes back to Exhibits? His hand drifted down her shoulder. He envisioned her with her dress hiked up, her tits squashed against the desk while he pounded her from behind. *She'd leave her glasses on and stifle her squeals so they don't reach the outer office.* He put his hand on her shoulder. "Don't cry. Can't you seek professional help? I think the benefits package covers such things."

"He'll say it's my fault!" She turned toward him and his hand brushed to her breast.

"Don't, don't," he said, putting his other hand on her thigh. He could feel the heat rising from her. He started to stiffen. *Pay attention!* His hands withdrew.

She rose. "I-I'd better be getting back to my desk. Mr. Lovelace will be here."

"Yes, of course, of course," said Willets, reflexively standing and going to the doorway. He was up before he realized he was tenting, fully sprung. *Down, boy! Damn thing's got a mind of its own.*

She noticed. As she walked by him her hand brushed his booming trouser front. She took another step and turned. "I'd be pleased to work in whatever way you wish," she said in a husky voice. "Any way at all."

He remained standing, in full display. "Thank you," he said. "I may need you tomorrow." *Game on.* He recalled a time with a young intern back in Dayton, blouse open, skirt up, panties down, wet slapping sounds in a small broom closet during working hours. Her eyes had crossed when she came. The memory still excited him.

Clare smiled provocatively. "Unfortunate we couldn't begin right away, Mr. Willets." Her glance lowered to his ballooning trousers, "But Mr. Lovelace is coming down the hall."

"Yes," he said, moving behind his desk. "Make sure my calendar is wide open tomorrow after eleven."

"Already done," she said.

Willets pushed his chair under his desk to block the view of his crotch. *I'll put the lumber to the wife tonight. She loves a roll in the hay as much as I do. With this new job and the demands of Nick Jackson I haven't banged her recently. How about straight from no nookie in over a week to a twofer in twenty-four hours? One of life's scheduling advantages. Lovelace is coming in; this hard-on better deflate.*

***

They listened to the Willets-Duckett dialogue. "Sounds like Willets will be busy at eleven," Donnelly said. "Did you hear the stuff about her husband?"

Collins made no response. He lit up and stared into the distance. "What're you thinking?"

"Cal Duckett," said Collins and waved the cigarette. "You know, I can't blame him, the poor bastard."

Donnelly's eyes widened. "Of course. Damn, I missed it; I was too wrapped up on the possibility of Willets doing Clare Duckett." He took a sip of Coke. "Should we do anything?"

307

Collins inhaled. "He had means; he had the electrical knowledge. He had motive. If I read between the lines he can't get a stiffy and he somehow found out Rawley was porking his wife." He blew a stream of smoke. "He had opportunity. The Christmas party and the chair and the distractions caused by the dwarfs."

"Gluing Rawley to the chair was a spectacular stage effect." Donnelly drained the Coke and reached for another can. "What now?"

"I don't know." He took a deep drag. "Suppose Cal finds out about Willets and his wife?"

"Impossible," laughed Donnelly. "Pacelli won't let him inside; no gate pass." He frowned. "Seriously, I'm not sure what we do. Any ideas?"

Collins stubbed his cigarette. "Talk to Jimmy McGarry, get his take after we're finished here."

"Agreed. Now let's listen to Lovelace and Willets. Find out who's who in the A&P Department…"

***

"A journey to Kenoten is something of a pilgrimage for the select employee," said Lovelace, "and is a transformative learning experience, a defining career event."

"Here's the risk, Len," said Willets. "The people who get selected for Kenoten Island Management Center are the ones Nick Jackson hopes will drive change. This is why we're sitting here; whomever we select are the future leaders of Ilium. If they go and can't embrace Jackson's philosophy, it will reflect badly on us. At Kenoten the wrong people are found quickly and are out of the company in short order. Did A&P ever send anybody to Kenoten?"

"No," said Lovelace. "Sorry, yes. Joyce Locker went, shortly after Jackson became CEO. Three years ago."

"Didn't seem to do her much good," said Willets.

"So we know how Willets feels about Locker," Donnelly said, turning to Collins.

"You're not surprised, are you?" Collins muttered. "Wait a minute, wait a minute." They clamped the headsets tighter.

"...Joyce Locker nominated Collins and Donnelly?" Outrage in Willets's tone. "They're still on the program, they flaunt rules and regulations, and they're disrespectful to authority..."

And she'd nominated me before we were together in the hotel.

Donnelly stopped the tape. "Willets dislikes us, wouldn't you say?"

"Well put. Eloquent. No doubt where we stand." Collins sat back and absent-mindedly cracked his knuckles. *Time for a smokescreen.* "I'll bet Locker entered our names before the LA trip, considering the contretemps in New York."

"No argument." Donnelly hit the play button.

Lovelace's voice. "...okay, okay, later." Crinkle of papers, a match striking. "...here are others...ah, Bob Dingmann put Quentin Rhodes forward."

"Good recommendation," said Willets.

"A no-talent butt-sucking asshole," said Collins. Donnelly nodded.

They listened as more names were suggested and discussed.

Collins stopped the tape. "Willets is dismissing the hi-pot recommendations left and right. I wonder if he wants anyone going to Kenoten other than Rhodes?"

"Lovelace did say he would come back to us." Donnelly hit play.

"I think we're finished," said Willets. "Right, Len?"

"If you say so," said Lovelace, "but the only name you've put forward is Quentin Rhodes. Did you contemplate Donnelly and Collins?"

"Unacceptable. The standards must be observed. Anything else?"

"No, we covered everything," said Lovelace. Sounds of leave-taking and doors closing. Willets muttered "shit," and the door opened again. Silence on the tape.

"I guess," said Collins, "we don't run out and get fitted for a Star Fleet uniform just yet, cadet."

"To think what could have been." Donnelly sniffed loudly. "To paraphrase the immortal Groucho, I don't care to enter an elite management center which might take people like me."

"Yeah. The larger question is do we want to work in an organization where the top guy wants to squelch us?"

"We hold that truth to be self-evident. A further incentive to finish those treatments Jentzky asked for." Collins gathered some papers. "Let's get out of here. We need to meet with Jimmy McGarry."

"And have some food," said Donnelly.

***

"Well, at least we got something to eat," said Donnelly, holding his glass. "Too bad your pal Jimmy wasn't manning the bar."

"Maybe for the best," said Collins. "All we have is conjecture."

Donnelly poured another beer. "Will Lou Willets be safe as he and the good Mrs. Duckett play hide the salami in Lou's inner sanctum?" Collins's lip curled. "Seriously, Jim. Remember Burt Rawley."

"Alert Pacelli," said Collins, deadpan.

"Up yours." Donnelly laughed. "Maybe we should talk to our fathers."

"Are you going to tell your father you're bugging offices? I know I'm not."

"Right. Plan B is our course of action," said Donnelly. To Collins's raised eyebrow, he said, "An anonymous phone call to Maqua's finest?"

Collins slowly nodded. "Worth a shot. When?"

"No time like the present," said Donnelly. "We'll call from the phone booth on the corner." They finished their drinks and walked out.

***

Sergeant Bill O'Malley of the Maqua police had pulled night shift for this week. He had barely settled into his chair when the switchboard lit up. The loud buzz startled him. "O'Malley," he blurted, his coffee splashing to the floor.

"Is this the Maqua police?" said the obviously disguised voice on the phone.

O'Malley sighed. *A drunk? They're starting early tonight. Doesn't sound like a drunk, though.* "Yes." He fiddled with a pencil. "What can I do for you, pal?"

"Is the Burt Rawley homicide still active?"

We've been getting heat from Ilium for not closing the Rawley case. O'Malley began to pay attention. "It's an ongoing investigation; all our unsolved crimes remain open," he said, spouting proper police-speak. "Who's calling?"

"That's unimportant...pal..." the voice said. "Here's something you need to know. Rawley was banging the secretary to the manager of Ilium's Exhibit Operation. Her husband is the operation's chief electrician."

This was news, O'Malley knew. Those details weren't uncovered in the original investigation. "Go on," he said, and began taking detailed notes.

"He's a Vietnam vet," the voice said, "who's returned with some kind of syndrome." Nothing else was said; O'Malley thought for a second he'd lost the call. "Maybe the poor son of a bitch can't get it up. Maybe it's something else. Whatever, he might be one angry fellow."

"Yes," O'Malley prodded. "Being angry doesn't make him a murderer."

"No," said the voice, "but having the knowledge and skill to wire the chair gives him the expertise. Plus, he was involved in the set-up of the chair and the other staging for the party. Should I spell things out for you...pal?"

"Now listen..." O'Malley did not like being mocked, even though he knew the caller was correct.

"Better get cracking, because nowadays she's banging someone else." The caller disconnected.

What a grand, colossal fuckup. Who the hell caught this case? Much of this, if true, involves basic investigative procedure. Our guys mailed this in. Was the screw up out of laziness or stupidity or something more insidious? Check who the original detectives were. There've been too many political promotions of rank incompetents recently. I hope one of them gets his ass nailed. He made a note to talk to the captain in the morning.

Collins replaced the receiver. "How'd that sound?"

"You led him to the water," Donnelly said. "Hope he's smart enough to drink it. Let's get out of here."

***

At a little after two in the morning, O'Malley's phone rang yet again. After the first call, a succession of drunks and pranksters had worn O'Malley's patience to a frazzle. "O'Malley," he hissed.

"This here's Lester at the Hogtied Heifer," the caller yelled. "They're wrecking the goddamn bar! Send a van full of cops!" Shouting and crashing sounded.

O'Malley could tell from the background commotion and Lester's voice he wasn't exaggerating. He punched the general call button. "All units in the vicinity of Hogtied Heifer." He reeled off a series of codes: disturbance with possible assault, everyone involved intoxicated, and possible lewd conduct.

He set off the heart-thumping klaxon in the garage and rebroadcast his message over the intercom. *That'll rouse 'em. At two in the morning the cowboys and cowgirls at the Heifer are more than likely drunk and disorderly. Okay, pretend cowboys and cowgirls. Of course when the good ol' boys from the local dairy farms get a couple of drinks, they lose their sense and manners, which is a recipe for mayhem and a headache for us. We'll have a shitload of occupants for the van before everything gets sorted out.*

***

Officers Johnny Montini and Al Luciani were having a comfortable coffee behind Grand Union when the call hissed and

313

sputtered over their radio. "Let's roll," Montini said, and flipped on the light bar. They pulled across the front parking lot and on to Uncas Boulevard. They were only a quarter mile from the Heifer.

The police piled out. An unkempt thirty-something-year-old man sat against the Heifer's front wall holding his head. "Bastards," he moaned. Montini and Luciani left him for the van officers.

Inside the Heifer a kaleidoscope of flying bottles, chairs, articles of clothing, hats, paper, and assorted liquids greeted them. "A real pier sixer," said Montini. He unholstered his nightstick and tapped a guy about to swing at a fat cowgirl.

Luciani was the first to notice. "Look at all the midgets," he yelled. They seemed to be everywhere, in ten-gallon hats, chaps with fringe, and shirts with embroidered flowers and cactuses.

Two dwarfs sat on a local "good ol' boy" wearing engineer boots, and hit him repeatedly with a broken chair leg. Three others had a pair of buxom cowgirls backed into a corner by the jukebox and were trying to grab their breasts. The cowgirls were beating the dwarfs back with beer mugs.

Lester Finch poked his head from behind the bar. "Those little fuckers started it," he shouted. "Kick their asses!"

Luciani chuckled. *Lester doesn't typically get involved in bar brawls. The dwarfs must have really pissed him off.*

"Holy shit, maybe these are the dwarfs the chief's been screaming about for that Ilium manager's murder from last Christmas," Montini shouted.

"Round up the little bastards," Luciani shouted. *Maybe we'll get a medal.*

The inside of the Heifer turned a pulsing pale blue as the van plowed up to the doorway, its blinking light bar level with the front windows. A metallic boom sounded as they threw the sidewalk drunk into the van and three officers erupted through the front door.

"Get the midgets first," yelled Montini.

The van crew gathered the dwarfs and hurled them into the van like hay bales. They subdued and zip-tied the remaining brawlers.

"We didn't do nothing," one of the dwarfs hollered.

"They started it," another howled, pointing at the cowgirls.

"Yeah, we did," one of the cowgirls screamed. "What did you expect when you grabbed my tits?" She laughed derisively. "You shrunken perverts can barely reach them."

A dwarf in chaps gripped his crotch. "As soon as you see my anaconda you'll beg for it."

A cowgirl in sprayed-on looking jeans cackled. "You little twerp, we'd need a microscope and a pair of tweezers." Laughter erupted.

***

The commotion was worse in the station's tiled holding cells, which stank of old vomit and stale urine. At least one cowgirl and one dwarf were barfing into the toilets.

One of the cops watched. *This is only the beginning.*

Sergeant O'Malley, a hefty man with the bulbous nose and broken veins common to the heavy drinker, stood outside the crammed holding cell where the dwarfs were being held. "We're going to hang you guys by your nuts," he said in a raspy tone. "Your voices will be so high your kids will think you turned into women."

The dwarfs regarded each other. The crotch grabber stepped forward. "Let's not get all worked up here now, Sergeant," he said. "I'm sure we can make a mutually agreeable deal. When the detectives come in later we should talk with them."

O'Malley, red-faced, yelled, "Deal? Deal? You wrecked the place, you crazy pipsqueak. The deal you'll get will be up your Hershey's highway when you're in the slammer!"

"You're upset," said the dwarf. "We'll talk when you calm down." The group moved toward the back of the holding cell. They sat and closed their eyes. The crotch grabber began to turn away.

O'Malley remembered the anonymous caller. "Hold up," he said. "We've got you on drunkenness, assault, public lewdness, and wanton destruction of property. We also have you for fleeing and resisting arrest from the Ilium Christmas party warrant. So why would we ever let you go?"

"Can we talk in a more conducive location?"

"Why should I?"

Because," said the dwarf, "we may have an answer to something that's been eluding the Maqua police force."

The Ilium case? Worth a shot. "I suppose so," said O'Malley, unlocking the cell and letting the dwarf slip though. "You better have something, pal. We'll go into this room. Wait here." He closed and locked the door and corralled one of the officers to sit at the main desk and another to stand outside and witness the interrogation.

The dwarf sat across from O'Malley. "So, Bond? James Bond?" O'Malley said.

"A stage name," the dwarf said. "None of us have what you'd call real names anymore. My mother named me after someone in a book. She thought the name was cute, clever, you know? Me, I don't give a shit. Call me Jim or Jabo.

"Okay, Jabo, tell me why we should let you go?"

Bond sat back. "Give us a pass on the Heifer dustup and the Ilium Christmas party, in writing, and we'll give you the goods on Rawley's death on a silver platter. We got a witness, and a corroborating witness to back him up. What do you say?"

"Why should I believe you? You clowns are the prime suspects."

"When you check our backgrounds you'll see we can barely screw in a lightbulb, much less wire a chair."

O'Malley considered what Jabo said. *He makes a good point. There's also what the voice on the phone said last night.* He signaled for Jabo to continue.

"We saw the guy who wired the chair and put the glue down." Bond crossed his diminutive legs.

"Right," said O'Malley. *I don't want to believe him but I'll hear him out.* "We'll need additional detail."

"If I give you a statement without written and verbal assurances, we have no leverage," said Bond.

"What is it you want?" asked O'Malley.

"Simple," Bond replied. "All of us out of here. In addition to the pass, in writing, on the Christmas party and the Heifer, a phone call from my boys after you let them out telling me they're clear. Then a colleague and I will provide you with all the details. Trust me, it's incriminating. We'll need written, guaranteed immunity for any of us who might have to testify." He sat back, legs dangling a foot above the floor.

O'Malley lit a cigarette. He walked around the table and loomed over Bond. "No tickee, no shirtee."

"I'll give you this much," said Bond, shifting aside. "The individual is a *he* and he's an Ilium employee."

"How do I know if you're telling the truth?" O'Malley questioned again.

"Look, it's not just me; as I mentioned, there's a number of us that witnessed the same thing."

O'Malley took a few seconds to ponder the request. "I'll talk to my captain and get with the state prosecutor on your requests." O'Malley checked the clock on the wall before exiting the interrogation room. O'Malley was halfway out when he turned. "If the captain and state agree, I'd suggest once this is all finished, you and your crowd get out of Maqua and come back only for any pending trial. Clear?"

"Crystal," said Bond. "Crystal."

"And if what you say doesn't pass muster," said O'Malley, "we'll throw you in a place where they'll wait in line as you guys grab your ankles."

***

After several hours O'Malley returned.

"Here's the deal," he said, and pushed the signed document across the table. He lit a cigarette.

Bond skimmed it. "I may need to talk to my lawyer."

"Don't be such a wiseass, you little shit," O'Malley said. "This is everything you asked for. Prosecution's office said you'll get the immunity only after you provide a sworn statement and agree to testimony at trial. Take ten minutes and study it. Don't go anyplace."

"Possible but not probable." Bond smiled.

O'Malley returned and Bond handed him the papers. "Your buddies need to sign this too. All of them."

Bond made assurances and was released from custody.

Chapter Thirty-Two

The head of the patrol unit came puffing up to O'Malley. "Okay, where does this guy Cal Duckett work again?"

"Like I told you," said O'Malley, "the Exhibits Operation."
"Are they located at the Works?"
"No. They're on the other side of town near the river." O'Malley's patience was wearing thin.

"Thanks," he said. He turned to his unit. "Okay, guys, let's go.
"Don't you think you should call Exhibits and find out where Duckett is?"
"Don't worry, we'll handle it."
O'Malley shook his head in exasperation and went to his desk. He laughed to himself and picked up the phone.

***

Collins made a notation on the layout and pushed the page aside, muttering, "If I get another meaningless change to these stupid spec sheets, I'll scream."
"Ah, Frank." Pat came around his partition. "Ms. Locker would like you and Jim to come to her office."

More shit raining down on us? "When?"
"Now, if you don't mind," she said.

He and Collins shuffled into Locker's office. "We're here," said Collins.

She waved them to chairs.

"What's up?" said Donnelly as he and Collins sat.

"Leeson tells me you two are current on your assignments and are attending your training course classes."

"Yes," said Collins. *I wouldn't mind conducting a training course with you right now.*

"Good." She glanced at some papers on his desk. "I've—" The phone rang and Locker paused.

His intercom flashed and Pat said, "Ms. Locker, a Mr. O'Malley is on the phone for you."

"Thanks," said Locker. She picked up the phone. "Hey, Bill, how are things going?" They talked for several minutes. "Thanks, I'll tell Pacelli. Too bad your boys rushed off; it'll take them awhile to drive over here." She sat back, frowning.

"If those furrows in your forehead get any deeper, Joyce," said Donnelly, "they'll start planting corn. The mere mention of Pacelli gives Jim and me indigestion."

Collins patted his pockets for a cigarette, which remained back on his desk.

Locker smiled and took her time lighting a cigarillo. "I need to call Pacelli." She pressed the intercom. "Pat, can you get Gino Pacelli for me, please?"

Donnelly chuckled quietly. *It's great to be king. One does not sully one's fingers dialing a number.* A minute later Locker picked up.

"Pacelli? Joyce Locker here. Are you aware the Maqua police are descending on the Exhibits Operation? They're looking for Cal Duckett." She explained why and heard Pacelli sputter. "You might want to find out where Duckett is at this moment." She listened again.

"His wife, Clare, is here at A&P subbing for Lou Willets's secretary while she's on vacation. Keep me posted."

Locker leaned back and savored her cigarillo. "O'Malley is a sergeant in the Maqua police. I went to high school with him."

Well, well, pieces are beginning to come together. "Something going on with Cal Duckett and the police?"

Locker puffed. "O'Malley told me they caught the dwarfs last night during a brawl at the Heifer. An anonymous tipster called earlier in the evening and said Burt Rawley had been banging Clare and the husband found out. Said the husband had some kind of condition from Vietnam. The dwarfs pinned Rawley's murder on Cal."

"You think Cal's coming over here?"

"Apparently," Locker said and rested her cigarillo in an ashtray. "Why?"

Collins examined the ashtray: black enamel and near the top was an Ulster flag. *Donnelly and I are on the wrong side of the border. Is this wha. Joyce thinks of guys like me? Am I just a romp in the hay?* "Because if Willets's door is closed and Clare is in there with him, they're doing the old rumpy pumpy."

"Ha, ha." *Sniff. He's seen the ashtray. I can read his mind. Will he walk away from me? Play it as it lies. Anyway, to business.* "Any recommendation?"

"If I were Pacelli," Collins said, "I'd have someone intercept Duckett before he gets to Willets's office." He winked. "Just in case Clare's not at her desk. Do we charge for our professional opinion?"

"We should," said Donnelly.

Her laugh filled the room.

Collins looked out the window. "Pacelli isn't listening to you, Joyce. He's got his guys giving tickets in the back parking lot, not patrolling the hallways and preventing a capital crime."

Locker cursed and picked up the phone again. The conversation with Pacelli was one-sided and terse. She slammed the receiver down. "As useless as a Ping-Pong ball in a bowling alley!" She pressed the intercom. "Pat, walk down to Willets's office and check things out? Don't talk to anyone and come right back, please?"

"Um...okay."

"Take a camera," said Donnelly. "No joke," he added.

Locker grunted approval.

"Okay," Pat said. "Got the one from the file cabinet."

***

Cal Duckett staggered, emotions whirling with a thousand conflicting feelings as he approached Lou Willets's office. Deep in his head the fog hung, keeping thoughts out of focus. The tenseness between him and Clare had grown worse. *Have to do something, gotta talk to her—make things better between us; she hasn't been answering my calls at work lately. Why the heck would someone direct me over here? This is not where her desk is...*

Rounding a bend he came to Willets's office and the secretary station outside. *Empty. Door shut.* Flashes of Clare and Burt Rawley behind another closed door flooded his awareness. He stepped forward, tentatively. He could hear muffled sounds coming from inside. The hair on his arms tingled. *I've been on a long journey from 'Nam to here and a short one from Burt Rawley to Lou Willets.* He reached for the door.

He slowly turned the knob. The slap-slap and urgings of the sexual act reached him first. The unmistakable odors of carnal rut

323

followed. He took his hand off the knob, afraid to go any farther, more afraid not to. The sounds and smells swept past him to a small crowd gathering behind him. Oblivious, he again gripped the knob.

None of Pacelli's people were near.

Duckett took a deep breath and swung the door open.

Lou Willets hunched over Cal's wife, pants around his ankles, buttocks pumping back and forth. She sprawled on the desk, her legs on Willets's shoulders. Her bra, skirt, and panties were on the floor, covered by papers and files.

Oh my god, it's Clare and Willets going at it. Pat pushed her way forward and shoved her camera between two onlookers. With a clear field she squeezed off several frames. The repeated illumination caught Clare Duckett gasping and Lou Willets pulling out.

Cal Duckett stood, immobile, in shock.

***

Pat sat in Locker's office with Donnelly and Collins describing the events she'd witnessed. "So by the time Duckett was at the doorway the outer office was filled with gaping people. They had the opportunity to watch their department general manager going hammer and tongs with his substitute secretary." She giggled. "You know, his thingy is kind of small."

"Matches his common sense," Locker murmured.

Pat coughed and continued, "Finally, Pacelli and his people arrived, grabbed Cal Duckett, and led him away. Poor guy, he was mumbling to himself."

"Thanks, Pat."

She took her cue and went back to her desk. "Opinions?" Locker said.

Collins said, "With the right lawyer he'll be in the psycho ward, third straitjacket from the left. Then they'll give him a vacation on citizens' money."

"For a year or two," said Donnelly. "Afterward, he'll be out. Combat fatigue."

Collins nodded agreement. "Willets?"

She rubbed her lips with a forefinger. "Good question. Pat said the staff caught him in action with another man's wife. If this gets to Jackson, he may not have much choice but to get Willets out of here."

One can hope. "Was there something else you wanted to discuss?" said Donnelly.

Not the time to talk about Kenoten with these two. "Later."

"We look forward to later," said Donnelly and they walked out. Collins held back and handed Joyce a note. *This is a test, see if things are real or if the ashtray told us the story.*

She read: "Are you available for dinner at my place tonight? I'm a pretty good cook. Seven?" She read the address. "Yes," she mouthed and smiled. She pointed outside.

Donnelly was at Pat's desk. He opened the file drawer and took the roll out of the camera. "We'll need to get the film back fast," he said.

"How do we pull this off?" said Collins, stepping in.

325

Donnelly shrugged. "The only easy way to put previously exposed latent images on to unexposed film is to photograph a print of the original image on a copy camera."

"And?"

"Load the cassette containing the film with the new latent image into the camera."

"This is sounding like Sanskrit," said Collins. "What you're really saying is we find someone who can do this for us."

"Yeah, sounds right," said Donnelly. "How about Tucker Photo?"

"Perfect. I'll messenger the film and get it back tonight and into the file cabinet early in the morning."

"What'll we do with the pictures?"

"Nothing," said Collins. "We hold them in reserve; you never know."

***

"Well, hello there," said Collins as Joyce Locker entered his home. "Glad you could make it." He gave her a peck on the cheek and took the bottle of wine she handed him. "Nice, thank you."

"You're quite welcome," she said, removing her coat and putting it over a chair. She looked around. "You have a lovely place here, very tasteful."

"You're very gracious," he said. "I'm sure your place is light-years nicer." He gestured toward the living room.

"Don't be too sure, Jim. I live with my parents." To his questioning look, she said in a subdued voice, "I'm the youngest, I'm not married and, given that, I stay and look after my folks."

That's a tough hand she's dealt herself. Wait. If she gets married, she's out of there? Does she think I'm her ticket out? He flashed a smile. "You sure you're not Irish and come from my old neighborhood?"

She laughed her deep, throaty laugh. "Not likely."

"Come keep me company," Collins said, "while I fix our dinner."

***

"Everything was delicious." Joyce licked her lips. "The Mongolian beef, the shrimp fried rice, the spring rolls, and the dumpling soup." She raised her wineglass.

Collins raised his glass. "Thank you. I have some ice cream, which we can have in a cone, if you'd like."

"Perfect."

As they sat eating the cones, Joyce asked, "Did you almost play professional baseball?"

"Yeah. So did Frank." Collins licked the cone. "He was first team all-city. Both of us had the decision made for us by our parents to go to college." He laughed. "His story is more interesting than mine. You should ask him."

"I may sometime."

***

"I'm glad you liked the meal," Collins said, as they cleared the table.

"You are a man of many talents," she said, handing him the last dish. She paused. "One other thing. I have a gift for you. It's in my purse." She stepped into the living area and took a package from her purse. "Here, Jim, consider it a late housewarming gift."

327

He opened the package and took out the ashtray with the Ulster flag that had been on her desk. "Erin Go Bragh," she said.

"Interesting gift," he said, straight-faced. "Thank you." He burst out laughing. "Brilliant, and you do notice things."

"Couldn't miss the two of you," she said. "It shouldn't have been on the desk in the first place."

"I know." He put his arms around her, drew her close, and kissed her.

"How about I provide some more dessert," she said, pulling back and taking his hand. She led him toward the bedroom.

She never sniffs when we're alone together.

Chapter Thirty-Three

A tense Lou Willets sat in Nick Jackson's office mentally preparing for summary dismissal.

"As you may suspect," Jackson began, "the power of my position enables to me to do almost anything. The one exception is I cannot do is save a fu-fu-fucking idiot from himself."

"I'm fully aware I've been foolish..."

"No need for bullshit," Jackson snapped at him. "I'm not angry about what you did. I'm only mad you left the goddamned door unlocked and made a public spectacle of yourself to a hallway full of those A&P degenerates. If I were mad at you snagging a little snatch I'd be a fu-fucking hypocrite." He paused and took a deep breath. "But I can't overlook the incident..."

My career is over.

"...everybody's banging somebody. It's the human condition. Joyce Locker's father caught me in a similar situation once. He kicked me and the secretary out of the building. Luckily it was after hours and he let it go." He slammed a fist on the desk. "But you screwed somebody in full view of an entire peanut gallery with the husband coming through the door."

So that's why he's so tight with Locker. "I'm very..."

"...I'm still n-not finished. I don't need you to be f-fucking sorry. I hired you because we thought you were the right guy. Now we have a problem with your location. The price of this stupid act is you're going to be transferred. I'm not sure where we will be putting you, but you'll be a long way from Maqua and New York. Let's hope this blows over."

"Thank…"

"Guys like you, and even me," said Jackson, "we, we get thinking with our w-wieners and suppose we can do whatever we want. More often than not that's a recipe for trouble. Meanwhile, your ass is gone immediately from Maqua. We'll give you a new posting; shouldn't take too long. Oh yeah. Tie a knot in your dong when you're on company property."

This time Willets barely got his mouth open.

"Don't s-say another th-thing! Rumor around the office is that someone took pictures of your little orgy. If that's the case and those are shown around, your career at Ilium is *o-over!* Got it! But in the meantime g-g-get packed. Tell Florence I want her."

Willets exited Jackson's office quickly and quietly. He gave Florence Jackson the message. She did not look up from her desk. Willets reached the hallway and his posture collapsed slightly, as much a slump of relief as any other emotion. *Pictures? I hope they stay buried somewhere. I was sure this was going to be the end of me. Jackson must be a real Billy Goat to let that one go by. No matter; I'll just count my lucky stars, do my penance, and rise again. Still, better update the old résumé.*

"You wanted me?" Florence stood in the doorway.

"Yeah, get me Walt Sukeforth," Jackson said.

***

"You told me Willets was a pussy hound," Jackson said to Sukeforth, "but Christ, I never expected a public spectacle. I should have listened more closely."

"Nothing wrong with a little nookie, Nick," said Sukeforth, "but what happened was a bit excessive."

"Christ on of a fu-fu-fu-fucking crutch. Did I ever d-d-do anything to deserve this shit?" Jackson said, staring out at the New York skyline. He took a deep breath. "What about the pictures? Have any of them circulated?"

"None I'm aware of," said Sukeforth.

"That's one in our favor."

"Right, Nick." Sukeforth made to rise.

"Not so fast. Draw up a list of those openings in the upper Midwest and throw in that one in New Mexico if that's still available. Match Willets's experience and make me a recommendation. Any way you slice it, Willets is gone from Maqua no later than Friday."

"What type of person do you want?"

"I'm going to put Joyce Locker in his place on a temporary basis so I'm not in a rush. Work with Len Lovelace up there in Maqua. Who knows, Joyce may like being the general manager. Meanwhile, look for somebody who can make the job take off."

As the door closed Jackson pressed the intercom. "Florence, get me Joyce Locker."

Sniff. "Hello, Nick, How're things going?"

"F-fucking great, Joyce. That stupid bastard Willets made a public spectacle of himself." Jackson fumbled for some papers on his desk.

"Indeed he did," she said.

"Isn't the husband the one who did in Burt Rawley?"

"Needs to be proved. But probably. Rawley was doing his wife. He'd just gotten fingered and the cops caught up with him as he was entering Willets's office." *Sniff.* "Lucky for Willets. What's going to happen to him?"

"Willets? He'll be toxic in Maqua; I'm shipping him out pronto. Joyce, I'd consider it a personal favor if you take over as general manager until we find someone permanent. You still don't want the job full-time, do you?"

Sniff. "No, Nick, I don't. I'll do it until you get someone."

"I owe you, Joyce," said Jackson and hung up.

***

"A clusterfuck," said Collins, sipping his martini as he and Donnelly sat at L'Fey's half-empty bar. "Our general manager, with flashbulbs popping, is pulled off his temporary secretary by her husband."

"The upshot," finished Donnelly, tossing back a Jameson's, "is the husband is arrested, the general manager gets his ass shipped out to Upper Nowhere, and the secretary goes back to her day job."

"As the Hester Prynne of the A&P Department," said Collins. "And Joyce is the temporary big kahuna until Jackson ships in another Willets clone."

"You realize we have a novel in all this stuff, don't you?"

"The thought crawled through my frontal lobe. Might make a better movie, though."

They watched Drake and Hogg come in. "Wonder where Shepherd is?"

"Banging Hogg's wife, I'd suspect," said Collins. "Do you think Hogg will find out?"

"Eventually. With them two good ol' boys at each other? A cinch for the evening news."

"A film-at-eleven evening newscast deal. Wonder if we somehow fit that into our oeuvre," said Collins, finishing his martini.

"Don't see why not," said Donnelly. "Widen the aperture."

"Speaking of apertures, you keeping track on how our Electric Chair is doing?"

Donnelly mentally counted. "They're not wasting time; we're already up to twenty in just a couple of months. The ones they've televised had good ratings. A few got toasted in the right-to-work-capital-punishment states. Elsewhere, where the sensitive folk live in gated communities and rally for the cause of the week, they've tied them up in the courts."

The commercial ended and the screen filled with a soundless picture of an extended van rolling slowly along a desolate street past rundown houses with plywood sheets nail-gunned over windows and doors. After ten seconds the voiceover intoned, "Next on GBS, *Felon Hunters*; truth and justice come to the mean streets. Now these messages."

"That's our show," smiled Collins.

"Points for pride; even better the boatloads of cash we're getting for the concept."

The screen lit with an interior shot of the van. The driver and shotgun rider had the windows rolled down. The camera panned to the back. The narrator spoke. "Silent people on a mission; the judge, jury, and the officers of the court sit in the dim van, on the search for an errant felon. Today, Linus Parkrind, freed on a technicality while serving fifty years to life. His bald head and swastika-decorated body quickly disappeared into these slums before the DA could issue paperwork for another murder they had had him pegged for.

Parkrind's sworn mission: the eradication of people of black, Indian, Asian, and Pakistani descent, along with any other color Parkrind does not recognize. The dumpster-body count in this neighborhood has spiked."

The camera switched to a street lined with decrepit brick row houses. "Outside, the oppressive odors of garbage, whiskey, and urine prevail. A tipster described a house with a white door and white shutters on the bottom floor windows. The white paint is Parkrind's not-so-subtle boast of his presence, police say."

"What you boys watching?" Hogg asked, as he and Drake joined them.

"New show, been on about six weeks," said Donnelly. "*Felon Hunters.* Short version: they go after bad guys and toast them in Ilium Electric Chairs."

"Can't be more interesting than Joyce Locker being the new GM," said Drake. "Anything for us?"

"You won't kiss Dingmann's ass anymore," said Donnelly.

"Your transfers to Outer Mongolia get delayed?" asked Collins.

"Har, har, har," replied Drake. "Funny."

"You two plus your pal Shepherd wanted to be on Dingmann's team even though you were on Joyce's." Donnelly finished his beer. "You didn't apply for a transfer. Way to read the tea leaves, guys."

"Where is Shepherd, anyway?" asked Collins. "Don't tell me he's still at his desk."

"Don't know," Drake said. He turned to Hogg. "You?"

"No idea." He pulled out a cigarette. "Ask Locker; she's right behind you."

"Round for the group, Tappy," Locker said, reaching for the just-poured martini. "Maybe he's at your house, Hogg." *Sniff.*

333

Closer than you think, Joyce. Collins reached for his drink.

On the TV screen a pair of SWAT teams arrayed themselves on the sidewalk. The van driver and shotgun rider walked, 16-inch barrel-pump shotguns parallel with right legs so as not to expose a silhouette. The two groups came toward each other, the white door between them.

Drake wondered whether to follow up on her comment. *Nah, he thought.* "Thanks for the drink." He picked up his glass. "Congratulations on being the GM."

Locker nodded. Donnelly made a kissing sound. Collins laughed. Drake flushed.

The SWAT team breached the house and charged up the stairs. A man with a battering ram got in position and again swung the steel door-breaching tool. The door shattered. The flash of gunshots boomed from the gloomy interior. The lead team member poked a shotgun around the jamb and pumped off five rubber rounds, and the team stormed in. Parkrind lay stunned on the floor. "At ten feet the rubber rounds knocked Parkrind down. He appears to be alone. More after these messages." The picture faded with men wearing gas masks dragging Parkrind down the stairs and out the front door.

Hogg was distracted; Locker's offhand comment had given him pause.

"I guess they're using that new technology to tape this show," said Drake.

"Yeah," said Locker. "They can edit down to time constraints. It does lose some of the spontaneity, though." *Sniff.* "What do you think, Rufus?"

Hogg climbed off the stool. "I think I'll head out." He stubbed out his cigarette, threw a few bills on the bar, and signaled Tappy. "A round for these guys. Catch y'all tomorrow." He went to the door.

"Where's Shepherd?" said Donnelly.

"No idea," said Drake.

"Is he with Anna May?" said Collins.

"For everyone's sake I hope he isn't," Drake said and took a drink.

Locker's attention focused on the screen. Parkrind was wrestled into the van and cuffed into a chair. The judge stared at him and said, "For evil to triumph it is only sufficient for good men to do nothing." They went right to the charges. The prosecution offered its invective; the public defender had no objection.

Locker turned to them. "What's going on?"

"After more exchanges the jury declares him guilty and the judge sentences the bad guy," said Donnelly, sipping his beer. "I suspect they'll strap him into an Ilium Electric Chair and toast him."

Locker glared. *Sniff.* "Next question. Hogg got a bug up his ass?"

Donnelly and Collins glanced at each other. Drake lit a cigarette. No one said anything.

"Well?" Locker tapped her fingers.

Collins puffed his cigarette. "Joyce, you're the big dog now, at least for a while. You don't need to be digging into personal minutiae not affecting a guy's work performance."

"It could," said Locker. She swallowed the rest of her drink. "Ah, what the hell." She turned to Donnelly and Collins. "I'll be out for several days. I want you two in my office Tuesday morning."

"Career goals and objectives?" asked Donnelly.

"You'll find out then," said Locker. "Good night."

Donnelly said to Collins, "Is Joyce married?"

Collins toyed with his coaster. "She's never mentioned a husband." *No. she told me she hasn't been.*

"Look, they polled the jury," said Drake. "Here comes the sentence."

The judge asked, "How do you find?"

The beak-nosed jury foreman read from a notebook. "The jury finds Linus Parkrind guilty on all counts."

The judge banged his gavel on his collapsible bench. "By the power vested in me by the State of Michigan I sentence you to be strapped into that chair, the switch thrown, and you will remain seated until you are deceased and no longer a threat to society."

Parkrind spat, straining to loosen his manacled hands.

"Another triumph of the GBS network and national publicity for the Ilium Electric Chair," muttered Donnelly. Collins smiled.

The judge asked, "Mr. Parkrind, any last words?"

Parkrind   yelled, "…uking…uking…ew…oving…other…uckers!   Mmmph!"   The bailiff had stuffed a rubber ball into his mouth.

"We're sorry you feel that way," said the judge. "May the Lord have mercy on your soul." The judge signaled and Job Slaughterthorn threw the switch.

Fire crackled out of Parkrind's toe-tips. His scream dopplered though the acoustic range. Smoke trickled from his ears and nostrils as his hair shriveled. The picture shifted to the crowd, who yelled, "Los pollos están pagando las consecuencias, hijo de puta." (The chickens come to roost, motherfucker.)

Christ, Cox must've cranked up the juice.

"This is top-flight television," Drake said.

Slaughterthorn plucked Parkrind out of the chair and shoved him into the bag. He hooked the desiccating hose to the bag and was busily turning Linus into nascent plant fertilizer.

"Don't touch this bag," he warned the crowd. "If you let air in Parkrind will reconstitute. I can't be responsible for how badly he mucks you up." Laughing, Slaughterthorn climbed into the van and they sped away, leaving the bystanders open-mouthed at the swiftness of the process.

The announcer cut in, "*Felon Hunters.* Street Justice, swift and fair. Next week: Oakland. Now these messages."

***

Nick Jackson pushed his chair back from looking at the list of executives not making their quarterly numbers. Red lines ran through several names.

He handed the report to Walt Sukeforth. "Fire these people and get their successors in place within two weeks."

Sukeforth made a note.

Jackson turned to another folder.

"Holy shit, Bella Madonna Bidet is going to license the electric toilet!"

"Bel who?" said Sukeforth. "Sounds like a question at a spelling bee."

"Bella Madonna, Walt, is one of the finest manufacturers of porcelain and stainless steel toilet furnishings in Europe, is who they are. We'll be on every yacht in the Mediterranean and the master baths of mansions in Monaco." He stared at the report. "The unit's still in Milan for testing. Some Italian got his or her rocks off as soon as they plugged it in." Jackson drummed his fingers. "Too bad we can't market the toilet here."

Sukeforth snorted. "They'd hang Ilium out to dry if we tried it. Too many already in an uproar over the 'chair' we produced. The Temperance riots would look like Bible camp."

"The Italians should embrace this toilet like a plate of anchovy linguini." He turned a page and laughed. "They've already ordered a dozen additional prototypes, the fucking perverts. Ride 'em, Luigi. What was the name of the engineer who worked on this? "

Sukeforth thought for a minute. "Harold Cox; works for George Kelso."

Jackson pressed the intercom button. "Get me Kelso up in Maqua, Florence."

Florence connected him. "Kelso, Nick here. I want you to talk to your engineer, Harold Cox. Transfer me; I want to talk to him now. Just thought I'd give you a heads up."

***

Harriet Cox rubbed the thumbs of each hand against her index and middle fingers waiting for Nick Jackson to come on the line. She was startled by the timbre of his voice. "So you're Harold Cox?" he said.

"Yes, sir. Good afternoon, Mr. Jackson," said Cox.
"Let's get over the Mr. Jackson stuff," said Jackson.
"Yes, sir."

"You've had more than one good idea in a row; I like that." *Son of a bitch sounds a little fruity but we'll overlook it and we'll tune up the porno toilet.* "Call me Nick. You can consider your standing better than the cretins working for me this quarter. Profile these Italians who want to license the toilet for me."

"Well…Nick…I supplied Bella Madonna's name. Your people did the deal. I discovered Bella Madonna while looking for high-end manufacturers of some, ahem, feminine hygiene products little known or even used in the US. They were consistent with the A&P strategy of getting in at the top of the market and trickling the product down. Europe and Scandinavia are much more open to an orgasmic product. In the US people would have a hard time seeing June Cleaver or Harriett Nelson riding the clit clouter."

"Clit clouter! Marvelous!" Jackson's face turned purple he laughed so hard. "Jesus, Cox, that's a good one. You and I are going to get along fine."

"Collins and Donnelly came up with it," said Cox.

"Before we go any further, Cox, and I bust a goddamn gut, let me tell you why we're talking. Donnelly and Collins are sharp and I love 'em. But you're an engineer and I'm an engineer. I believe one thing in my dark little engineer heart. You're nobody until you make something, and that's what engineers do."

Cox's mind raced. *Where is this going? This guy fires on extra cylinders. Like I'm talking to a pinwheel.*

"I want you to start brainstorming. I'll clear this with Kelso. Work on your ideas up in Maqua and keep me in the loop on what you dream up."

"Yes, sir. George Kelso will give me the details?"

"Yes." Jackson slapped his palm on his desk. "Crank up your testosterone, Cox, and let's rev this baby up!"

"I look forward to it, sir." Testosterone? If you only knew, Mr. Nick Jackson.

After calming down and analyzing the situation, Cox called her sister, Emily. They talked for fifteen minutes. "Then we're agreed," Harriet said and hung up. She dialed Collins in his Maqua office. The phone rang three times before Collins picked up.

"Collins." He stared at the white drop ceiling tiles with its thousands of little acoustic absorption holes and speculated on the mutant life forms crawling out of them at night.

"Bella Madonna Bidet bought into the electric toilet," Cox said. "I just got off the phone with Nick Jackson himself. He wants me to develop new products." She chuckled to herself as she heard Collins's feet hit the floor as he yanked them down from his desk. His chair screeched as he sat up. Cox thought the screech sounded like a mouse that senses the boot heel coming.

"Are you kidding?" Collins almost bellowed.

"I wouldn't kid a kidder," said Cox. "Kelso will tell me officially, but we're off and running."

Collins exhaled. "Anything about A&P plans?"

"The toilet is international so I expect Advertising and Promotion won't be involved. It could never be on American television unless someone like Ozzie Nelson was the endorser."

"Very funny. This is big news; you're now on Jackson's radar."

"I plan to take advantage of that."

Joyce is out of town; I'm still a free man. "Can I take advantage of you tonight?"

"Yes, I guess that's a possibility."

Collins's radar pinged. *Guess? Uh oh. Better ignore it.* "Do you also plan to wear undergarments tonight?"

"They should all be off by six-thirty."

"Good I'll be over at six thirty-five."

"We have a lot to talk about," said Cox.

My radar was right. "Where will Emily be?"

"With Frank."

"Well, maybe I can be a little earlier and help you with those undergarments."

"Maybe you can."

***

Afterward, their cigarettes glowed as Harriet and Collins lay among the twisted sheets in the dimly lit bedroom.

With a deep sigh, Harriet reached over and turned on the light. "We need to talk, Jim."

Collins squinted. "What's wrong? The chair? The toilet?" *Was my radar correct? What the hell is going down here?*

"Neither. It's you and I. Jackson's call got me thinking. I'm becoming more anxious about my career than my current sex life. I don't want to sneak around Maqua anymore."

Am I hearing "Goodnight, Sweetheart" playing in my head? Be understanding; no flippancy. "I thought we were having a little more than just a sex life. I thought we were connecting." *God, that sounds lame.*

Cox smiled. "Connecting? Via your willie, perhaps, but not much more."

"Pretty harsh." He recalled those connections and began getting hard.

"Not harsh, just realistic. I'm an engineer; I deal in facts, not fairytales. I've become a good screw and I know it." She noticed his tumescence. She reached over and gave it a friendly wiggle. "You're a

341

good screw and I know that too. We enjoy ourselves. Where we part company is your idea of any permanence."

Say something, you idiot. Like I'd like you to do something with my rock-hard boner? Probably not appropriate. "Permanence? We're not seeing anyone else." *That is, presuming you're not aware of Joyce.*

Cox gave his erection another friendly tweak. "You guys are fun in the sack but involved in your own career games. Kind of impermanent, if you catch my drift."

I feel like the calf that found out where veal comes from. "You said we. Does Emily feel this way?"

"She does. Right now she's telling Frank." Another squeeze. Collins shuddered. "Emily's thinking of moving back to the Midwest. At heart she's a homebody; she'll probably wind up in Iowa, have a pile of kids, and gain sixty pounds in the process. Just like our mom did. But as for myself, I intend to keep moving up the Ilium ladder, and I don't want the continued temptation/danger that *we* as a couple would pose to endanger that future. I've already put my job on the line and broken laws, so to speak." She bent over and gave a lick to his quivering member.

Collins struggled to control himself. Marvin Jentzky's comments about Midwest girls morphing into boxcars flashed through his mind. *Thank you, Lord, I have dodged the porker bullet. Act surprised and disappointed. Don't jump up on the damn bed and tap dance out of here singing, "Fat ain't beautiful, fat ain't grand, fat ain't what'll keep this man."* His erection began to soften. *Say something.* "I'm speechless."

"Don't say anything." She stroked him, restoring his stiffness. "I just want you to know how it is."

"Um..."

"We'll go our ways; you and Frank will go yours. I don't think I need to go on, do I?"

"I guess not." *Just keep doing what you're doing; don't stop.* "This is kind of sudden."

"You'll get over it," she said. "Meanwhile, let's finish the evening with dessert." She tightened her grip and brought her lips to his.

I'll pretend it's Joyce. Christ, that's weak, even to me.

***

The next morning Donnelly came to Collins's cubicle. The wall shook as a freight train rumbled on the tracks behind the building. "Did you get the same 'so long it's been good to know you?' that I got from Emily?"

"Oh yeah. What do you think?" Collins lit a cigarette.

Donnelly took a sip from his tea. "I was surprised at first; we were kind of floating along in the relationship. Then Jentzky's comment about Midwest girls turning into boxcars popped into my head." He shrugged. "Actually, I was relieved."

Collins laughed. "Me too." *Are we bullshitting each other?*

"Well," said Donnelly, "at least we didn't get to the 'til death do us part." He finished his tea. "The hell with it if we can't take a joke." *And it clears the path for anything with Sue. Jesus, I'm an idiot; got to get it in my head; she's married, off-limits even to someone as perverse as me. But my oh my I am attracted to her.*

"Speaking of which," said Collins, "I read in the *Gazette* this morning Nick Jackson is on Crandall tonight."

343

"The PBS guy?" said Donnelly, wrenching his attention into the here and now. "Might be worth watching. McGarry's?"

"Sure." Collins considered his paper-strewn desk. "I've got these spec sheets to finish."

"Do you really want to?" said Donnelly.

"Hell, no." *I'd rather be with Joyce.* "I'll see you tonight."

Chapter Thirty-Four

"Nick Jackson is on Crandall tonight," said Abe Floss. He and Justin Hitchcock sat in a secluded area of Off the Record, the basement bar in Washington, DC's Hay Adams hotel.

Hitchcock inclined his head. "So they told me," he said, "did you read the editorial in this morning's *Times*? The folks on the Upper West Side are writing letters and chatting at cocktail parties about curbside justice and lack of due process."

"I'm not at all surprised," said Floss.

"Well, you should know, Abe, they're your people," said Hitchcock.

Floss chuckled. He signaled the waiter and murmured to him. The waiter nodded and spoke to the bartender, who switched the television closest to them to the PBS station. "Let's see how Jackson does."

Hitchcock shifted in his chair. "When the *Times* is tut-tutting, Brooks Crandall is harrumphing."

***

The PBS underwriting messages ended and the Crandall logo faded. The camera zoomed in on the host. He sat at a round oak table, a folded *New York Times* at his elbow. In a smooth, confident voice he began, "This is Brooks Crandall. Our first topic tonight is violent crime in America and the introduction of so-called curbside justice. We will explore reactions from various strata of society. Our special guest this evening is Nick Jackson, chairman of the Business Board and president and CEO of Ilium Electric. Good evening, Nick, and welcome to this table."

"Good evening, Brooks, happy to be here," said Jackson in a confident, stutter-rehabbed voice.

Crandall finished a brief biographical sketch. "…and its newest acquisition, the GBC network." He glanced at a notecard. "Since Ilium's takeover GBC is airing an unusual number of so-called punishment shows. The following is from the top-rated show *Felon Hunters*. Roll tape, please."

On the screen Job Slaughterthorn, identified by a caption, was strapping a convicted criminal into an Ilium chair. "I'm going to roast your arms and legs, you pedophile creep," he growled. "You're going to take a ride in this electric chair." Sweat beads boiled on the felon's forehead. Slaughterthorn stepped back and, with a flourish, threw the switch.

The narrator screamed as the prisoner thrashed. "His hair is on fire; may be a little difficult for the viewer to see, but the flame is blue." The blaze circled the condemned man's sneakers. A moment later his fingertips blew off. Wisps of smoke rose from the fly of his trousers. "Considering his lurid history of child abuse, he's getting his just desserts," the narrator said.

The clip ended. A stern-faced Crandall said, "Do you believe GBC's involvement in this very open pursuit of justice warrants such public violence?"

"It's the law of the land, Brooks," he said. "The clip, as edited and presented, is not quite fair and balanced. It left out a few salient details." Jackson raised a finger. "One, Chester Howard, the executed criminal, was a pedophile who specialized in Irish Catholic girls still in their First Communion frocks. Two, he was convicted five years ago and served time. Three, after his early release he was arrested three months later for four rape attempts. Four, a judge freed him on bail, which he promptly jumped. Five, by the time *Felon Hunters* caught up to him five months later he'd attacked and created seven more victims. Little, innocent girls." Jackson sat back.

Crandall worked his face and consulted an index card. "Do you believe the lurid aspects of this and similar GBC shows benefit the need for fair and equitable justice?"

"Well, Brooks, since we're pursuing this line, do you think it fair for a TV reporter to shove a microphone into the face of a grieving loved one? Or, similarly, for a print reporter to ask a father about his emotions regarding his daughter being violated by a pervert who'd been freed on a technicality? How about asking a wife her opinion of her husband being beaten by a youth gang? Those stories were in that paper today." Jackson fingered the paper by Crandall's elbow. "With photographs, I may add. Due process is wonderful but has become a recycling project, spiraling out of control with irresponsibility and unrestrained mayhem."

"Are you saying," said Crandall, "this necessity for justice warrants such publicly draconian measures?"

Jackson sighed. "I would point out the substantial drop in violent crime, something not mentioned by the editorial writers." Jackson smiled, all pretense.

Crandall interrupted. "So the felon hunting process will continue indefinitely?"

"I'm not in the prediction business," Jackson said, "but the statistics show it acts as an effective deterrent."

***

Hitchcock leaned across the table. "Your friend Nick Jackson left out the words, 'as long as it effectively sells electric chairs and our broadcast ratings hold up.'"

"Merely doing his job. I'd expect no less from Nick," said Floss. "He's getting better at these interviews. He seems focused and he hasn't stuttered. This could bode well for his address to the security analysts in two weeks. Crandall will make one last attempt."

***

Crandall pursed his lips. "GBC also won the rights for sole coverage of the executions. Isn't all of this a bit medieval?"

"We must deal with the reality of life today," Jackson said, "and the threats society faces. Public expressions of consequences for criminal action get attention." He sipped some water.

"How long will GBC continue this programming?"

"All the people who think they know are writing editorials." With an engaging grin, Jackson added, "Or doing TV interviews."

The camera focused on Crandall. "And that will have to be our final answer. Thank you for visiting with us this evening." He reached across the table and shook Jackson's hand. "We look forward to meeting with you again." He turned to the camera. "Next up, the rise of Buddhism in Hollywood and Washington. Is it because it promotes tolerance without demanding repentance? We'll have a discussion with the Australian philosopher and theologian, Burken Willis."

***

"Right across Crandall's bow with that last one," Hitchcock said.

"Do you think this frontier justice trend is starting to wind down?"

Hitchcock fingered the wattle on his neck. "You may be correct, Abe. Might be time for a slow, strategic backing away from the more extreme aspects of some current trends in law enforcement."

"You mean you're agreeing with the *New York Times*?" The corners of Floss's lips turned up.

"Hardly." Hitchcock stood. "We should coordinate our movements." He extended a hand. "Good night, Abe."

It wasn't until he'd left before Floss realized Hitchcock had stuck him with the bill. He laughed out loud.

***

"We were the only people watching the show," said Collins. McGarry's patrons were absorbed in conversations or the bottom of their drinks.

"We're erudite and they're not," Donnelly said.

Collins snickered.

"Okay, we have a vested interest," Donnelly said. He peered at the screen and the next segment. "You know, Jackson didn't stutter and he scored off Crandall." He signaled for another round.

Collins finished his drink and waited while the bartender filled his glass. "Yeah, he did. But if I'm reading the tea leaves correctly, I'm seeing the signs the try 'em and fry 'em days will start to wind down."

"Which means," said Donnelly, "our Jentzky treatments may be less marketable."

"Except for *Cops and Courts*," said Collins.

"Right. Joyce talks to us about Kenoten tomorrow."

"More than likely." Collins lit a cigarette.

"Suppose she offers it to us?"

"For four months we won't be doing the usual shit work."

"Then what?" Donnelly drank his beer.

"We don't get an assignment that appeals to us we bolt to LA?"

"Sounds like a plan. Thanks to *Felon Hunters* we'll have enough money for a while. Let's get out of here."

Collins stubbed his cigarette. "Tomorrow morning with Locker should be interesting.

"Game changer," said Donnelly.

Chapter Thirty-Five

The morning sun filtered through the grimy window of the general manager's office, Joyce Locker's new digs. *More space, chair's more comfortable, everybody wants to kiss my ass, including Dingmann. I could get used to this. Good grief, where's my head? Better than my "no sun" old office where the window overlooks the chain-link fence, crushed rock embankment, and railroad tracks. I don't miss the unmelted snow piles and high summer patches of orange day lilies and sumac clumps.* "Pat, get me a coffee, would you please, and grab something for yourself on me."

She had preferred not to work at Willets's expensive mahogany desk. *God knows the stains and bodily fluid embedded in that piece of furniture. No thank you.* She had moved another desk in. Her reflections were interrupted by the intercom. "Ms. Locker, Mr. Jackson's office is on the line.

After a minute she was connected.

"Hi, Nick."

"I want to talk about your Kenoten nominations. Donnelly and Collins. Sukeforth forwarded them to me. You realize what you've got. They're young for Kenoten but they think outside the box. Unusual for you A&P pussies."

"Hey!" Locker laughed. "Are you still interviewing each candidate?"

"Not so much," said Jackson. "Nowadays I send people to do that. In this case, your guy Lovelace, my guy Sukeforth, Tweed the top guy at Kenoten, and a clinical psychologist who can search out their motives. I've a feeling these two are worth it. We'll find out if they are."

"Don't worry about that," Locker said. "We only have to be careful they don't bring the whole place down around our ears." *And Collins between my legs.*

This got a chuckle from Jackson. "Worse could happen. The old guard needs something to come down around their ears. I'll tell the three guys down here about the meeting. We'll schedule for next week in Maqua. Regards to your folks; we'll talk."

Jackson was a piece of work, but brilliant. Locker understood Kenoten required corporate participation.

Sukeforth and his cohort might be a pain in the ass but Jackson sent me a clear signal of approval. She stared at one of the ubiquitous A&P section monthly project listing reports, over an inch thick, with more green and white stripes than the St. Patrick's Day parade. *This part of the job I could easily do without. Sniff.* She pulled the report toward her across the desk.

She pushed the intercom button. "Call Collins and Donnelly and have them come down right away."

"Will do," Pat said.

***

Donnelly and Collins stood before Pat.

"Good morning, Frank, Jim."

"Do you like the new digs? Is Joyce enjoying being the new Lou Willets and Burt Rawley?" Donnelly grinned.

"Ms. Locker is just getting off the phone," Pat said. "She'll be with you in a minute." She sat back. "I'll tell you in a week whether I like it here."

"Okay, Worker Bee," said Collins, with a laugh.

"Who's she talking to?" Donnelly winked at Collins. "Nick Jackson?"

Pat's head snapped up. "Who told you?" A second later she realized she'd been suckered.

"Don't worry," Donnelly said, "we won't say anything."

***

"You rang?" Donnelly sauntered in,

"Yes I did, gentlemen," said Locker in a tone of surprising formality. "Take a seat." She pushed the intercom again. "Pat, would you mind bringing us some coffee?"

"Tea for me, please," said Donnelly.

Sniff. "You two are doing a good job in spite of your unorthodox ways. Nick Jackson likes you, which can be a mixed blessing. Right now you're on the upside. Accordingly, I'm nominating you for the Kenoten management course. Your names came up once before but were not approved." Locker offered no further comment. They feigned mild surprise.

Pat entered with the refreshments. Locker took a sip of her coffee. "Okay, questions?"

Collins lit up, took a deep drag, glanced at Donnelly, exhaled, and said, "We don't deny this is a huge break for us and we appreciate being selected." He inhaled again. *We know all this; what I don't know is when you and I can be together again.*

Donnelly put his coffee cup down. "And after the four months at Kenoten? Do we come back here to a life doing spec sheets or to other possibilities?"

353

Collins checked Locker's new office. The oak desk, originally rescued from the depths of basement storage, appeared as old as the Works, carved at the corners and joined with leaf-and-vine motif. Clawed ball feet clutched at the dirty green carpeting inexorably continuing the color scheme of the linoleum halls and minion offices. Period wooden chairs matched the conference table. Gray metal-framed green vinyl-upholstered atrocities waited in Pat's office should a meeting require extra seating.

Sniff. "You'll be attending a meeting," said Locker. "As will Lovelace and I. Nick Jackson will send people. It will be a serious discussion, not an interview per se. We put a great deal of effort into who goes to Kenoten and bet big on their future performance. The guys from corporate and Len Lovelace will interview you but you should do okay with that. I want you to give the meeting some thought. This is a big step for both of you. The level at which you've been recommended will have immediate career implications."

"Okay, Joyce, how soon?"

"Next week. You guys know I'm a company person. Frankly, I can't imagine you not wanting to go, but I grew up here. Maybe for you it isn't the same." *Sniff.*

"We'll be ready," said Donnelly.

Collins puckered his lips.

Was that affection for me or a rank-out of Donnelly? Locker slurped her coffee. "And, if you decide to turn this down, realize you've made an even bigger decision. Turning Kenoten down sends the signal you're not staying with Ilium. If your thinking goes that way, for whatever reasons, tell me first. I don't want to find out after a bunch of other Ilium people." *Sniff.*

"Not to worry; you have our word," said Donnelly

"You stood by us," said Collins. "We'll make a good impression next week, do you proud."

***

Locker sat back and laced her fingers behind her head. *Those guys never fail to amaze. They didn't seem surprised I recommended Kenoten for them. Guess Lovelace's idea about hiring trainees with more experience achieved results. Hard to say if we'll be able to live with the outcome, but we got them.* She looked out the grimy window. *God I love this place. I hope they stay. I want Collins to stay, that's for sure. We have to figure what's after Kenoten. We need people like them so we don't get stuck spinning our wheels in the corporate bullshit.*

She picked up the phone and dialed Len Lovelace's extension. "Len, let's talk about Donnelly and Collins and Kenoten. Can you come down?" She turned her attention to an Ilium A&P revenue report.

***

As Collins exited, a worker was sliding a new nameplate into an aluminum extrusion screwed to the wall. "Joyce Locker, Interim General Manager." *Slide the old one out, slide the new one in. Like having sex. It's been swell to know you.*

Donnelly pulled up beside Collins, matching strides down the green hallway.

Collins was deep in thought. *It must be weird being trapped between two worlds. The Works is enough to drag anyone down. Its mere existence on the landscape is like some industrial Grendel waiting to bite the head off any warrior who shows himself. No way that won't eventually get you. She doesn't think she needs shit from us but the day will come when maybe we can watch over her from afar; save her from the monsters. Joyce is a good person at heart. Pretty damn good looking, too. Great in the sack, easy to get along with. I wonder how deep are her feelings for me? How serious are we getting? Do I care? Yes.*

"Hello, anybody home?" Donnelly nudged him.

"Sorry," said Collins. "Woolgathering." *And realizing maybe Joyce and I may be more than a romp in the hay.*

***

Lovelace and Locker sat at the oak table in Locker's office. When she had come across the table in the storage basement beneath the old Lightning Rod and Grounding Equipment building, she had turned it on the side to check its construction integrity. In ink, bled deep into the wood was written; *What are you looking under here for? The action's on the other side.* Whenever a meeting was boring, unproductive or frustrating, she thought of that sentence.

"I was always amazed how Willets shot them down out-of-hand," said Lovelace. "I argued, I pleaded…"

"I'm sure you did," said Locker. *Right.* "We're here to talk about now. I want these guys to stick around. Yeah, they can be annoying. Yeah, they're not the best for my sanity, but they've also given me the biggest laughs in recent years and they're superior to anyone I've seen around here in a long time. They've done the company some good. Their best is yet to come. They're made of the same stuff as Jackson with fewer deviant impulses." *And Collins and I have the beginnings of something special, maybe permanent. Permanent? What am I thinking? Something I should have thought of a long time ago.*

"Yes. Fewer deviant impulses. Well phrased."

"Don't like it enough to repeat it. I can say it. You can't."

"Yes, right. Sure, Joyce. I won't. I wouldn't."

"Don't forget."

"So what needs deciding?"

"I want a clear, attractive path for those two. A plan they'll want to chase after. Something to engage their love of combat and intrigue. A love I suspect most of us around here, including the recently departed Lou Willets, underestimated at their peril." *Sniff.* "I may even talk to Sukeforth or Jackson."

"Anything specific?"

"Yes. Nominations like this make everybody and his dog want to get involved. Happened when Nick Jackson threw in my name for Kenoten. Ten people must've been at the meeting to 'determine and clarify my interest.'"

"Yeah. Big job. Custom. Future." Lovelace scribbled notes.

"You need notes?"

Lovelace mumbled. "…trying to get all the high spots…" He finished a line. "When's the meeting?"

"I figure next week. Jackson told me I'll be with you and some of Jackson's folks, including Sukeforth, Tweed from Kenoten, and a clinical psychologist. Kenoten serves at the whim of the executive and they'll be aware of Nick's objectives. I put a note to him with my thoughts. Knowing him, he may already be a step ahead on the route plan. Make your proposal a good one. Custom, even. With a big, defined carrot. Specific jobs or tasks those two can really get into."

"Route plan…" Lovelace scribbled.

"For god's sake, Len! Quit writing down all this bullshit. Pat will send you a memo when the meeting date is set. Meantime, check the corporate organization charts. Draw up a little list of where these guys might fit. Impact jobs. Doesn't have to be the A&P department; probably shouldn't. "

Lovelace scribbled. Under his breath he repeated, "Impact jobs."

"That's all. Thanks, Len." She retreated behind her desk. Soon as you finish your notes give them to Pat. She'll type them up." *I'll read them as I die of frustration.*

***

Sue Costello had completed her rounds at Maqua Hospital and was writing up her notes. She put her pen down and sat back. *Okay, that's done. Another day, another round. All work and no play have made Sue a frustrated girl.* She sighed. *Stop avoiding it, Sue. You've a problem. My so-called marriage is the biggest mistake of my life. Two years wasted. I should have ended it as soon as I found out...Too proud to admit failure, too wrapped up in my career. No one's fault but mine. No! Damn it, damn him, he misled me, looking for cover. I was such a fool. Now someone's come into my life. Back into my life, really; I always had a thing for Frank, all the way back to grammar school. He's shying away because I'm married. Big taboo. Says a lot about Frank. Honorable. But I always knew that. I guess it's my turn to call him, keep the ball moving until I can figure out what to do about Bob. Who am I kidding? Frank is seeing me out of politeness, not out of any idea of a future for the two of us. Okay, he was aroused at that place, McGarry's, but that's a normal male reaction, and I was pushing it. Did he think I was forward? Am I acting too much like a schoolgirl?*

Her pager vibrated. She looked at the number. Frank? She called Directory Assistance to be sure. It was his home phone. *Do I seem eager and call immediately? Or do I play it cool and hold off? If I do that Frank'll be off doing something else. Maybe with the sister of that engineer he mentioned? Bob's off somewhere and won't be back until tomorrow evening. Don't be an idiot.*

She lifted the phone and dialed.

"Hello?"

"Frank, it's Sue. You called?"

"Uh, yeah." *Now what?* He took a deep breath. "Do you have any plans for tonight?"

"No. What do you have in mind?"

What I have in mind I won't do. "I thought you might like to come over; I can fix us something to eat and we can talk." *And maybe you can tell me why you're not really married even though you are.* "Do you have any food preferences?"

"Not really," she said. "I'll bring some stuff and we can do it together, okay?"

Is that a double entendre? "Sure, great."

***

Sue Costello walked into Frank Donnelly's flat and handed him a bag. "Here're some groceries. Let's get some things going and put the rest into the fridge and maybe talk inside." *Clean-shaved, khaki pants, nicely pressed subdued plaid collared shirt. Great looking guy.*

Wow, she looks great in jeans. Nice sweater. Love the sneakers. "I've a chicken in the oven," he said, "but that's pretty automatic. Would you like something to drink?"

"A beer, please."

"You are indeed from the neighborhood," he laughed.

The packages put away, Frank gave Sue a tour of his place. As they walked back into the living room, beers in hand, he said, "That's it—Chez Donnelly."

"Very nice," she said, "clean, neat, well-kept. I'm impressed." *And I am. He's not a slob. This place is immaculate. The flowers are a great touch.*

They sat on the long couch, their beers and some crackers and cheese on the coffee table in front of them.

"So, Frank," she said with a smile, "tell me what you're doing at Maqua and what you're doing to Bob." She picked up her longneck and took a pull.

"Yeah, right," he laughed. He then gave her the rundown on the Portable Electric Chair and how it had occurred. He added the details of Bob Dingmann's performance with Nick Jackson, the dinner the evening before that, and his subsequent attempts to undercut him and Collins at every opportunity.

"He pissed his pants? Oh good grief." She shook her head and covered her mouth. "Tell me, Frank, how did we get to this state?"

He blinked. "Dingmann and me?"

"Not really, Frank," she said. "Oh, he's part of it. I mean what's happened in the last ten years ago that's brought us to this place where we're legally electrocuting people in drive-up vans." She drank more beer.

"Where do you want me to start?"

"I'll leave that up to you." She looked down.

She's lonely. I've been blind. "Ten years ago there was a simpler unquestioning innocence. We've seen the almost blanket rejection of the conventional values we grew up with. The assumptions of the old order are undermined and…" *Over to you.*

"The counterculture looms largest," she said. "They've triggered the generational conflicts of the last decade." She turned to him. "I see them in and around the hospital. Their dress and behavior are in-your-face affronts to the more staid, traditional values of the old status quo and the government they are attempting to transform."

Sharp, but I knew that. "The silent majority," Frank said, "is uniting to force the civil authorities to act against these challenges. The local execution laws are a way to meet the 'movement people' with a fury of their own. The Portable Electric Chair is merely the means to the end."

"It's all about control, isn't it?" She took a cracker and put some cheese on it.

Perfect summary. "The battle lines are drawn and the inevitable bloody conflicts have come to pass. What's going on is an attempt to restore equilibrium."

"All you need is love," she sang.

He laughed. "I think the chicken's probably ready. Let's eat."

***

"Well, that was a great collaborative effort," Sue said. They had cleaned up the dishes and had walked back into the living room. "The chicken was delicious and all the accompaniments were perfect." They stood by the sofa, neither one sitting, both looking at the floor.

Better make the first gesture. "Have a seat, Sue. Can I get you another beer?"

"I'd love one." *I need the courage for the next conversation.*

Frank returned with the beers and he sat and clinked his longneck with Sue's. "Sláinte."

"Sláinte," she said. She drank some beer and cleared her throat. "I said I'd tell you why I don't think Bob and I are married." She glanced up at the ceiling.

"You don't have to do this," Frank said.

"I do. I at least owe this to you." *And to myself.*

Frank leaned forward and gave her a tender kiss on the cheek. "Go ahead."

"I think the best way to start is by telling you where we spent our honeymoon." She twisted her wedding ring.

"Where'd you go?"

"Cape Cod." She drank some beer.

"Cape Cod's nice. Where on the Cape?"

"Provincetown." Tears welled and she looked down. "It was horrible," she murmured. "I was paraded in front of his friends like a trophy. He was courteous and considerate, a poster husband. Until we were alone." She shook her head, fighting the memory.

"Do you…?"

"Yes, Frank, I have to."

"What did he do?"

"Nothing." She spoke in a rush. "He, he, never touched me. He said he couldn't bring himself to; that he wasn't wired that way. He thought being married would change things. It didn't. He admitted he was gay and how he now needed me for appearance's sake."

"It was a threat?" Below the table, Donnelly's fists tightened.

"It was and it wasn't." She shuddered, eyes brimming. "He said it was to our mutual benefit. Maqua Hospital likes people in stable relationships—marriage, if you will. And Ilium…well, you know how Ilium is up here. He hasn't touched me in our two years of marriage."

Two years? Why did she let that happen? He swallowed and wet his lips. "I have to ask, Sue, why have you let it go on so long?"

"I was afraid," she said. To Frank's quizzical glance she added, "I had accepted the job at Maqua Hospital; they would have frowned on a divorce so soon after a marriage and the new position. Moral turpitude is still a factor up here. I just let it slide…"

"For two years?" *I'm repeating myself, for Christ's sake.*

"I wasn't that experienced." She threw her hands up. "Oh, I wasn't a virgin, but barely not. Me, a doctor, in a profession where everyone plays grab-ass, I was Miss Prissy. Can you believe? There, there was no one else, Frank. I took the marriage vows seriously, fool that I am."

"Did Bob have a physiological problem?"

"No. He can get it up, but only for a man," Her eyes bulged. "He's a queer, Frank. I don't give two hoots about his lifestyle, but for Christ's sake why marry me?" She finished the beer, stood and went into the kitchen. She came back with two more.

She still needs to get sorted but I could get it up for her. Right now, as a matter of fact. "Thanks," he said as he rose and took the beer. He took a swig and put it down.

"My problem, Frank, is I got used to living that way." She stood, a foot between them, beer in hand. She took a drink and put it on the table. "I guess my two years in the convent prepared me. I dove into my work and sailed along. Until…"

"Until what?"

"Until the night I saw you at Bonta's Restaurant," she said, and pulled him to her.

Danger, Will Robinson. I could be lost in the embrace. He resisted for a second before he put his arms around her. They were two statues, not moving. After five minutes he whispered, "This isn't right."

"What isn't right is the last two years," she snapped, and put her tongue in his ear.

Oh that feels so good, I want to take her right now, I want to… He felt her hands running down his back and along his buttocks. His hands began to move along the same path.

Several minutes later she broke away and led him to the couch. She gently kissed his closed lips.

What's wrong with this picture? We're making out like sixth graders and I'm the one resisting. Scruples? I can't resist much longer. Do I want to resist? Her hand moved up his leg and rested on his crotch, moving back and forth. His lips opened and the resulting kiss was long, her tongue deep in his mouth.

Their hands were all over each other and clothes gradually came off. She was in her bra and panties and he was in a tee and boxers. He drew her close and looked into her eyes. "Are you sure, Sue?"

"I've never been as sure of anything as I am of this. Let's go inside." she said, smiling at his visible arousal.

Hand in hand they walked into the bedroom. They stood by the bed and finished undressing each other. "Hold me, Frank; I don't know why, but I'm anxious."

"You're so beautiful, you take my breath away," he said, moving into her embrace. "I don't want to let you go."

For a half hour they kissed and explored each other until Sue whispered into Frank's ear, "I want you. Now."

He obeyed.

Chapter Thirty-Six

"Well, that was interesting," said Donnelly. He and Collins walked out of Len Lovelace's conference room and started down a bustling corridor.

"Aren't career goals and objectives meetings always stimulating?" Collins lit a cigarette.

"Yeah, but this one was high-powered. Nick's personnel guy, Sukeforth; the head of Kenoten, Tweed; and the shrink, Dr. Kleinmann."

"At least we dressed up, not the usual slovenly Maqua duds." He turned to Donnelly. "The pocket handkerchief was a rather fastidious touch."

"Just trying to keep up. I noticed you ditched the Robert Hall suit for an upscale one."

Collins took a puff. "They thought they were asking tough questions," he said, "and being penetrating and determining our motives. I figured it'd be a lot trickier, but I faced more probing questions from Internal Affairs."

Donnelly laughed. "Oh, yeah. My father's questions about my nights out when I was in my teens would put these guys to shame."

"Do you think they got the answers they were looking for?"

"We struck the right note," Donnelly said, "between cool reserve and intellect and being gung-ho attaboy Ilium cheerleaders."

"Our Nick Jackson references told them he's the reason we're enthusiastic."

"Joyce can't complain."

"She shouldn't." They went through the door to the back stairs and started down. Little dust puffs rose with their descent. "Love the maintenance they do here."

"No one checks," said Donnelly. "The only people who ever use these are the managers who duck out early." He avoided some cigarette butts and gum wrappers. "Anyway, we knew Joyce put us up for Kenoten and Willets shot it down. Now we're back on the first string." They reached their floor.

"When does she want us in her office?"

"Tomorrow afternoon. Today they gave us the third degree. Then they told us about the phenomenal opportunity Kenoten represents and why we were fortunate to be given this chance so early in our careers, blah, blah, blah. She wants to tell us our options."

"What do you think they are?" Collins tapped an ash on the linoleum floor.

"We may be forced to make some decisions," said Donnelly.

"McGarry's tonight?" said Collins.

Donnelly nodded.

***

"Christ on a crutch," said Donnelly. He and Collins sat in a booth at McGarry's, a pitcher of Utica Club between them. "I can't believe they're out of Schaefer. Who runs out of Schaefer? This Utica Club tastes like the brewery is downhill from the panther cage at the zoo."

"True," said Collins, "but better than no beer."

"Not by much." Donnelly peered at his glass, watching the bubbles. "UC is not Schaefer. Or Rheingold, for that matter."

"Just drink one, then. Schaefer is the one beer to have if you're having more than one."

"Funny."

"I thought so. UC for me today, UC for me," Collins sang. "We didn't come here for a beer tasting. Get a pickled egg. Make you happy to be drinking any beer." He lit up. "Kenoten is ours if we want it, I suspect."

"We don't go, we're all but through at Ilium. Sounds to me like those gangster movies where they tell the guy if he tells the truth they won't kill him and you know they're lying. Joyce said we have a choice but I don't think we do. Once they decide, we don't get to decide. This is the part where you're in or you're out. So let's figure it like a business plan. Start with what we want. What do we want?"

"Make some dough, have some fun, meet some women, knock back a few drinks, travel the world." Collins blew smoke toward the web-encrusted ceiling. *Have I met the right woman?*

"Right. Live a reasonable life as asshole-free as possible." *Too bad Sue is married to one of the biggest ones. She could've been the one.* Donnelly drank his beer and made a face. "The problem is, as you rise in the ranks the asshole quotient expands."

"Maybe." Collins gestured with the cigarette. "Regardless, it's nice to get some appreciation for our accomplishments."

"Jentzky appreciates us," Donnelly muttered.

Collins tilted an eyebrow. "As long as we're a hit machine."

"Come on. He's from the neighborhood."

"He's also Jewish, as is anybody who's anybody in Tinseltown. Jewish is a way older neighborhood."

"So we stick with the goyim?"

"I'm not saying that," said Collins. "I'm merely trying to clarify which briar patch we'd be willing to dive into."

Donnelly leaned back. "I liked the feeling when we came up with *Felon Hunters*. Plus we made some serious cash. Don't forget, *Johnny Volt* is under contract."

"We can keep on writing shows and all that shit. I'm just saying we may not want to be in amongst the thorns and berries with those LA guys. They play by different rules."

"We could convert. Be the white Sammy Davis, Jr. and Jackie Wilson."

"This from someone whose father saw 'Irish Need Not Apply' signs?" Collins said. "Good luck. You'd never go home again. Your old man would tear you into the littlest pieces he could manage and scatter your remains all over Flatbush Avenue. And mine would do the same."

"You're right," said Donnelly. "Even Marv wouldn't like the conversion idea, cynic though he is. He busted our asses about Harriet and Emily becoming boxcars; he never mentioned those whiny, shrew princesses the gals from his synagogue turn into."

"Whoa! We're off track here." An ash flew from Collins's cigarette.

"You think? We've decided not to go to LA. Not to convert to Judaism. Keep writing pilots and not marry a Jewish American Princess."

"Well said. So, the next item is Kenoten? Another pitcher of UC?"

"After the first one and the goddamn pickled egg I can't taste anything anymore anyway."

***

Donnelly filled Collins's glass. "Do we hang with Nick Jackson's meritocracy?"

With a thank-you nod, Collins took a large gulp. "I'd say so. Hollywood is mostly inclusive or exclusionary based on money, hidden agendas, and, maybe, religion. Ilium, at least under Jackson, is easier to define. We can still consort with the Jentzky brothers and work out our creative muscles with less chance of being blackballed out of hand over something stupid."

"We'll have to be careful if we go down that path," Donnelly said. "Saul set up our dummy company with us nowhere near visible."

Collins laughed. "Bravo! Inside of a couple of pitchers we've considered three choices. One, Tinseltown. Two, Kenoten, and throw in with Nick. Three, into the woods somewhere and only come out once in a while when we produce a killer script treatment." He drummed his fingers. "And the decision is…?"

"We give Kenoten a shot."

"Deal." Collins took another drink. "In spite of the tech sheets and stupid ads for stuff nobody knows anything about, Ilium has been fun."

"Ilium maybe, but if I do well at Kenoten, part of my package is going to include getting out of Maqua. I'm sick of the dirty snow, tubby factory women, and drunken rednecks. I need my city back."

"A worthy goal to which we both aspire…"

"We're semi-agreed then," Donnelly said. "Bottoms up!" They clicked glasses. "Let's order some real food."

***

"To sum up, Nick," said Walt Sukeforth, "they are well-spoken and give a good impression in manner and appearance." He sipped his coffee. "Given their age, they're among the best candidates Tweed or I have seen."

Jackson made a note. "Where should they go after Kenoten?"

"I thought about that on the way down from Maqua," said Sukeforth. "Depends on how they do."

"Presume they're at or near the top," said Jackson.

"They will be," agreed Sukeforth. "I'm pretty sure they'll quit the company rather than go back to Maqua."

Jackson sat back.

Sukeforth spoke into the silence. "What do you think of Doremus's performance?"

"Adequate," said Jackson. "He hasn't developed a strong staff."

"Would you consider his reassignment in the next year or two?"

"Where?"

"Keep Joyce Locker in charge of the A&P department for a while longer. Bring Collins to New York, have him work with Doremus for a year and then send Doremus to A&P with an"— Sukeforth coughed—"'understanding' that within a year or so of working up in Maqua he's in line to be the next general manager. Collins would slot into Doremus's job and if he does well, the job expands."

He's taken time with this. Doremus is a bit of a stiff; Maqua might loosen him up. If not...might work. "What about the other one...Donnelly?"

"A little trickier," said Sukeforth. "He's a natural for GBC but a year in Washington under Stan Schuyler would round him enough to create an impact at GBC."

Makes sense. Networks are becoming embroiled in politics. "Good. I might add a wrinkle."

"Let me know," Sukeforth said. "These two are keepers. Either one of them could wind up running the company."

Jackson looked up. "I want to talk to someone about the Washington angle."

"Not Schuyler?"

"No," said Jackson. "I'm contemplating something else for both of them." He twisted his lips. "Thanks, Walt."

Sukeforth took the hint and left the office.

Jackson pressed the intercom. "Florence, get me Abe Floss."

***

"Okay, Nick." *Sniff.* "I'll speak to them." Locker placed the phone into the cradle and took a deep breath. *He wants me to stay as GM for at least two more years. Bring Doremus up here. Surrender the throne to him if…there was an if, wasn't there? An implication I can stay if I want to. I might just get to like this. Get real, Joyce. Well, we'll keep tabs on how things work out. Take the "interim" off the General Manager sign on my door.*

As for Donnelly and Collins, I felt they'd knocked it out of the park. The New York guys agreed; so did Lovelace. Their job rotation is well-thought-out. Better get Lovelace in here and we can tell them their possible futures at Ilium.

***

Locker placed her hands together. "Okay," she said, "let's begin." Collins and Len Lovelace sat opposite her at the table. "Len, why don't you summarize Sukeforth's recommendation?"

Lovelace put down his coffee cup. "You and Donnelly did well with Sukeforth, Tweed, and Dr. Kleinmann."

Collins smiled. *Kleinmann looked like a cross between Quasimodo and the loser in a dwarf toss. Smart bastard, though.* He lit a cigarette.

Sniff. "I guess you want to know what's in store for you."

"Might be helpful," said Collins, drawing in a lungful.

Lovelace finished his coffee. "Okay. First, everything is based on your doing well at Kenoten. You will be entering the four-month Future Executive Course. As you will find out, it's intensive as hell. The several segments focus on leadership, manager development, innovation, strategy and business impact, and external influences." He stopped and lit a cigarette. "You'll be up against the best and brightest at Ilium."

Is that supposed to intimidate me? Collins stared past Lovelace.

Locker said softly, "The assignments, Len."

"Jim," he said, "You will be transferred to New York and will eventually be working for Tyler Doremus."

"You said 'eventually.' Can you explain?" Collins tapped an ash.

"For roughly the next year you'll work in six-month segments for Abe Floss and Justin Hitchcock. You start with Floss and Frank with Hitchcock. After six months you switch. After that, you're assigned to Doremus.

The DC angle is the unusual part. "Floss and Hitchcock are the ultimate political power brokers. Whose idea was this?"

"Nick Jackson's," said Locker. "He thinks enough of you two that he wants you to have a broad perspective—a first for Ilium."

Nick Jackson? Holy shit, this is a good thing. Not too shabby a slogan either, minus the holy shit, of course. "Any plans for Doremus?"

Shrewd question. "He'll be your boss after you finish with Floss and Hitchcock," Lovelace said. "The rest remains to be determined."

Pretty obvious. Best not to pursue. "What about Frank?"

"We'll discuss that with him," said Lovelace. "The first year is the same for both of you. You and Frank will be based in New York. You're on expense account in DC."

Answers one big question. "Can you tell me this? Are we going to be in competition with one another?"

"No," said Lovelace.

Locker nodded. *At least not in the beginning years.*

Collins understood the fast-track opportunity with which he had been presented. "Not to be crass, but what is the financial side?"

For the next ten minutes Lovelace laid out the financial package: pay grade jump, bonuses, stock options, and other perks. He sat back and stubbed out his fourth cigarette. "Questions?"

"When does Kenoten start?"

"Six weeks," said Lovelace. "You can finish up here, get a place in New York, and take some vacation."

Neither Lovelace nor Locker added anything. "I'm honored. I'm sure I'll have more questions." *Like what about you and me, Joyce?* Collins took a final puff on his cigarette, shook hands with Lovelace and Locker, and walked out.

"Joyce, were we listening to the same wiseass Collins?" said Lovelace, "Or was he replaced?"

"He's practicing for Kenoten and New York," said Locker with a chuckle. "Let's get Donnelly in here."

***

"Let me summarize," said Donnelly. "I start Kenoten in six weeks, during which time I finish up here, get housing in the city and use up some vacation, and do Kenoten for four months. Jackson bypassed Stan Schuyler and his crew; Jim and I spend a year on six-month alternating assignments with Abe Floss and Justin Hitchcock. After, Jim goes to Doremus. I go to GBC in a position yet to be determined but on a level with Jim's. Either News or Programming. Neither one of us has to relocate to the Washington office." He glanced at Lovelace.

Lovelace nodded.

Sniff. "There are no two sharper guys who know the political scene and how the system works than Floss and Hitchcock. Mr. Democrat and Mr. Republican. You're lucky, Frank."

"I'm aware of that," said Donnelly, "and am grateful for the opportunity." He sipped his Coke. "What about remuneration?"

Lovelace repeated what he said to Collins.

"Acceptable," Donnelly said, straight-faced.

"Anything else?" said Locker.

"I'm sure I'll have questions, said Donnelly, standing. "Thank you for the opportunity." He shook hands and left Locker's office.

"Same as Collins," said Lovelace. "Took a politeness pill before he came in here."

Sniff.

Chapter Thirty-Seven

Outside the Pittsfield, Massachusetts, courtroom, Donald Quite brushed back an errant hair. The director signaled and the camera's red light went on. "In the seemingly unending weeks of his trial, a shackled Guy Pearson sat as the prosecution built its case. The trial continues despite countless interruptions by the defense, objections by the prosecution, one sidebar conference after another and the sometimes amusing, sometimes annoying theatrics of Pearson's defense attorney father, the estimable Clint Pearson. Now the 'Trial of the Decade,' as some call it, appears to be drawing to an end. The closing arguments are made, and Judge George Robertson has instructed the jury."

The camera showed a large group of people across the street. Signs saying "Fry Guy" and "Hang Guy High" were prominent. Quite spoke over the images. "The crowd outside the courtroom, held back by the barricades, has reached its own verdict. The prosecution seems to agree; they argued for the death penalty."

He spotted Clint Pearson coming down the steps of the courthouse. He gestured to his cameraman and called out, "Clint, how do you feel now that the case is gone to the jury?"

Pearson recognized Quite. "We are confident, Don, they will acquit my son of these false and heinous accusations."

"What did you think of the atmosphere in the courtroom?"

Clinton shook his head, his ponytail whipping behind him. "This courtroom had the appearance of an armed camp. I noted to Judge Robertson the Supreme Court ruled the appearance of an armed camp is a reversible error. It can be deemed prejudicial and the verdict overturned."

"What was the judge's response?"

"He considered the security precautions adequate and appropriate." Pearson stifled a cough.

"Any comment on the exchange between Guy and the prosecutor when Guy was being led back to his cell? I believe your son informed the prosecutor his entry on Who's Who was three times longer than the prosecutor's. The prosecutor's response was, 'I hope you get a better obituary.'"

"I heard no such comment," Pearson said.

Quite's director moved his hand across his throat, signaling him to wrap up.

"Thank you, Clint. And now these messages."

***

Abe Floss's phone rang that evening.

"Did you watch GBC's televising of the Guy Pearson trial?" Justin Hitchcock asked.

"A ratings smash," Floss replied. He sipped his scotch. "It's the highest-rated show on daytime TV. Their prime-time summary is ranked number one. Not too bad for Quite's career either."

"Indeed," said Hitchcock, "Quite returns from limbo." Floss heard the tinkle of ice. "How do you think the jury will find?"

Floss thought for a minute. "The evidence against Guy seems overwhelming and despite Clint Pearson's antics, the judge rules with a firm hand. I say guilty."

"I agree," said Hitchcock. "The jurors didn't respond well to Pearson's style of defense. This is Pittsfield; the jury is not urban and sophisticated, and the prosecution correctly speculated women would be sympathetic to a woman as the victim. I also say guilty. Meanwhile the judge is being criticized for allowing TV cameras into the courtroom."

"The newspapers I'm reading," said Floss, "say the trial is a media circus and the judge isn't doing enough to regulate the court proceedings."

Hitchcock laughed. "Yet they continue to report on the story. For all their whining the newspapers are giving heavy coverage. The *Boston Globe* has the case on the front page every day of the trial. It's on the front page of the *Times* every other day. The coverage in the New York tabloids is excessive. Even with the GBC lock on the live coverage, the other networks' nightly news broadcasts give more airtime to the case than to anything else."

"Which means Nick Jackson's bet paid off big."

"And the two hotshots who dreamed up the idea will be working for us for a year after they finish the Ilium management course. Give me their names again?"

The sound of a rustling paper could be heard through the phone. "Jim Collins and Frank Donnelly," said Floss. "You read the files Nick sent over?"

"I did," said Hitchcock. "The Bronx and Brooklyn, Catholic commuter colleges; those young men have gone far beyond their education."

"A very Republican assessment," said Floss drily.

"Got me," chuckled Hitchcock. "To be serious for a moment, they seem cut from a different cloth."

"They're smart, clever, and with good political instincts," said Floss, "the primary one being how not to get mad but to get even."

"So how will we handle them?"

"Show them the ropes, be open, trust their discretion, and hope they'll be powerful allies down the road." Floss finished his drink.

"Perhaps we should talk with them before they leave for Kenoten," said Hitchcock.

"Good idea, Justin," said Floss. "I'll give Jackson a call and make arrangements."

"Good," said Hitchcock. "I anticipate meeting them. I'll set something up at the Union League Club." More ice tinkled. "If I remember correctly, their plan also included a public execution of Pearson in an Ilium Electric Chair."

"Under the new laws the judge could rule that way," said Floss. "It could happen rather quickly; within days of the verdict."

"The audience would be huge," Hitchcock said.

"A Harvard man would be getting the volts, not some low-life career criminal." Floss chuckled. "Yes, proof the new laws apply to all classes."

"A mildly amusing interpretation, Abe," said Hitchcock. "Let me know Jackson's thoughts about our meeting those fellows." He broke the connection.

***

"You're running late. Locker wants us in her office."

"Did you watch Guy Pearson's electrocution last night?" Collins put his coffee on his desk and leaned over the wall.

"Pearson surprised me when he started crying for his mother," Donnelly said.

"Brought a tear to the eye," said Collins, coming out of his cubicle. "Happened right before he started twitching and shuddering when they threw the switch. Think the Pearson hot squat made ratings go off the charts?"

"Given the public's newfound lust for frontier justice, I can only presume so."

"Agree," said Collins. "What's Locker want?"

"Don't know. She's the big kahuna now; she needs to pay attention to all sorts of crap." They walked down the hallway.

Joyce Locker sat behind her desk as Donnelly and Collins stood in the doorway. She waved them in. *Sniff.* "When do you two leave for Kenoten?"

"In five weeks. Why?"

"Your dance card's filling up. Nick Jackson called me last night and told me he'd gotten a call from Abe Floss." She hesitated.

"Is this a test?" asked Collins.

Sniff.

"Democrat power broker," said Donnelly.

"Unbeknownst to most people, Floss joined up with his Republican counterpart, Justin Hitchcock." Collins lit a cigarette.

"To ease the way to fight crime and or evil with special laws, thus allowing dirtbags like Guy Pearson to get fried *magna cum celeritate.*" Donnelly sat back.

"Loosely translated, Joyce," said Collins, "really fucking fast with minimal bullshit."

Sniff. "Well, at least you know the background since you'll be having dinner with them."

"Oh?" asked Collins.

"Messrs. Floss and Hitchcock told Nick they'd like to meet you two. With Nick's blessing you'll be dining with them at the Union League Club in the evening of the Wednesday after next."

"Tells us Hitchcock is the host," said Donnelly. "The Union League is old money, which Hitchcock is."

"If Floss hosted it'd be the Harmonie; after all it's designed by Sanford White, the second most historic social club in the city, more ethnically appropriate while still allowing for discreet screening during application," said Collins. "Who else will be there?"

"Just the four of you." *Sniff.* "You guys'll be in your comfort zone." *Sniff.*

Collins and Donnelly walked out of Locker's office, bemused looks on their faces. "Well, well, the Union League Club," Collins said. "We've landed on the private runway and are taxiing to the privileged hangar." He stopped and lit a cigarette.

"With the Hitchcock imprimatur they'll even let us in the door."

"Will wonders never cease?" Collins exhaled a stream of smoke toward the dust-inlaid ceiling tiles. "Think they'll let Floss in?"

"A day pass, I'm sure." They reached their cubicles. "Back to the mundane." Donnelly picked up a folder. "I'm heading down to get together with the guy who's trying to build an electric tractor."

"Five hundred pounds of batteries and a range of fifty yards or fifteen minutes, whichever comes first, right?"

Donnelly grinned. "Pretty much."

Chapter Thirty-Eight

A car horn blared as the taxi cut it off and pulled to the curb on East 37th Street outside the Union League Club. Donnelly and Collins stepped out. "Pretty impressive exterior," said Collins. The symmetrical Georgian red brick façade replicated familiar motifs from Park Avenue brownstone mansions but on a grand ten-story scale.

"Built in the thirties," said Donnelly. "Even during the Depression these folks could afford something like this."

"Nice entrance. Plenty of dark wood."

"Better stairs," said Donnelly, looking at the dramatically curved twin stairways. "Rather grandiose; nothing symbolizes power, wealth, and status in this town more than open floor space. Definitely built to impress."

"Or intimidate," said Collins. "They flatter their sense of their own good taste. Perhaps like Hitchcock and Floss?"

A white-gloved attendant approached and scanned them through rheumy eyes. "May I help you gentlemen?"

"Mr. Donnelly and Mr. Collins to see Mr. Hitchcock," said Collins.

He glanced at a list. "Yes, he and Mr. Floss await you in the library." He turned and another white-gloved attendant materialized. "Roger will escort you."

They nodded.

"I'll inform Mr. Hitchcock you are here." The attendant picked up a phone and spoke softly.

"We're early, aren't we?" said Collins, glancing at this watch. "Five minutes," said Donnelly. "Better early than late."

***

Roger ushered them into the library. He guided them past floor-to-ceiling bookcases to a table by the fireplace where two white-haired men sat, a cane propped by the chair of the older man. The other one rose. "I'm Abe Floss. Justin and I are pleased you could join us." He gestured to the two remaining chairs. "Please, take a seat."

"Excuse me for not rising, gentlemen." Hitchcock signaled to Roger, who approached. "Drinks? Abe and I are working on a couple of Maker's Marks."

This is an interview. Rule number one: don't drink during an interview. "Thank you, Mr. Hitchcock, I'll have a club soda with a twist of lime, please," said Collins.

"I'll have the same, Mr. Hitchcock," said Donnelly.

Hitchcock acknowledged with an ironic curl of his mouth and a glance to Roger.

They exchanged pleasantries while the drinks were served. With a liver-spotted hand, Hitchcock put his glass down. "I'd like to set some ground rules before we begin."

"Of course."

"You are aware," said Hitchcock, "Abe Floss and I come from different segments of the political spectrum. We talk from time to time and maintain a cordial relationship. Nick Jackson brought your names to our attention, and we agreed it could be good for all of us to have you work with us for six months each upon completion of Kenoten. You'd give us some fresh thinking; we might afford you some perspectives on the political process." He paused. "We prefer you not discuss this meeting or your assignment with anyone other than Nick Jackson and"—he took a note from his pocket—"Joyce Locker. Do you concur?"

"Yes," they both said.

"Glad that's settled," said Floss, with a smile. "You gentlemen are off to Kenoten soon. What do you hope to achieve?"

"I liken it to officer training," said Donnelly. "We've been through basic, which is the program we were on. Among other abilities, Kenoten should sharpen our leadership and managerial skills."

"And the more important?" said Floss.

"Leadership," said Collins, "although aspects of that cannot be taught. Management techniques are what I would call a mechanical skill, more easily absorbed."

"Sartre said 'hell is other people.'" Donnelly sipped his drink. "Leadership skills allow one to take a disparate group and unite them toward a given set of objectives."

"Kenoten should," said Collins, "let us build relationships with Ilium's future movers and shakers." He smiled. "That's Realpolitik."

"And exposure to its current executives," added Donnelly. "One of Kenoten's singular advantages. There's a name which applies, but not in polite company."

Hitchcock chuckled. "Interesting analysis."

"More cogent than most we hear," said Floss, straight-faced.

***

The fire crackled, the small flame exuding gentle warmth. Hitchcock and Floss were on their second round of drinks. Donnelly and Collins sipped club sodas.

Floss tossed out an open-ended question. "What do either of you think of the state of politics today?"

This is a test. Donnelly glanced at Collins and said, "Television is changing the game. The Nixon-Kennedy debates proved that. Kennedy won on TV and Nixon on the radio. Over time the more physically unattractive the candidate the less viable he will be. Lincoln or FDR couldn't run in this day and age."

"Negative advertising is replacing civil discourse," Collins said. "Remember when the Democrats ran the Daisy ad, the atom bomb mushroom filled the screen? Unbelievably successful. They positioned Goldwater as someone who would lead us into nuclear Armageddon."

"Politics will become more divisive," said Donnelly, "and single-issue politics will drive the process. You saw the beginnings with the riots in Chicago."

"My way or the highway," Collins said. "Political parties will cooperate less and less." He sipped his club soda.

"The increasing use of opinion polls is another trend," said Donnelly. "They'll turn candidates into platitude-mouthing androids. Every verb and sentence will be parsed and neutered. The press will seize on mistakes, personal idiosyncrasies, and gossip. The media, particularly broadcast journalists, will become the kingmakers."

Collins puffed. "This may take a while to come about, but it will."

"You paint a dark picture, gentlemen," said Hitchcock.

"We thought we'd be candid; this is the way we look at things." Donnelly shrugged.

"We're glad you do," said Floss; Hitchcock nodded in agreement. "Too often all we get are clichés and requests for favors. We need hard-nosed analysis."

"Do either of you have any comments about the Guy Pearson electrocution?" Floss asked.

Collins took a deep drag on his cigarette. "Many people were surprised Pearson was actually electrocuted. No one ever thought that someone with his family wealth and social position would be sentenced to death."

"Mr. Donnelly?"

Inwardly, Donnelly sighed. *Do I give my real opinion? Yeah. We'll soon be working for them.* "This might be the beginning of the end; the laws are achieving their effect. Crime is down and balance is being restored. Not immediately, but the pendulum will swing back. Hollywood will produce movies and TV shows themed with the renegade aspects of this new approach. Not enough due process, for example. The media will go back to its old ways. Attitudes will begin to shift."

"Anything to add, Mr. Collins?"

"Too many lawyers are in Congress and the trial lawyer lobby is too powerful to let all the lost paydays go for too long."

Floss glanced at Hitchcock. "An accurate breakdown, I would say."

Hitchcock nodded. "Quite. What triggered these draconian laws?"

Collins rested his cigarette in the ashtray. "The Nixon assassination attempt. Its unintended consequence was to energize the country, the so-called silent majority if you will, into forcing the issue about doing something about crime."

"Indeed," said Hitchcock. "If I'm not mistaken, it also created a market for Ilium products like the Portable Electric Chair." He reached for his cigar. "Of which you gentlemen played a prominent part."

Floss turned to Donnelly, inviting a comment.

"The silent majority achieved," Donnelly said, "the successful pursuit of justice, something long denied them, in their opinion." He picked up his drink. "We believe you gentlemen played a part in making that happen."

Hitchcock turned to Floss and winked. "Mr. Collins, do you have any other thoughts regarding the attempt on Nixon?"

"I thought the shooting ill-conceived; the perpetrators didn't think logically."

"Why?" Floss lit a cigarette.

"Kill Nixon and Agnew becomes president." Collins sat back. "Probably not something those folks considered; Agnew would have jacked up the effort in Vietnam."

"What about Nixon?" asked Hitchcock, blowing smoke toward the fireplace.

"Nixon wants out; doesn't think it's his war," Donnelly said. "He campaigned in '68 to end the draft. He wants to pin everything on the Democrats."

"He's signed draft extensions," said Floss.

"The war is costing the country a fortune," said Donnelly. "Guns and butter aren't viable. It is being attempted, though, with no apparent consequences." He waited a beat. "Yet."

"What consequences?" said Floss.

"Expansive social programs combined with a massive military effort mean enormous debt for the country, which could lead to very high inflation," Donnelly said.

"Well," said Hitchcock, "politicians, whether they are the president or in Congress, come to power to stay in power, and to the extent they can, keep control of the money. The corollary is they need votes and will do what is expedient to get those votes."

Floss put his drink down. "Everyone wants to feed at the trough. Inflationary deficits are built into the federal budget. They're for the next guys to worry about."

"Meaning no disrespect," said Collins, "but Mark Twain's observation seems correct."

Floss and Hitchcock traded bemused glances. Floss looked up. "Which was?"

"'There is no distinctly native American criminal class.'" Collins paused. "'Except Congress.'"

Floss and Hitchcock burst out laughing. "We should write that down," said Hitchcock.

"Twain already did," said Floss.

Hitchcock took his cane and thrust himself up. "On that note, let us adjourn to the dining room and talk of more general things."

***

"What did you think?" asked Floss after Donnelly and Collins had said their good-byes and left.

"I liked them." Floss took a pull on his cigar. "They're not quite what one would have thought, given their backgrounds."

Hitchcock smiled. "That's the kind of stereotyping one would attribute to me, not you." Floss wagged his cigar in acknowledgment. "Quoting Sartre and Mark Twain in the same conversation is noteworthy, Abe."

"I thought," said Floss, "the most entertaining part of the conversation was the dinner discussion of the most evil people of the twentieth century."

"Yes. A remarkable perspective. Hitler, Stalin, and Walter O'Malley. Even Collins, the Bronx boy, said Horace Stoneham and the Giants would never have gone West if he'd been sober and understood what O'Malley was getting him into."

"A fundamental truth in all that," said Hitchcock, "but Mayor Wagner and Bob Moses also caused it. Moses turned O'Malley down cold because he wanted to build a parking garage where O'Malley wanted to build a new stadium. Wagner didn't intervene."

He sipped his wine. "Our future employees are everything we thought they were and more: smart, analytical, articulate, well-mannered."

Floss, raising his wineglass. "And witty, tough and charming. I look forward to their arrival."

***

"An interesting time," said Donnelly, "great food and two noteworthy people."

"Stimulating discussion. They seemed genuinely surprised about our response to the most evil people of the twentieth century."

"They may have even come round to our way of thinking."

"I guess we'll work for them then?"

"Yeah. Now let's get a drink. I'm parched."

Chapter Thirty-Nine

Morning, kemosabe." Donnelly leaned on the end of Collins's cubicle partition. "You seem overly busy."

Collins's chair squeaked as he rolled back. "I'm laboring mightily on a brochure copy for the new core-wrapping feature of Ilium DC motors. Film at eleven, in case you want to tune in." He pulled a cigarette from a pack. "Your thoughts on anything this fine day?" Outside, a cold rain spattered down.

Donnelly waved away the smoke. "Something we may have forgotten, a detail we should deal with before we depart these sodden shores for Kenoten."

Collins puffed. "Let me take a wild guess. Dismantle our clandestine surveillance network. It's occurred to me as well. We've just been so damn busy…" He blew smoke. "Shit."

"Empty for fifty years," said Donnelly. "Now we have to get up there again in the same decade with all the dirt and mutant bugs."

"Do we leave the wires, pull the microphones and recording equipment and call it good?" Collins stared up at the ceiling.

"Suppose some maintenance guy working on the phones finds the wiring and figures it out?"

"Yeah, you're right." Collins shrugged. "Let's set a tear-down date. The less of a trail, the safer we are in our new hideout."

"What's with the Lone Ranger dialogue?"

"Sorry, I was noodling an idea for a TV series. Kind of a modern day sheriff in New York City. I was calling it, *Sheeney's Bluff,* but I'm stuck. I don't know what perverted muse made me think I could write a goddamn Western."

"Sheeny? A rather insensitive slang term given the ethnicity of the power brokers and decision makers in New York and LA, don't you think?"

Collins grunted. "I wasn't even thinking of slang terms. More like a play on Sheehan or some similar name."

"Dangerous, Jim." He stopped while a freight train rumbled noisily outside.

"Back to current reality. I told Locker I'd sit with her and discuss the lawn tractor campaign tonight at Bonta's." To Donnelly's look he said, "She's buying." *Maybe we can talk about us. Or maybe I'll be delivering a little bit later at my place.*

"Okay," said Donnelly, "we'll remove the taping system tomorrow night. Won't take us any time at all. We'll stick the wires in the basement archive room."

Collins nodded. "Cox can turn all the electronics back into whatever she made them out of and we're done. If anyone else comes along who's as smart and nefarious as us, at least the wiring will be precut for them."

Donnelly chuckled and went silent.

Collins had seen Donnelly's thousand-yard stare often enough to recognize something was up. "Uh, Frank?"

"I'm contemplating your elegant phrasing, 'anyone as smart and nefarious as us.' No such animal in the trainee group, but in management? Leeson, Dingmann, and some of the other midlevel guys are idiots, true. But Burt Rawley was a crafty, manipulative son of a bitch. I can only presume his predecessors also were. Gifting that capability to carry on the S-O-B tradition in Maqua would be a superb last hurrah."

Collins stubbed his cigarette. "A vision approaching the divine." He pounded his desk. "You're not thinking about..."

"Bingo. Woman of the hour, Advertising and Promotion's fearless leader, Joyce Locker." Donnelly grinned. "I'll bet she's liking the power chair. Let's give her some help so she stays."

"Good idea." *Do I want her to stay? Do I want her with me or at least close to me?*

Chapter Forty

Joyce Locker sat at her desk. The bright light of a cloudless morning slanted through her newly cleaned windows. Staring at the sun-blotched carpet she drifted, daydreaming. She shook her head and turned her gaze to the furnishings and trappings.

Bad time for Pat to take vacation. She got Clare Duckett to fill in for her; she's got excellent administrative skills. Those bastards assigned full blame to her for the actions of the higher-ups who enjoyed her charms. No one's aware I interceded on her behalf. They were going to make her take sex addiction counseling until I reminded them they were wide open for a lawsuit. I hope she's figured out that "Clare, give us a suck, would you?" is not part of a secretarial job description. Wonder if she feels awkward about being back here. Husband will be gone for a long time; someone said she's already filed for divorce. Don't blame her.

She lit a cigarillo. *This job brought some surprises, like the headaches of a department head. I underestimated the constant whining and jockeying, the tedium of the endless green-striped computer printouts and the incessant budget review meetings. Even so, I think I could get to enjoy this. Willets was stupid. Couldn't keep it in his pants. I wonder what challenges will come my way? Something out of the blue like the maneuvers of Donnelly and Collins? Especially Collins. I'm the Big Dog now, like they said. I should tell Lovelace to find more guys like them. If we don't, we won't see their like anytime again soon.*

She puffed on the cigarillo and basked in the welcome warmth. *What am I hearing? Annoying. Low. Mechanical. Insistent. A train? Some new process or test in the next building? No sounds nearby.* She turned, her bracelet jangling, and tried to pinpoint the strange intrusive noise.

She zeroed in on the wall-mounted bookcase behind her desk. She opened the doors of the cupboard at the base. Nothing. She cocked her head to listen better.

The sound came from behind the second row of books. She picked up a magazine, rolled it and swept several volumes off the second shelf, poising to strike. A compact metal box hunkered in the space she'd cleared behind the books strewn on the floor. *Okay, a reel-to-reel tape recorder.* She moved the box and found the wire threaded through the back of the bookcase. She pulled more books off the shelf. *Ah, the headset. Let's do a random check.* She put one of its earphones to her ear and plugged into the jack on top of the recorder.

A door closing and muffled conversation. She fiddled with the controls and a burst of sound followed. "...Bob, you said Kenoten was certain. You promised." *Whiny voice. Sounds like Quentin Rhodes. Must be in Dingmann's office.* "After all we've meant to each other." *Christ, he's talking in clichés.*

"Quentin, it was a done deal." *Dingmann.* "Willets had signed off. You were on your way. But Lou was caught banging Burt Rawley's leftover, Clare Duckett, and all bets were off. Joyce nixed my recommendation."

"And she endorsed those two unwashed creatures, Donnelly and Collins. Oh, Bob, I'm so, so, bereft." *Bereft? Code between these two? Will this lead to something else?* "Kenoten would have so helped my career."

"There, there, Quentin, everything will be fine." *He sounds soothing. So unlike him.*

"You're so strong for me, Bob."

"Nothing I wouldn't also do for Spencer and Chase." *Hmmm, Spencer Holdsworth and Chase Winchester.* She fiddled with the headphone. "You know you're my special one, Bob." *Oh no, don't tell me Rhodes is…*

"The office is not the place for this type of discussion. What we say and do in private should not be discussed here. Walls have ears, Quentin." *Dingmann too?*

"Thank you, Bob, of course you're right. Decorum is all-important. It's just so frustrating. Arrgghh. Donnelly and Collins? Anyone but them."

"Perhaps we should handle this off-site, Quentin, where we can both be more comfortable."

"I could use some comforting, Bob. I'm sure you need some too."

She stopped the tape and put the headphones down. *Dingmann's dirty little secret. I wonder if his wife is for show?* She went to put the headphones back on. A noise came from the outer office. *Must be Clare. She's early, nothing else for her to do. Better put this stuff away and come back later.*

She sat back and laughed to herself. *I wonder how many of my predecessors used this tool? Now, whenever I hear Dingmann's arrogant and condescending voice I'll visualize him and Rhodes. That stuff won't fly in this day and age and in this place. Dingmann better play ball with me.*

Locker realized the value of her discovery. The odd decisions and byzantine maneuverings of Rawley and his predecessors took on a new light. She decided to allot time to review the tapes and to keep fresh ones. *Forewarned is forearmed.*

There was a knock on the door. "Come in."

Clare Duckett entered, memo pad in hand. "Anything you'd like me to set up for today, Ms. Locker?"

"Not right now, Clare, thank you."

"Can I get you some coffee and a pastry?"

"Black coffee and a plain donut. Get the same for yourself." She handed her some bills.

"Thank you," she said.

I wonder if any of these horny males out there will ask her out. She's also warm and zaftig and has a good heart. Rawley had her, Willets had her. They took advantage? She's good-looking, lonely, and available. Maybe I can get her an introduction to some gentlemanly companion from Maqua who doesn't work for Ilium. Someone who will show her some love and respect. Would that be appropriate? She made a note in her day timer.

We all deserve a little happiness, me included. God knows Collins and Donnelly's antics have turned my life upside-down. But I have to say I'm in a better place. I'm numero uno now. I think I'm almost content. At least professionally.

What about personal happiness? Well, there's Jim, whom I am getting to really care for. I had no life outside this company until he came into my life, I have needs, too. I wouldn't mind a few innings on the inner spring with him right here and now. Careful, Joyce, at least not on company property.

Chapter Forty-One

L'Fey was filling with the nighttime crowd when Collins arrived. He spotted Rufus Hogg staring mindlessly at the bar mirror. A cigarette dangled from his lips and an empty glass perched in front of him. Subdued conversations buzzed nearby.

"A beer for me and whatever my man Rufus here is having, Tappy," Collins said.

The tinkle of the drink splashing a double Jack Daniels over the ice cubes broke Hogg's reverie. He rested the cigarette in an ashtray, lifted the glass, and downed half. "Hey, Jim, thanks."

"No big deal." Collins took a first taste. "Where're Shepherd and Drake?"

"Said they'd be here; not yet, though." He sipped the Jack Daniels and picked up the cigarette. "No Donnelly?"

"He's back at the office; had an attack of industriousness. I expect he'll be through the door in a couple of minutes"

Hogg grunted and lapsed into silence.

Hmm, not the garrulous Rufus we all know. Something's bugging him. Collins finished his beer and ordered a martini.

Hogg had stewed since Joyce Locker's offhand crack about who could be at whose house while they downed drinks at L'Fey. Did he want to find out if innuendo was literal?

Mike Drake gave a wave and strolled over. "Rufe, my man, how ya doin'?" Drake was giving the full hearty: voice, backslap, and head rub.

"All raht, all raht." Hogg didn't have his heart in it. Not for the first time Collins wondered if Hogg learned to speak in some time-warped bayou.

"Jim," said Drake with a head bob, "a brew here and a round for my friends."

"Where's ol' Shepherd?" Hogg asked, jangling the ice in his glass.

"Off someplace." Drake stared at his drink.

Suspicion bloomed again in Hogg's mind. "Did he say where?"

"I'm not his momma, Rufe."

Collins sipped his drink. *Hogg's too interested by half.*

"Another round," said Hogg, "before I set out for home."

Sounds like Rufus is heading out. Collins frowned. *I hope Shepherd's not at his house with Anna May.*

Hogg finished the Jack Daniels in two gulps. Grim-faced, he said his good-byes and left.

I smell trouble. Do I follow him and prevent mayhem or do I stay and hear the headlines tomorrow? Damn. Collins threw some cash on the bar. "Tell Donnelly I had to go. Catch you later." He hurried out to the parking lot.

When Hogg related at L'Fey how he had done Bonnie Bilbie in his car and ranked the deed an enthusiastic six, Shepherd and Drake had pursued the titillating details. Collins figured Hogg wasn't laughing now as he contemplated Shepherd getting a piece of Anna May. *It was all hahaha until it was you.*

Collins had barely heard of Fireball Roberts and stock car competitions until he joined Ilium and came into contact with Hogg and the other good ol' boys. He soon learned that Fireball Roberts drove Fords. So did Hogg, who popped the trunk to his Ford Falcon. *Oh, Jesus, a shotgun? Where's Donnelly?*

Headlights wheeled into the parking lot. *Donnelly.* Collins hustled over, motioning for Donnelly to get back behind the wheel. "Follow that car," Collins yelled, as he piled in.

"Points off for the cliché," said Donnelly. "Who're we after?" he added, as he followed the taillights.

"Hogg. He suspects Shepherd is at his house with Anna May."

"So?"

"A moment ago he took a shotgun from the trunk and put the damn thing on the front seat."

"That's serious shit," said Donnelly. "Play it by ear?"

"Yeah. He lives in Old Town so we should be there in a minute."

"You know," said Donnelly, as they pulled into the neighborhood, "Shallenberger Lane here is named for the man who invented the watt hour meter and made electricity a paying proposition. Locker told me Old Town has a ton of such streets: Fermi Circle, Tesla Boulevard, Edison Way, Westinghouse Street, and the like. City management pictured itself magnanimous in these nods to industry greats. Nick Jackson thinks otherwise, since they founded Ilium competitors."

"Thanks for the lecture; you've told me everything I could give less of a crap about." Collins watched Hogg park, a house away from his flat. "My turn. That black wrought iron streetlight, now electrified, was no doubt candle or gas lit when Ben Franklin was almost fried by his kite. Oh, and Rufus isn't moving."

"He's debating his next move," Donnelly said. "And your bullshit was more inane than mine." He switched off the lights and pulled in several car lengths behind Hogg. He turned to Collins. "You want to distract him?"

"Sure."

"Good. I can check the house and if Shepherd is inside, get him the hell out the back door."

"Let's go." Collins got out and ambled toward Hogg's car. Donnelly slipped under the gloomy nighttime shadow of an elm tree and headed to Hogg's flat.

Collins was tapping on Hogg's passenger window and Donnelly was twenty feet from Hogg's house when the front door opened. Anna May Hogg lingered in a pool of light, an air of melancholy surrounding her. Her sorrowful countenance bestowed a strange dignity. A minute later Austin Shepherd appeared, buttoning his shirt. He pulled Anna May to him, kissed her passionately, and gave a fond squeeze to her crotch. She hesitated, and pushed herself into him.

Hogg banged his head on the roof and again on the doorframe of his car as he stormed out screaming, "Shepherd, step away from my wife, you slithery sumbitch." He lifted a 410 Mossberg shotgun.

Donnelly ducked and yelled to Shepherd. "He means business, Austin."

Shepherd's head shot up, fear changing his face as he disengaged from Anna May.

Hogg advanced, waving the shotgun, his eyes blazing. "Off my porch."

"Rufe, Rufe, slow down," Collins hissed, "before you do something really stupid."

Hogg glanced over. "Get out of my face, Jim."

"Hey, Rufe, this isn't what it seems." Shepherd's voice cracked.

An evil chuckle mixed with anger, and sorrow spilled out of Hogg. "I know; it's worse. The guy I thought was my best friend is humping my wife." He leveled the gun and Shepherd came one step down. Hogg racked a shell into the Mossberg. Shepherd scampered to the sidewalk.

Anna May Hogg stood transfixed. *How have I gotten to this place? Why? It's Rufus. Damn you, Rufus, with your wandering eye and unzipped fly.* She started yelling at him.

He cocked an ear toward her. "You should've thought of that before…" He shrugged. "You got no dog in this hunt, so shut up."

Anna May's mouth slammed closed.

Donnelly whispered to Collins, "And now?"

"I'll talk to him." Collins took a step toward Hogg. "Rufus, you made your point. Let him go."

"Like hell. I should make him wipe his ass with poison ivy. But I've got something better." Hogg brought the shotgun to his shoulder.

Anna May shrieked, "No, Rufus, don't!"

Tears leaked down Shepherd's cheeks. "Rufe, please, I'm begging you," he sobbed.

"I don't want to see your face, you low-life. Turn around, bend over, and prepare to kiss your miserable ass good-bye."

Shepherd stood, arms out, face contorted with tears. "Rufe, please," he whimpered.

Donnelly sidled toward Anna May and heard her mutter in disgust, "Sweet Jesus, he's nothin' but a yellowbelly crybaby."

"Do it!" Hogg barked. He waved Collins away with the gun. Shepherd bent to his knees.

"No, Rufus!" Anna May clasped her hands and yelled again, distracting Hogg.

Shepherd seized the opportunity and bolted down the sidewalk.

Hogg turned and fired the shotgun, twice, in rapid succession. He racked the slide once more but did not fire. Shepherd shrieked as he ran from the cordite-tinged air, the seat of his trousers in tatters. He rounded the corner and disappeared behind a hedge. The drifting shell smoke floating under the streetlight added a surreal quality to the eerie silence.

On the porch Anna May Hogg began to laugh. A beat later it morphed into a high-pitched hysterical cackle.

Hogg let the shotgun fall to his side and nodded to Collins. "In case y'all were wondering, the gun was loaded with rock salt."

He turned to his house and his eyes rested on Anna May. She trembled, knowing their marriage was floundering. He walked up the steps. In a quavering voice she said, "Well, you just gonna stand around or are you gonna help me wash that man out of my life?" She took a deep breath and continued, "And I'll wash that Bonnie bimbo out of yours." Hogg flinched. Anna May gave a slight wheeze as she collapsed against him. With a remorseful smile he put his arm around her and they walked into the house, the door closing behind them.

"So," Donnelly said, "your impression?"

"Hillbilly opera comes to Maqua. Shepherd needs to have his rock-salted ass examined without identifying how it happened. Hogg might get a misdemeanor ticket for disturbing the peace, but not much more. The toughest will be dealing with Shepherd at the office." He looked down the street. "Where are the cops?"

Donnelly unlocked his car. "I guess the neighbors figured Shepherd got his just desserts. The Hoggs took their passion play inside, so no harm, no foul, and maybe a little entertainment for their humdrum existence. Let's get out of here in case the cops do come. Speaking of hillbillies, why don't we cast people like Hogg and Shepherd in a revenge flick series about the Grand Ol' Opry?"

"Perfect," said Donnelly. "You want opera?" he laughed. "Think Joyce discovered the tapes yet?"

"Been five days," said Donnelly, opening the door. "She should have them by now."

"Wonder if she's listened to Dingmann and Rhodes?"

Donnelly laughed. "I sure hope so. Too bad we won't be around to see how she uses it."

But Joyce could still be using me and vice versa. Collins waved and went to his car.

Chapter Forty-Two

Frank Donnelly sat at his desk staring at the work he should be doing. *The more time I spend with Sue the more I realize how much I enjoy her company. It's more than the physical side; she's great to talk with, has a great sense of humor, she's smart.* He looked up. *And she's officially married. Meanwhile, I'm soon off to Kenoten, on to New York, and out of Maqua. What will Sue do? She says she's determined to end the marriage. Will Bob go along with it? Things for us to talk about. Maybe we should go out to dinner so we're not distracted. Did I read something about a new restaurant near Bend? It's far enough away that the usual suspects shouldn't be there. What's the name of the place?* He snapped his finger. *Galore, that's it. Yeah, good reviews. High priced. Almost guarantees that no one from Maqua will be there.*

He paged Sue and ten minutes later she called back and said she was available and that Bob would not be home until late in the evening. He said he'd pick her up at the hospital. He called the restaurant and made a reservation.

***

Jim Collins was running his hand across Joyce Locker's perfect backside as they reviewed a rough layout in her office. She gently moved it aside with a whispered, "Not here."

Collins smiled, rubbed once more, and removed his hand.

"A friend of mine mentioned a new restaurant," she said, "over on the river near Bend. It's called Galore. All fresh ingredients, local grass-fed meat and fish from a couple of lakes up north. Its main feature for us is it's out in the boonies and expensive." She adjusted the layout for a better perspective. "Clientele are mostly tourists on their way up to the lakes or mountains. We'll be able to have a nice meal in private without getting stared at and talked about by god-knows-who from Ilium. We can go Dutch treat or maybe," she returned his hand to her buttocks, "I'll even put it on the expense account for services rendered."

"Jesus, Joyce."

"Just kidding," she moved his hand away again, "although, I probably do owe you one. Maybe after dinner."

"Sounds good to me," Collins said. "All of it. I could stand to get out of Dodge, someplace where we can relax a little without worrying what kind of rumors we're hatching. When do you want to go?"

"I'm thinking tonight," she said. "It's bound to be less busy on a weeknight. I'll pick you up at your place at five. We can be on the highway before the Works lets out at the end of the day."

"I'll leave early and be outside."

***

Galore stood, a stately old converted country farmhouse, atop a winding driveway. An addition on the back of the house, visible from the tree-shaded parking area, held the kitchen, identifiable by a large vent-fan installed in the side wall.

The home's vestibule had been retained for service access with four rooms on one side and three on the other, all connected to the entrance area through sliding pocket doors with beveled glass panels. A large, ornately framed mirror hung on the left wall. A stand with a leather-bound reservation book was on the right.

"Reservation for Locker," Joyce said to the maître d', who checked his book, nodded and smiled.

"Different than in Maqua," murmured Collins, "not as formal."

Locker checked the dining areas. *Linen appointed tables, two-, four-, and six-place settings with substantial silver utensils. Tables spaced apart for privacy, unlike the tight seating in many Maqua restaurants.*

Collins wandered over to look at a picture of Bend. *Looks like it was taken when the main street was still dirt.* He stepped to the next picture when a familiar voice said, "Reservation for two, Donnelly."

Oh, no, oh no! Collins hesitated. *Maybe he'll go into another of the dining rooms. Not going to happen.* He turned and was presented with Frank Donnelly and Sue Costello, both with shocked expressions matching his own. "Jesus, Mary, and Joseph," he said. Sue laughed, more out of shock than humor

"I believe," said Frank, "you've met Sue?"

"Yes, yes, of course," said Collins, recovering, and holding out his hand. He turned to Donnelly. "What brought you here?"

406

"Apparently the same as you, Frank. Having dinner. But why would a guy like you come all this way?" He raised an eyebrow. "Are you with someone?" His voice trailed as Joyce Locker stepped out of one of the dining rooms. He laughed. "Well, well, Jesus wept."

"Frank, for heaven's sake, don't be sacrilegious," Sue whispered.

"You're right." He turned. "Jim, tell me what the hell is going on?"

"I think, after a moment's thought, we both know what's going on," said Collins. "Joyce," he said, "have you met Sue...?"

"...Costello," Sue supplied.

"I have," Locker said. "Hello, Dr. Costello."

"Sue, please," she said.

Collins turned to the maître d'. "Can you make it a table for four, please? These folks will be joining us."

"I guess we will," said Donnelly, offering his arm to Sue. "Shall we sit?"

Locker held up a hand. "A moment, please. I'm going to visit the ladies' before we sit down; be right back. Care to join me, Sue?" Sue joined her and they walked down the hall.

"So, our boss, Joyce Locker?" said Donnelly. "I mean, she is hot, but you're playing with fire, Jim."

"Me? Fire?" Collins laughed. "Dingmann's wife? You're with Dingmann's wife and I'm playing with fire? Hah!" He lit a cigarette. "Okay, what happened?"

"Sue and I have been friends since first grade," said Donnelly. "We went through grammar school together. We ran into each other a while ago; she needed someone to talk to and we drifted back together. She's been having a little marital trouble. Her husband turns out to like men more than he likes her. Much more, as a matter of fact."

"A bit light in the loafers?" Collins blew out smoke.

"Exclusively," said Donnelly, "and I mean exclusively."

"Aha, I understand." Collins shook his head and inhaled. "Okay, Joyce. Our situation is a tad different. We discovered a mutual attraction in New York and acted upon it. This is a difficult situation for both of us so we snuck out here to have dinner, where no one would see us, where we could be alone to talk." The smoke poured out of his nostrils.

"Sounds familiar," said Donnelly. "Here come Joyce and Sue. I'm sure their discussion was similar to ours."

No one spoke until they had been seated and ordered a drink. "Let's start simple," said Donnelly. "What's been said tonight and at this table stays here and goes no further. Agreed?" Solemn nods of agreement. He leaned over to Sue and said softly, "What did you tell Joyce?"

Sue hesitated, twisting her hands together. "Practically everything. It just poured out of me." She put her hand on his thigh.

"She's a good listener, Sue. You can trust her." He paused.

"A toast." Collins clinked his glass. "May God bless and keep in good health your enemies' enemies," he said, raising his glass to Frank and Sue.

Turning to Collins and Locker, Donnelly responded, "God is good, but never dance in a small boat."

The table chuckled. Joyce asked, with glass still raised, "And since I think we all know what's going on, maybe we can have a relaxed meal?"

They all drank. Collins put his hand over Locker's.

"Dingmann," she muttered. "I knew he was a lowlife, but sucking your own wife into a sham like this. How cruel can you get?"

"Not much more than Dingmann has," said Collins. "If there were a way to get him…"

"Well, one thing is sure, folks," said Locker, "all of us have a lot at stake here. If I ever saw a pile of dynamite with a fuse lit, this is it. We better work out what we're going to do very carefully or, as Nick is prone to say, someone not involved is going to do it for us."

Tough, smart, and decisive. Glad she's on my side. Collins smiled.

"Defining the playing field before it's defined for us," said Donnelly.

"Couldn't have said it better myself," said Sue, with a chuckle.

Locker laughed.

"What I mean," said Donnelly, "is I think we have a best-selling book here. It would have to be fiction, of course."

"Because no one would believe it was the truth," said Collins. He picked up the menu. "Let's order; we can get into more detail during dinner."

***

Donnelly placed his fork on the table. "Here are the elements." He raised a finger. "One, a law-and-order crisis in the country. Two" —two fingers—"an outcry from the everyday people essentially saying enough is enough."

"Three," said Collins, wiping his mouth with a napkin and spearing another piece of meat, "an industrial or technical solution to speed justice."

"Four," said Donnelly, "an Ilium-like company providing the solution." He drank some water.

"Political actors," said Locker, sipping her wine, "working the system to speed the judicial process while making it all legal."

"Newbie change agents come into the company and create the idea and upset the process," said Collins, lighting up again.

"Inside-the-company jockeying for credit and plaudits," said Donnelly.

"A hard-charging company CEO," said Locker, pushing her plate away. "Should we order dessert?"

Joyce Locker raised a hand. "Maybe we should continue this

conversation somewhere else."

"We can come back to my place," Collins said. He signaled the waiter for the check.

***

"I promised you some comfort, Quentin," Bob Dingmann said, as they drove in Rhode's car on a road inside the Ilium Works.

"Where are we going, Bob?" Rhodes said.

"Over to the Research and Development building. I promise you, Quentin, an experience you won't soon forget."

Dingmann had Rhodes park near the front door of the building and turn off the headlights. He turned off the ignition and they were about to get out when a car pulled up and a man got out. They watched him hurry into the building.

"Who's that?" said Rhodes.

"Cletus Gustafson," said Dingmann. A minute later a light winked on in a window of the top floor.

"He must be important," Rhodes whispered, "he's got an office with a great view."

"Of course he's important," said Dingmann. *Why do I put up with these simpering minions? Indeed? Be honest, Bob, Quentin has the most magnificent package you've ever had the pleasure to deal with.* "He's the best conceptual model maker on the east coast, if not the entire country. He carried something inside, so he may not be long. We'll wait."

Five minutes later the light in the window went out and shortly thereafter Gustafson came out, got in his car, and drove away.

"Let's go," said Dingmann.

At the building entrance Dingmann swiped his managerial card, flashed it again to the security guard rather imperiously, and signed himself in as James Collins and Rhodes as Francis Donnelly. *Chew on that, you street trolls.* They walked to the elevator and the guard went back to reading his fishing magazine.

Dingmann used a passkey he had gotten from Gino Pacelli, of Ilium Works security, during the inside-the-main-gate parking fiasco, for which he knew Pacelli had been demoted on the direct order of Nick Jackson.

When he opened the door to Gustafson's work lab he and Rhodes caught their breath. The electric toilet gleamed in all of its prototype glory in the center of the room. To its right sat an elegant armchair, appearing to be upholstered in leather. On the left were several unidentifiable items consisting of various gears, metal blocks, and colored wires.

"Damn," said Dingmann, casting a look at the electric toilet. He disengaged. "We have to try that steed; maybe find out what the fuss is about."

"Afterward we can relax in that chair," said Rhodes.

***

They sat in Collins's apartment eating ice cream. Donnelly pushed his plate aside. "Okay, do we want to continue the conversation we were having at Galore?"

"What will the book be about?" said Sue

"The book will pretty much parallel everything that's gone on since Frank and I joined Ilium," said Collins.

"Everything?" said Sue.

"Well, not everything," said Donnelly.

"The names will be changed to protect the innocent," said Collins.

"And the guilty," added Donnelly.

"Will there be a Portable Electric Chair?" said Sue.

Collins and Donnelly exchanged glances. "No," said Donnelly. "We can't duplicate real life. We came up with a different way to deal with the bad guys.

"Quick-freeze technology," said Collins. "Ice the criminals and put them in a kind of suspended animation. If they're really bad guys, keep them in permanent stasis."

"Our fictitious company, Ekelnarr, is big in refrigeration equipment, building and HVAC systems, including security." He grinned. "Otherwise, it bears a vague resemblance to Ilium."

413

"What's the title?" said Locker.

"*Cold Play*," said Donnelly

"*The Cooling Game*," said Collins. "Or *The Cool Gambit*."

"*The Change Agents*," said Donnelly. "I'm getting some beers. Anyone want one?" They all raised their hands.

"*Justice for All*," said Collins.

"Quite a list," said Sue, with a smile.

"How do you plan to get this opus published?" asked Locker.

Donnelly returned with four opened beers and put them on the coffee table. He took a drink and said, "We've come up with a new strategy for the writing game, to be played from the author's side."

"We're always with the new strategies," joked Collins.

"Isn't the normal process," said Locker, "to submit queries, outlines, excerpts and synopses, hoping sooner or later some starving agent or small-time publisher will pick you up? Why destroy yourself with hope and dreams with the fiction market the way it is?"

"Good point, Joyce," said Donnelly. "But there's no fiction here. We developed this approach after we read a quote from a writer, or someone claiming to be a writer, stating, 'If your work is good, you will get published. Just keep at it.'"

"Sounded solid to us," said Collins. "We took it to heart. The quoted sage did not say what he meant by 'keep at it.' So we construed this as a way to 'keep at it.'"

"Most writers," said Donnelly, "consider the words, and enter
414

the polite denial in a tattered notebook. They try to avoid burdening any agent by sending their same pitiful entreaty twice. I'm sure it occurs to them to send the same agent the same package one hundred times." He laughed. "That's after they've decided not to commit suicide."

"That's desperate. Isn't it," said Sue, "an excessive expectation, too pat an approach?"

"Once again, how do you get it published?" said Locker.

Collins went over to his briefcase and pulled out a folder, from which he extracted a piece of paper.

Donnelly nodded. "We'll send it," he said, "to an agent or publisher or whomever."

"Who's we?" Locker poured herself a beer.

"Frank and I," said Donnelly, "writing under the nom de plume of Gregory Ellis."

"Am I to understand that this book is already written?" asked Locker.

"Pretty much," said Donnelly. "Except the ending, which we're working on." He glanced at Collins, who rolled his eyes.

"I see," said Locker. *Well, well, those two have been very busy. Jim and I need to have a serious talk.*

"Anyway," said Collins, "the letter goes something like this: I have recently completed a 90,000-word manuscript, titled *Cold Play*, a wonderful ride through political and corporate life, chock full of disguised truth, tall tales, and homespun wit.

"The storytelling caresses the synapses. It's funny, smart and different. The plot spins smartly along to an unpredictable ending.

"The characters do not look past life; they look through it. They may be otherworldly. Heroic, somber, awe-inspiring, and ruefully comic, they engage with the tremendous questions of life and death and have the weight to take them on and bring things to a deeply satisfying conclusion.

"Genre, setting, plot, are inconsequential in this sprawling tale of debauchery, revenge and redemption. Romance, thriller, and literary readers alike will be caught up in the intensity of this story.

"Although several publishing contacts have expressed an interest, we prefer to work on this project with people of high reputation and integrity. If you find this proposition of interest, send us a mailing address to keep us out of the piles of inane queries we are sure you receive every day and we will rush the manuscript to you."

Collins placed the paper back in the folder. "What do you think?"

"We believe," said Donnelly, "it'll rack up a better response than Edgar Allan Poe, Joseph Heller, and William Golding's letters managed. They were all ignored, slighted, and rejected, a bunch of times, and not always politely either."

"I don't know," said Locker. "Your letter's a bit unusual; are you being too honest?"

Collins laughed. "Of course it's honest. We used actual blurbs from respected writers and reviewers found on the dust jackets of best-selling novels. If nothing else, the letter will stir an agent's primeval olfactory epithelium for a creative load of dreck capable of causing a stampede of bad taste when waved in the winds of popular culture. We've used their own lingo…"

"…kind of like a duck call," said Donnelly.

"I don't know about this," said Sue. "I mean it sounds interesting…" she trailed off.

"Our fallback plan," said a straight-faced Collins, "will be to add a zombie, a vampire, a witch, and a sadomasochistic religious extremist to the story. This may require a rather extensive rewrite. We're not sure we want to embark on that journey. We've already made the head of the Black Ops Team a sexually frustrated woman with a lust for herd animals; her Number One is a hermaphrodite. I mean what more can we do?"

"Follow the *Chicago Manual of Style*? Start every dialogue paragraph with a quote regardless of the flow?" said Locker.

Sue's pager buzzed. "May I use your phone?" she asked Collins.

"Sure," he said. "Use the extension in the bedroom."

***

417

Ten minutes later Sue walked back into the room. She smoothed her dress and sat. "The call," she said in a shaky voice, "was from the Ilium Works police." She took a deep breath. "Bob is dead."

"How?"

Sue took a deep breath. "They found him, naked slumped on, in what turned out be, a vibrating electric toilet Bob had talked about." Donnelly walked over and put his arm around her. She leaned into him.

"Where?" he murmured.

"The Research and Development building."

"Gustafson's space, I'll bet," said Collins.

"Yes," said Sue. "The officer, I think his name was Pacelli, mentioned that name."

Collins and Donnelly exchanged glances. *Pacelli? He'll find a way to screw us.* "What does he want you to do?"

"Go there and identify the body."

"We'll take you," said Locker. "I'll drive Sue; and Jim, you and Frank take his car."

Collins drew Joyce aside. "I smell trouble." To her questioning glance he said, "Dingmann didn't climb onto that toilet without someone else around. Hell, he shouldn't have even been there. Pacelli has scores to settle and who knows what he's got up his sleeve. Let's be careful what we say and do when we get there."

"I agree," said Locker. "I'm sure the Maqua police will be there."

A half hour later they arrived at the Ilium Research and Development building to a ragged line of Ilium security and Maqua police vehicles.

"I see Gino Pacelli," said Locker to Sue. "He was the head of Ilium security until he tried to cross Frank and Jim. As a result of that encounter he was demoted to head of night security."

"Vendetta against Frank?"

"And Jim," said Locker.

Sue opened the car door. "Let's get this over with."

"I think it best that I go with you." A Maqua police officer approached, Sue identified herself, and they entered the building.

***

"Hello, boys." A smiling Gino Pacelli came up to Collins and Donnelly. "What brings you here?" He raised his voice. "Or, more appropriately, what brings you back here tonight?"

"What do you want, Pacelli?" asked Collins.

"It's not what I want," replied Pacelli, "it's what the Maqua police want." He raised a hand and waved. "Officer Roncalli, I have Donnelly and Collins here." His smile was cold. "Seems you two signed the after-hours logbook tonight and all that remains is a dead Ilium executive that you two had a grudge against."

"Mr. Donnelly, Mr. Collins?" They nodded. "Would you please come over here? I have a few questions for you."

Collins turned to Donnelly. "Lawyer?"

"Let's see what's on his mind," said Donnelly.

***

A shaken Sue Costello came out of the R&D building with Joyce Locker. "Awful," she said. "Even Bob didn't deserve that."

"Where are you staying tonight, Sue?" asked Locker.

"I, I don't know," she replied.

"Why don't you stay at my house? I live with my parents and there's plenty of room." She glanced at the Maqua policeman talking to Donnelly and Collins. "It would be best for appearance's sake. We'll go back to your place and you can pack a suitcase."

"Shouldn't we say something to Frank and Jim?"

"I'll do it," Locker said, and walked toward them.

As she was passing, Gino Pacelli said to her, "This is one your two hotshots won't get out of, Joyce."

"Why?"

420

"Their names are on the sign-in sheet." He leered. "Motive, opportunity, presence."

"Oh," said Locker, "was Mr. Dingmann murdered?"

"We think he was electrocuted, Joyce."

"On a toilet? You wish. Doesn't seem like Dingmann was murdered, does it? Was Dingmann's name on the sign-in sheet, Gino?"

"No," Pacelli said, scowling.

"I think you've done it again, Gino. Shoot, ready, aim. Great career move." She headed toward Donnelly and Collins.

"Hello, Joyce."

"Bill!" said Joyce. Maqua Police Sergeant Bill O'Malley was with Officer Roncalli. "Are you here on this?"

"Yeah. Some of your guys involved? Pacelli," O'Malley said, "told me he's sure they put Dingmann on the toilet and flipped the switch. They have a sign-in sheet with their names on it."

"For the record, Bill," said Locker, "the dead guy, Dingmann, was one of my managers. Those two work for me and were with Dr. Costello and me all evening."

"All evening?" said Bill.

She leaned in. "Bill, take it from an old friend, Gino Pacelli is a conniving liar and has a vendetta against those two." She jerked her thumb in their direction. "Check the folks at Galore, that new restaurant up in Bend, Bill. They'll confirm all this. Someone else was up there with Dingmann."

421

Donnelly and Collins turned to her.

"I'm taking Dr. Costello to my place," she said. "I've spoken to Sergeant O'Malley. They'll bust your chops, check a few things, and release you in a few hours.

"What about Pacelli?" said Collins.

"If I have my way he's worked his last days at Ilium." She glanced at O'Malley. "We'll talk tomorrow, Bill."

***

Donnelly and Collins entered L'Fey and into a pall of acrid cigar and cigarette smoke that mingled with the odor of beer and whiskey. "What a night." Donnelly coughed. "Does the place always stink like this?"

"Yeah," said Collins. "We're usually in here and acclimated so we never realize the buildup. And you're right, this has been the night from hell." He looked around. "Crowd seems to be thinning out."

They went to the bar and ordered their drinks. "Where is everyone?" Donnelly asked the bartender.

"I don't know; just some guy in the booth over there snuggling with some girl…"

"Sweet Jesus, Clare Duckett," choked Collins. "With Dick Leeson." He jerked the martini away from his mouth.

"Our ideals are crumbling around us," said Donnelly. "Dick Leeson and Clare Duckett? What is life at Ilium coming to?"

Collins laughed. "There's me and the General Manager."

Donnelly snorted. "Yeah, and I'm with a now-dead boss's wife."

"Well," said Collins, looking over at Leeson and Clare Duckett, "our Clare has an active libido. Her husband's in the slammer and won't be out for a long time. Burt Rawley is dead and Lou Willets is in exile. Leeson must feel he's next in the line of succession"

"I guess Leeson decided he needs a life and a new set of memories."

"Right now, they're two lonely people having a conversation. It's the stuff of romance novels."

"In L'fey?" Donnelly made a gagging sound. "Leeson's radar must be inoperative. He's lucky no one's here tonight."

"Or maybe he thinks he's lord of all he surveys, it's gone to his head, and he's exercising droit du seigneur."

"Not possible; she's anything but a virgin," said Donnelly. "And I'll bet this blushing maid won't want to go home if his lordship droits his senior. Even if it is Leeson." He sipped his drink. "Well, a woman is only a woman."

"But a cigar is a good smoke," said Collins, lighting one.

"We can't get out of here and off to Kenoten fast enough."

"Yeah, if they'll still let us, but there're some things to sort out," said Collins. "Like Joyce and me, and whatever the cops, urged on by Pacelli, have in store for us. We sort of can't leave town."

"I need to sort out Sue and me," said Donnelly. "I hope whatever Pacelli tries to pin on us blows up in his face."

"If Joyce has anything to do with it, absolutely," said Collins.

"You realize," said Donnelly, "with what just happened, we now have an ending for our proposed novel."

"We do," said Collins, "we'll leave the use of the Vibrating Electric Toilet as a crime stopper for the politicians and the lawyers.

That's not even getting into the Portable Electric Chair"

"Right," said Donnelly, "and don't forget the silent majority. Meanwhile, we have to find out who was with Dingmann and called our names in to the police."

"Until we do, we'll have a cloud over our head."

"I guess we go back to being investigators," said Donnelly.

"Only to save our asses and advance our careers."

"And love lives."

"Sounds like a plan," said Collins.

They clinked glasses.

About the Authors

Lawrence J. Strattner is author of the novels *The Geek Assassin, Nurse Maggie Cooper and the Shaman Dawn, Lola and the Raven Queen of Hornets, Real Men Love Dynamite Hot Extract, Homeless Children of the Redwood Forest, and Four of Swords* his collection of shorter stories dedicated to visions of intrigue and mayhem.

Larry's work has appeared on line numerous literary e-magazines. He is a member of fictionaut.com. His story, "Exit Strategy," was published in the Deadly Ink "best of" paperback collection.

He served in several management positions for major corporations, with on-site business experience in most of the industrialized world and project work in the Middle East and British Hong Kong.

Reading, and writing are among his many interests.

He lives in the far northern California Coastal Redwood forest.

About the Authors

Thomas J. Keller has worked as a house painter and done shape- up work on trailer trucks and on the Brooklyn docks. After college and military service he was a claims adjuster for an insurance company.

He was accepted to a highly regarded three-year corporate training program for advertising and public relations. He ran a number of successful mission critical advertising and PR programs. At their conclusion he accepted a Madison Avenue advertising executive position.

Five years later he joined a European-based international company for a two-year project and at its conclusion was recruited by a major, diversified international company as their corporate officer for advertising, PR, government relations, and marketing programs.

Mr. Keller has published several short stories and has won an award for a one-act play. *Ilium* is his first published novel. He lives with his family in Connecticut.

Credits

T Denise Clary | Editorial and Plot Consultation
Charmaine Taylor | Editing and Continuity
Eureka Writers Group | First Readers
Janis Strattner | Cover Designer
Thomas J Keller and Lawrence J. Strattner | Concepts and
Color US Corporations | Unbelievable unvarnished
truth

www.ingramcontent.com/pod-product-compliance
Lightning Source LLC
Chambersburg PA
CBHW071409180526
45170CB00001B/30